Threatened Peoples, Threatened Borders

THE AMERICAN ASSEMBLY was established by Dwight D. Eisenhower at Columbia University in 1950. Each year it holds at least two nonpartisan meetings that give rise to authoritative books that illuminate issues of United States policy.

An affiliate of Columbia, the Assembly is a national, educational institution incorporated in the state of New York.

The Assembly seeks to provide information, stimulate discussion, and evoke independent conclusions on matters of vital public interest.

CONTRIBUTORS

SERGIO DÍAZ-BRIQUETS, Casals and Associates

TOM FARER, American University

CARL KAYSEN, Massachusetts Institute of Technology

CHARLES B. KEELY, Georgetown University

KATHLEEN NEWLAND, Carnegie Endowment for
    International Peace

SHARON STANTON RUSSELL, Massachusetts Institute of
    Technology

MICHAEL S. TEITELBAUM, Alfred P. Sloan Foundation

MYRON WEINER, Massachusetts Institute of Technology

WARREN ZIMMERMANN, RAND

ARISTEDE R. ZOLBERG, New School for Social Research

THE AMERICAN ASSEMBLY
Columbia University

Threatened Peoples, Threatened Borders

World Migration and U.S. Policy

MICHAEL S. TEITELBAUM
and
MYRON WEINER
Editors

W. W. NORTON & COMPANY
New York   London

First Edition

The text of the book is composed in Baskerville
Composition and Manufacturing by the Haddon Craftsmen, Inc.

Library of Congress Cataloging-in-Publication Data
   Threatened peoples, threatened borders : world migration and U.S. policy /
Michael S. Teitelbaum and Myron Weiner, editors.
      p.   cm.
   At head of title: The American Assembly, Columbia University.
   Includes bibliographical references.
      1. Emigration and immigration—Government policy. 2. Immigrants—Govern-
ment policy. 3. Refugees—Government policy. 4. United States—Emigration and
immigration—Government policy. 5. Immigrants—Government policy—United
States. 6. Refugees—Government policy—United States. 7. United States—Foreign
relations. I. Teitelbaum, Michael S. II. Weiner, Myron. III. American Assembly.
   KV6271/T47   1995
   323.1′73—dc20   95-4160

   ISBN 0-393-03777-0

W. W. Norton & Company, Inc., 500 Fifth Avenue, New York, N.Y. 10110
W. W. Norton & Company Ltd., 10 Coptic Street, London WC1A 1PU

1 2 3 4 5 6 7 8 9 0

Contents

Threatened Peoples, Threatened Borders

Preface

International migration has risen rapidly to the top of the agenda for both foreign and domestic U.S. policy. As a foreign policy challenge, migration has joined a list of critical global issues that includes the environment, population, and the international economy. Human dramas involving millions of refugees from Rwanda, Haiti, Cuba, and Bosnia, among many others, have been the focus of much media attention, and international migration has also become a decisive element in U.S. domestic politics, as in recent California and Florida elections.

This volume was commissioned to help identify policy guidelines for these urgent and growing challenges. The chapters were first used as background for an American Assembly program held at Arden House, Harriman, New York, November 10–13, 1994, where a distinguished group of authorities representing government, academia, religious and other nonprofit organizations, the law, and the media convened to make recommendations to U.S. policy makers. Their names and the report of their findings and recommendations are included as an appendix in this volume.

To provide intellectual leadership for the Arden House meeting and to edit this volume, the Assembly retained Michael S. Teitelbaum, a demographer at the Alfred P. Sloan Foundation and vice chair of the U.S. Commission on Immigration Reform, and Myron Weiner, Ford International Professor of Political Science at the Massachusetts Institute of Technology.

We gratefully acknowledge support for this book and the Arden House Assembly from The Pew Charitable Trusts and the Pew Global Stewardship Initiative.

It is our belief that this book continues to fulfill the mandate of The Assembly's founder, President Dwight D. Eisenhower, "to illuminate public policy." We hope it will help both citizens and policy makers to understand more fully what is required to develop coherent guidelines for U.S. policy that will both protect American interests and values, and secure the support of the American public.

Daniel A. Sharp
President

Introduction

Threatened Peoples,
Threatened Borders
Migration and U.S. Foreign Policy

MICHAEL S. TEITELBAUM
AND MYRON WEINER

T he growing worldwide flow in the number of people leaving
their country has created a major foreign policy challenge to
the United States and other population-receiving countries. These

MICHAEL S. TEITELBAUM is a demographer at the Alfred P. Sloan
Foundation. He has been a member of the faculties of Oxford University
and Princeton University, served as professional staff member of the Ford
Foundation and the Carnegie Endowment for International Peace, and
been one of twelve commissioners of the U.S. Commission for the Study
of International Migration and Cooperative Economic Development
(1988–90). At present, he serves (via appointment by the congressional
leadership) as one of nine commissioners of the U.S. Commission on
Immigration Reform, and in 1993 was elected vice chair of the commission. Dr. Teitelbaum is a regular speaker on the subjects of immigration
and demographic change, a frequent invited witness before committees of
the United States Congress, and author of several books on demography
and migration. He publishes extensively in scientific and popular journals
and in national op-ed pages.
MYRON WEINER is Ford International Professor of Political Science at
the Massachusetts Institute of Technology. From 1987 to 1992 he was
director of MIT's Center for International Studies. He is the author of
numerous books and articles on South Asian politics, including *Sons of the*

flows are largely the consequence of deteriorating political and economic conditions among many countries in the Third World, in the former Soviet Union, and among states that were within the Soviet orbit.

In the last few years we have witnessed a torrent of people in flight from or within Somalia, Rwanda, Iraq, Bosnia, Croatia, Cuba, Haiti, Afghanistan, Tajikistan, Azerbaijan, and Armenia. In addition, the United States has been concerned with an influx of illegal migrants from Mexico, Central America, the Caribbean, China, and elsewhere; Japan with illegal migrants from China and Southeast Asia; and Europe with asylum seekers and illegal migrants from North Africa, sub-Saharan Africa, and Eastern Europe. Population-receiving countries within the Third World feel no less threatened. Zaire is burdened with hundreds of thousands of refugees from Rwanda, Pakistan with an influx from Afghanistan, India from Bangladesh, Bangladesh and Thailand from Burma, and Thailand from Cambodia. And the successor states of the former Soviet Union watch with anxiety the treatment of minorities by their neighbors.

This chapter reviews the foreign policy issues posed for the United States by worldwide migration. It is divided into four sections. First we consider how and why the prevention of unwanted migration into the United States by large numbers of refugees, asylum claimants, and illegal migrants has become a domestic and foreign policy objective in the post–cold war era. The older dominant view of refugees and asylum claimants as people who needed humanitarian assistance has increasingly given way to perceptions of threat to the American economy, social order, and welfare system and to the view that many who now seek asylum are not bona

---

Soil: Migration and Ethnic Conflict in India, The Indian Paradox: Essays on Indian Politics, and *The Child and the State in India: Child Labor and Education Policy in Comparative Perspective.* He is chair of the MIT Inter-University Committee on International Migration and editor of *International Migration and Security.* He is a member of the American Academy of Arts and Sciences. His most recent book, *The Global Migration Crisis: Challenge to States and to Human Rights,* was written with the aid of a grant from the MacArthur Foundation.

fide claimants for protection. A similar public turnabout has taken place with respect to illegal migrants, once described by some as valuable additions to our labor force but now portrayed as burdens upon schools and hospitals and competitors for jobs.

We then examine how the U.S. has responded to the perceived threat of an unwanted population influx, including efforts to control borders and interdict boats; measures to persuade sending countries to prevent their citizens from leaving; trade, aid, and investment policies intended to affect the economic conditions within sending countries; and, in one recent instance, military intervention. We note that the U.S. response has been confusing and inconsistent. The U.S. government has found it politically difficult to move away from a refugee policy based upon cold war assumptions. It has also been pressed on one side by human rights activists, by employers of illegal labor, and by ethnic groups not to become restrictive, and on the other by state and local governments concerned with the financial costs of illegal migrants and refugees and by a public anxious over uncontrolled borders. The public appears to be increasingly unable to distinguish among legal and illegal immigrants, refugees, and asylees, and it remains ambivalent as to how many legal immigrants should be admitted and how best to deal with illegal entries and asylum claimants.

In a third section we consider how other countries and international institutions have reacted to migrant flows across their borders. Again, we note that humanitarian concerns have increasingly given way to security considerations. The result is that many countries are now pursuing a dual policy, first by adopting tighter control policies to prevent illegal migrants and asylum claimants from entering and by increasing deportations, and second by considering measures of prevention and intervention in countries that generate refugee flows. International institutions are increasingly expected to take on responsibilities shunned by national governments, but they are constrained by a lack of resources and limited authority to deal with the internal affairs of states.

In a concluding section we consider what some of the policy options are for the United States. First, how can the United States protect its own borders while not departing from its obligations to protect those in need of asylum? Second, how can the United

States best respond to the concerns of other countries that they too are threatened by unwanted entries? And finally, what might the United States do to strengthen the capacity of international institutions to cope with the conditions that lead millions of people worldwide to attempt to leave their country?

Changes in U.S. Attitudes toward Refugees, Asylum Claimants, and Illegal Migrants

In August 1994 the governor of Florida declared an immigration emergency, and called upon the federal government to provide assistance to cope with the growing influx of rafters from Cuba. The governor's request precipitated a decision by President Clinton to interdict the rafters, arrange for their accommodation on U.S. bases at Guantanamo and in Panama, and negotiate with the Cuban regime in an effort to persuade them to halt the exodus.

This sequence of events dramatized the relationship between migrant and refugee flows, domestic American politics, and U.S. foreign policy. It also highlights the change that appears to be taking place in the United States away from the view, once widely held and embodied in U.S. refugee law, that refugees from Communist countries were welcome, since their flight demonstrated the lack of legitimacy of Communist regimes. Under this policy, the United States readily admitted individuals from Vietnam, Laos, Cambodia, Nicaragua, Cuba, Russia, and the countries of Eastern Europe, and, moreover, pressed Communist countries to permit freedom of exit. Policy makers paid little attention to the ways in which emigration from these countries may also have benefited our cold war adversaries. The departure of political dissidents often weakened opposition to the regime and may have made political change less rather than more likely. Communist regimes were also strengthened by the flow of remittances from refugees settled abroad, in some instances (as in Cuba) providing millions of dollars annually to improve their balance of payments.

Paradoxically, while policy makers argued that refugee flows undermined the regimes of our adversaries, they also reasoned that migration and refugee flows strengthened the regimes of our friends. The government of El Salvador, for example, successfully pleaded that its citizens residing in the United States (who constituted an estimated one-sixth of the El Salvadoran population) should be allowed to remain, since they relieved employment pressures and provided much needed foreign exchange. Similarly, the Mexican government persuaded some Americans that Mexico's economy was strengthened by the continuation of an irregular flow of migrants across the border.

In recent years the view that migration to the United States could both weaken our adversaries and strengthen our friends has been shifting toward a new view that a large influx of asylum claimants, refugees, and illegal migrants can impose unacceptably high costs upon the United States itself. While some Americans willingly employ illegals, others regard them as competitors for jobs, since many illegals are prepared to work at low wages and for employers who violate labor standards. Were the government willing and able to stop employers from hiring illegals, the critics say, there would be more opportunities for the unemployed, especially for those who belong to minority communities.

Beyond the issue of employment, American fears of a large influx of asylum claimants, refugees, and illegal migrants have deeper roots in the structure of the welfare state; the distribution of financial resources among local, state, and national governments; uncertainties over the prospects for immigrant integration; and a concern over the loss of governmental capacity to orderly manage the flows.

In regions of the country with large numbers of illegal and asylum claimant children, local communities resent federal requirements that they use property taxes to pay for the costs of the children's schooling. Similarly, some state governments view migrants as unwarranted financial burdens on public services. Texas, California, Arizona, Florida, and New Jersey have filed suits against the federal government seeking financial redress for the billions of dollars they have spent on educating illegal aliens, paying their Medicaid costs, and imprisoning illegal aliens convicted of crimes. By its failure to control borders, to punish employers who hire illegals, and to deport aliens, the critics argue, the federal government has permitted more than 3.5 million illegal aliens to stay in the United States—but passed on much of the welfare cost to state and local governments.

Public perception of asylum claimants and of illegal migrants is also shaped by a concern that governments of some sending countries are engaged in "dumping" their unemployed, political dissidents, and ethnic minorities to relieve themselves of unwanted populations. In 1980, 125,000 Cubans arrived in the United States by boat from Mariel harbor, including a minority who had only recently been released from prison. In mid-1994 the large emigration of Cubans was widely regarded as a Cuban government strategy for pressuring the United States to end the embargo. The use of emigration as an instrument of foreign policy was also demonstrated by the Haitian government in the early 1980s when large numbers of Haitians came by boat to the United States. The Jean-Claude Duvalier regime halted the flow when the United States agreed to augment its foreign aid. In the Cuban cases it was clear that the Castro government had engineered a flow to suit its own domestic or foreign policy needs, while the Haitian case demonstrated how a government could use the flow to influence U.S. foreign aid policy.

In recent years there has been a significant increase in the number of asylum claims by individuals who are fleeing neither from political persecution nor from violence. These include ethnic minorities, women, homosexuals who report that they have suffered discrimination, and young unmarried Chinese who claim they fled their country because the Chinese government violated their human rights by denying them the right to have more than one child. Unable to gain entry under existing migration laws, many would-be migrants looking for economic opportunities attempt to enter as asylees, aware of the loopholes in the law, the lengthy adjudication procedures during which time they can work, and the opportunities to slip into the labor market without being detected and deported.

Some of the policies intended to reassure the public that migrants do not constitute a threat, that illegal migration will be reduced, and that refugee and asylum flows can be managed have been ineffective. Studies have shown—and these have been widely reported in the press—that employer sanctions against illegals have not been effectively enforced. More recently, the Commission on Immigration Reform proposed establishing a national registry to ensure that individuals who sought employment were citizens or green card holders with authorization to work, a proposal that received support from the White House in early 1995. Asylum claimants from Central America who did not qualify under existing refugee law were granted protected status described as "temporary," but few have been repatriated, notwithstanding an improvement in political and economic conditions in El Salvador and Nicaragua. Moreover, in 1990 Congress passed legislation increasing the number of legal migrants admitted each year in response to demands by some ethnic groups and employers, with the adopted increases taking effect at a time when large numbers of Americans were unemployed.

In the minds of some Americans there is also a linkage between crime, drug traffic, terrorism, and migration. Though there is little hard evidence to support this linkage, the bombing of the World Trade Center by a group of Middle Eastern immigrants and asylum claimants played an important role in increasing public anxieties over immigration. There is, however, hard evidence that some of the illegal migration to the United States (and elsewhere) is now part of a worldwide trafficking business, with dealers earning substantial fees by forging documents and arranging illegal entry and employment of migrants. Upwards of $30,000 to $40,000 is paid by Chinese migrants who are then forced to repay their loans by bonded employment in restaurants and sweatshop industries.

Public opinion polling data suggest that public concern over migrants, refugees, and illegals is growing. The concerns are particularly great in some regions of the country and among some social classes and ethnic groups. Less clear is whether these perceptions are short-term reactions resulting from the recession and unemployment or reflect longer-term concerns over the cultural, social, economic, and financial costs. It is not clear, therefore, that public attitudes will necessarily change if unemployment significantly declines and wages increase.

In any event not all Americans share the concern that migrants constitute a threat. A.M. Rosenthal, former editor of the *New York*

Times and a long-time advocate of refugees and both legal and illegal migrants, described as a falsehood the view that immigrants, legal and illegal, are an economic burden.[1] They are, he wrote, an economic boon to America. He cites an Urban Institute study that migrants contribute $25 billion to $30 billion more money in taxes and jobs than social benefits paid out. The "anti-illegal crowd," Rosenthal fears, will soon move against immigration itself and "the concept of America as a haven for refugees and place of economic hope for some of those who stupidly failed to be born in America." Few public figures, he wrote, have been willing to defend immigration. One is former New York Governor Mario Cuomo, who said, "I love immigrants. Legal, illegal—they are not to be despised." New York City Mayor Rudolph Giuliani is quoted as saying, "If you come here and you work hard and you happen to be of undocumented status, you are one of the people who we want in this city. You are somebody that we want to protect, and we want you to get out from under what is often the life of being like a fugitive, which is really unfair."

With the end of the cold war many Americans have come to regard the prevention of illegal migration and large-scale refugee flows as a major foreign policy objective. Haiti and Cuba presented the first post–cold war refugee crises for the U.S. government. In both instances the government's response has been to interdict boats heading for the United States. While a few politicians, many journalists, virtually all human rights advocates, and members of the Congressional Black Caucus objected to the policy of interdiction, there was little public outcry and no objection from a majority of members of Congress. Some of the opponents of interdicting Haitian boats called instead for a stronger embargo and, if it failed, military intervention. Although some supporters of interdiction were unenthusiastic about military intervention, they often remained silent on the question of where large numbers of interdicted Haitians could be housed and for how long. In the Haitian case the interdiction policy was accompanied by an embargo, aimed at forcing the military government of Haiti to resign. In the Cuban case, the United States refused to end its longstanding embargo but was prepared to negotiate an agreement with the Cuban government under which the United States agreed to a legal immigration process that would admit 20,000 Cubans each year in return for a Cuban policy of preventing its citizens from leaving by boat.

The Cuban and Haitian situations raised the larger question of how the United States could affect conditions in countries that produced large-scale migrant and refugee flows. Interdiction was a reflexive response to a large flow when the United States government was concerned over the domestic political effects of admitting large numbers of people whose lives did not appear to be at risk. Persuading the Cuban government to halt the flow, through coercion if necessary, was a second reflexive response.

The U.S. government was clearly initially hesitant to use the entire range of instruments at its disposal to bring about a change in either Cuba or Haiti, ranging from ending the embargo in one and imposing a more effective embargo on the other, to coercive persuasion or, if that failed, direct military intervention. The embargo imposed upon Haiti was intended to bring down the government, but its impact was to worsen conditions so that it induced more Haitians to emigrate to the United States. Similarly, the embargo on Cuba was intended to weaken support for the Castro regime, but Castro apparently won considerable domestic support in his own country by arguing that it was the embargo (not Cuban government economic policies) that accounted for the deteriorating economic conditions. When it appeared that the embargo on Haiti was having little impact, and the administration's credibility was undermined by the disparity between its rhetoric and its policies, the U.S. government decided that military intervention was needed. However, public opinion surveys reported that most Americans did not regard the threat from migrants or, for that matter, the goal of reestablishing a democratically elected president as sufficient grounds for the use of military force.

U.S. Policy Responses to Perceived Threats

No one would describe U.S. responses to perceived threats arising from migration as coherent, or consistent, or orderly. Nor have they been uncontroversial.

A major source of incoherence has been the palpable momentum of the past—immigration and refugee policies created under circumstances now transformed beyond recognition. As with many other sectors of U.S. foreign policy, the hallowed assumptions of more than four decades of cold war die hard. In some cases (e.g., the Cuban Adjustment Act of 1966) these have been formalized into federal legislation or judicial interpretation for which formal repeal or reversal would be required. It is in such cases especially that the blocking capacity of focused interest groups can be most effective.

Yet responses there have been, in recent years rising to the very highest governmental levels in both administrative and political terms. It is helpful to consider such responses in two parts: those related to uncontrolled migration by boat, and those to movement by land and air.

In terms of threat perception, the most problematic migrations seem to be those taking place in boats—not because the numbers involved are higher than those crossing land borders (the reverse is true), but because of the greater concentration, vulnerability, and "tele-visibility" embodied in mass movements undertaken in small boats and homemade rafts. The principal U.S. responses to such movements—again hardly coherent or consistent, but the underlying thrust is clear enough—have been in three rough phases: an initial phase of toleration so long as numbers are small; a second phase of deterrence as numbers become larger; and a third phase of interdiction if perceived as necessary to halt large flows or deter potentially large flows from occurring. Hence the past decade has seen three presidents move sequentially to the third phase of interdicting migratory movements via boat from Haiti, from China, and most recently from Cuba.

Moreover, in all three cases, U.S. diplomats ultimately have undertaken negotiations to encourage the governments of such source countries to deter departures at their origin; in the cases of Haiti and Cuba, such negotiations produced formal agreements to this end. It is worth noting that such agreements embody a nearly complete reversal of past U.S. diplomatic positions: the cold war use of refugee departures as propaganda to discredit communism, and the humanitarian support of people's "right to leave" enshrined within the International Declaration on Human Rights and later in the Helsinki Accords.

Such shifts in longstanding policy have attracted energetic criticism from several directions. First, those concerned about the protection and extension of international human rights have strongly protested the shift toward interdiction post-departure, and have also denounced the bilateral agreements to deter such departures before they occur. From this perspective, the ability to depart one's own country without governmental obstruction is a basic human right, and the right to reach U.S. territory to claim political asylum without being impeded by the Coast Guard is equally fundamental. From another direction, echoing the cold war, has come criticism of any efforts to impede the movement of people seeking to depart Communist states such as Cuba and China (though not Haiti). Finally, each implementation of policies embodying at-sea interdiction and/or predeparture deterrence has evoked criticism from others whose concerns emerge from a sense of shared ethnicity/nationality with would-be migrants, rather than from belief in universalistic human rights or anticommunism.

For reasons perhaps best explained by psychologists, unregulated movements by equal or larger numbers of people via land or air have not evoked the same level of threat perception. The mass legalization of illegal aliens embraced by the 1986 Immigration Reform and Control Act (IRCA) applied primarily to (literally) millions of persons who had entered mainly by land routes over the preceding decade. A smaller proportion were represented by those entering by air, often on valid visitor visas the terms of which they subsequently violated.

Although U.S. policy initiatives to deal with such land and air movements have by no means reached the political levels engaged by mass migrations involving boats, there has been a gradual increase in policy attention nonetheless. The most notable involve the recent transformation of immigration politics in California and the Border Patrol's 1994 experiment with a new border strategy in El Paso.

California politics and politicians have been a leading force in the development of U.S. immigration policy. The 1980s California economic boom, fueled by the Reagan defense build-up, produced a parallel boom politics surrounding immigration—supported with heavy lobbying and finance by the largest employer of illegal alien labor, California agribusiness. When it became apparent that employer sanctions could no longer be blocked, California politicians took the lead in developing a hasty compromise that assured California growers a continuing supply of migrant labor via the Special Agricultural Workers (SAW) program, which produced well over 1 million legalized illegal aliens taking advantage of provisions allowing a notably high level of fraud.

But when—for perhaps the first time in living memory—the California boom economy turned into a bust and fell into deep recession, the boom politics of immigration shifted into reverse thrust. Since the early 1990s California politicians have taken the lead in seeking to reverse those trends in U.S. immigration policies that in many cases they themselves had promoted. A few examples should suffice: the state's 1994 lawsuit seeking $377 million in federal reimbursement for the costs of incarceration of criminal illegal aliens; the November 1994 ballot initiative to prohibit access of illegal aliens to public services including education and nonemergency health care; deployment of the California National Guard in support of the Border Patrol in southern California; the new counterfeit-resistant California driver's license; and so on.

The federal response to land/air irregular migration has, to date, been far more muted than that in California. The most visible effort was begun as a local initiative led by Sylvestre Reyes, chief patrol officer of the Border Patrol in El Paso, Texas. Reyes concluded that the longstanding strategy of allowing illegal border crossers to enter rather freely and then seeking to apprehend them within El Paso or at its airport and outskirts might be good for apprehension statistics, but was an ineffective means of deterring border violations. He proposed an experiment of visible deterrence: repositioning of available personnel visibly at the border and within sight of one another, so that any would-be illegal crosser would be able to see a Border Patrol officer looking at him or her. There is some dispute as to whether Reyes had support in this effort from Washington, but no dispute that the experiment has been largely successful and wildly popular with the population of El Paso, itself heavily Mexican-American. The result has been increasing calls from state and local officials for similar federal efforts in California and other border areas. In response partly to the apparent success of the El Paso experiment and partly to California politics, the federal government on October 1, 1994, initiated a new border management strategy in San Diego, albeit one with only limited similarity to the El Paso effort.

Finally, there has been growing interest expressed in measures aimed not at deterring departure of migrants per se, but instead at changing the circumstances in their countries that motivate them to seek to leave. These have taken economic form (trade, investment, and aid aimed at increasing employment and wages in the sending country), and politico/military form in the Haitian intervention intended to reverse political directions deemed to be producing unacceptable outflows of desperate people.

An example of the economic form is represented by the arguments emanating from North American Free Trade Agreement (NAFTA) proponents that adoption of the free trade agreement would reduce unauthorized migration from Mexico. While these were largely rhetorical points, since proponents were well aware of strong evidence that such effects could not be expected to emerge for decades, they nonetheless indicate a political judgment by NAFTA proponents that such migration-restraining effects would be perceived as an important positive contribution of the proposed NAFTA agreement.

It is important to recognize, however, that policies related to trade, investment, and aid have been little affected to date by concerns about migration. Trade policies especially are driven by a constellation of political and economic forces quite remote from the perceived threats from migrations, and indeed are largely controlled by regions and industries that see themselves as economic beneficiaries or victims of such measures. This is hardly a uniquely American phenomenon; the disconnect between trade and migration policies is more conspicuous in Europe, where alarm about migration influxes is combined with highly damaging trade restrictions addressed to the same source countries. These carry special force for agricultural commodities protected by the Common Agricultural Policy noisily defended by agricultural interests in

France and to a lesser extent in other member states.

On the politico/military side, there is the evocative example of Haiti, in which presidents and secretaries of state and national security advisers have long invoked the prospect of forceful U.S. intervention to reverse the coup against Aristide. Such action was justified on general humanitarian and democratic grounds, but also in no small measure in terms of reducing the unmanageable and deadly migration of poor Haitians in unseaworthy boats. After numerous unrequited threats and warnings, such concerns culminated in August/September 1994 in a UN resolution authorizing "all appropriate measures," and direct military intervention by nearly 20,000 U.S. military personnel.

Ethnic Groups and Foreign Policy

Considerable attention has been paid in recent years to two related phenomena: the degree to which political constituencies comprised of immigrant/refugee and related ethnic groups have sought, successfully or not, to influence U.S. policy positions regarding both migration and foreign relations; and the extent to which immigrant/refugee groups have been successfully integrated into receiving societies. As emphasized in the chapters of this volume, these two questions are not only closely related to one another, but the relationships involved can be double-edged: successful integration is a necessity if efforts to influence public policy are to be at all effective; yet full integration may diminish the intensity of interest among such groups in their ethnic groups and/or countries of heritage.

There is little dispute that ethnic groups have been significant actors in the development and maintenance of immigration and refugee policies in the United States. In contrast, such groups appear to have been far less effective in Europe.

American ethnic groups can claim considerable success, since the 1960s at least, in the framing and resolution of public debate about the criteria for immigrant and refugee admissions, the elements of law underlying control of immigration, and the feasibility and seriousness with which immigration enforcement efforts have been pursued. Only a few examples will suffice to illustrate this

point: the Jackson-Vanik Amendment intended to use trade preferences to pressure the USSR into allowing Soviet Jews to emigrate freely; the Morrison-Lautenberg Amendment, which lowered the definitional barriers for "refugee" only for Soviet Jews
and Evangelical Christians (but not for Soviet Armenians, given
that Armenian-American advocacy groups did not want to encourage their departure from Soviet Armenia); passage of the Refugee Act of 1980; the Cuban Adjustment Act of 1966, which gives
special admission and permanent residence preferences to Cubans
only; "diversity" visas of the 1990 Immigration Act directed toward Irish would-be immigrants; the "floor" on family based visa
numbers incorporated in the 1990 Immigration Act intended to
benefit the most recent immigrant groups, i.e., those with immediate family members still to be "reunified"; the legalization of 2.7
million illegal aliens, heavily from Mexico, under the 1986 Immigration Reform and Control Act; and so on.

The reasons for the responsiveness of U.S. politics to such ethnic lobbying are multiple. First, the relative openness to immigration in the United States, and the perception that it represents an
economic gain, or at least is cost free, has meant that additional
immigrant numbers sought by particular ethnic groups do not
require the politically difficult trade-offs of reducing visas available
to other groups. In effect, additional benefits to organized groups
can be provided with no apparent budgetary cost, in either economic or political terms. Such perceptions are not shared in most
of Europe, where the costs of immigration tend to be emphasized
more than the benefits. In contrast, the European political debates
have tended more toward denial that substantial immigration is
allowed or occurring, often in the face of clear evidence to the
contrary (the German asylum experience over the past fifteen
years is a good example of such a policy debate).

Second, ethnic groups are viewed as legitimate political forces in
the United States (unlike in much of Europe), and many members
of Congress are well practiced in the arts of ethnic politics. All view
the "demographics" of their districts as central to their electoral
chances (hence the energetic politicking about redistricting), and
congressional candidates routinely make the rounds of ethnic social organizations, picnics, clubs, churches, and so on. When this

congressional sensitivity to organized ethnic lobbies is combined with the well-established congressional predominance in immigration and refugee matters, the successes of ethnic lobbying on these subjects are relatively easy to understand.

American commentators tend to urge Europeans to embrace more of the U.S./Canadian/Australian perspective of immigration and ethnic groups: to recognize the legitimacy of ethnicity in political action; to adopt policies of a more multicultural form; and to be more open and explicit about the reality of substantial immigration taking place. Many Europeans demur, noting (sometimes passionately) that they do not wish to see their societies become more like those of the United States, Canada, and Australia.

Few would argue with the proposition that the offspring of the very large immigrant groups who entered the United States before 1930 have been successfully integrated. The attainments in many spheres of American life by recent generations of ethnic groups such as Italian-Americans and Jewish-Americans offer one of the great success stories of integration of immigrant groups.

What is not known—indeed, what cannot be known—is whether the offspring of the post-1965 immigrant groups will experience similar integration success. This is a question that has attracted a great deal of discussion, and not a little posturing on the basis of poor evidence. What we can say, with little reservation, is that public perception of the degree of immigrant integration taking place, and assessment of the prospects for future integration, is an important factor underlying the perception of threat or nonthreat posed by such immigration.

To some extent, the prospects for successful immigrant integration depend upon the nature of the labor markets into which recent immigrants have been moving. Unfortunately, there is great unpredictability attaching to such labor markets, and there is also a real lack of fit between the temporal experience of labor market shifts and the temporal patterns of immigration flows and immigration policies. As labor markets shift (unpredictably) from loose to tight to loose over the relatively short periods of the business cycle, pressures arise for concomitant shifts in immigration policy responses to expand or contract migrant inflows. Yet the familial and intergenerational structure of U.S. immigration has a far longer time horizon—family reunification policies may produce commitments to admissions stretching out decades into the future, when no one can know what labor market circumstances will be.

Finally, public and political responses to immigration tend not to make the kinds of fine distinctions among migrant categories that are the stuff of public policy debate. U.S. immigration law makes sharp distinctions between legal immigrants, illegal immigrants, refugees, asylees, nonimmigrants, those with "temporary" protected status, and so on. Yet all the available evidence suggests that public concern stimulated by illegal immigration has extended to legal immigration numbers, and that refugees and asylees are considered to be in the same category as legal and illegal immigrants. The 1990 Immigration Act embraced dramatic increases in legal immigration numbers on the assumption that illegal immigration was under control. These increases in legal immigration, conjoined with evidence that illegal immigration has not been controlled, have together produced a rise in public worries about immigration writ large.

This American Assembly session took place during the same week as a potentially formative set of elections in which such public concerns about immigration have become prominent. The issue resonated electorally in the gubernatorial and congressional elections in California and Florida in particular, and in California ballot referendum #187 focused on shifting that state's policies regarding public benefits for illegal aliens. It is too early to say what will be the fallout of this sudden entry of immigration issues into electoral politics. All we can do is note that such an entry has occurred, and flag the issue for assessment that may become more feasible months or years hence.

Responses by Other States and by International Institutions

Concerns over the effects of unwanted migrant and asylum flows are even greater in Europe than in the United States. Virtually every country of Western Europe has an antimigration political party, and the leaders of all the major parties are acutely aware of growing public opposition not only to continuing migration, but to the very presence of migrants and their children who have been living in Europe for several decades. The French are particularly concerned that growing Islamic influence in North Africa will result in an exodus to France by many secular middle class Algerians, and by the growth of Islamic fundamentalism among Arabs presently living in France. German policy makers regard their country as a front-line state, no longer standing against Soviet tanks, but against asylum seekers and illegal migrants from Eastern Europe and the successor states to the Soviet Union.

Refugee flows are regarded by governments as a humanitarian issue if the refugees are going to another country, but as a security issue if the refugees are crossing their own borders. For the United States, Canada, and Western Europe, the large increase of refugees and internally displaced persons in Africa, most recently in Somalia and Rwanda, has aroused humanitarian concerns. But neighboring African countries receiving refugees are concerned with the impact on the local environment, food, shelter and health services, jobs, and relations between the local population and refugees. Many African governments have been burdened by large-scale refugee flows from Rwanda, Burundi, Liberia, Sudan, Somalia, Mozambique, Angola, and Ethiopia. The movement of people across one's own border is thus more than a matter of humanitarian concern; it is an unavoidable foreign policy issue. The refugee influx from Afghanistan, for example, is a foreign policy issue for Pakistan; refugees from Sri Lanka are a foreign policy issue for India; illegal migration from Bangladesh is also a foreign policy issue for India; the expulsion of ethnic Albanians from Greece is a foreign policy issue for Albania; and the expulsion of ethnic Turks from Bulgaria has been an issue for Turkey.

Few governments regard refugee flows across their borders as purely a humanitarian issue. At a minimum they must often turn to international agencies to provide tents, food, and medical facilities. They may provide transit facilities to international agencies and nongovernmental organizations providing humanitarian assistance to internally displaced persons. They may provide arms to those seeking to overthrow the regime responsible for the refugee flows. They may play a negotiating role aimed at bringing together conflicting groups with the country producing the refugee flows.

And, as a last resort, they may move toward military intervention. For the United States the flow of refugees and asylum seekers in much of the Third World is usually sufficiently remote from U.S. interests that it is not high on the foreign policy agenda—unless the flows are to the United States or they raise the specter of war. Rwanda and Somalia were regarded as humanitarian issues by Americans, not matters of national interests. However, there are refugee movements in the world that would be regarded as more than a matter of humanitarian concern. Were the Baltic states, the Ukraine, Georgia, Kazakhstan, or any of the other former republics of the Soviet Union to engage in the "ethnic cleansing" of Russians, the United States and its European allies would be concerned if there were a Russian military response. Similarly the forcing of non-Russians out of Russia by ultranationalists would raise the prospect of internal and international conflicts within a critical region of the world of great security concern to the West.

Members of the European Union have sought to protect themselves from the internal disputes and violent conflict within countries that lead to refugee flows. Germany, for example, declared that it will not accept refugees who come through a "safe" third country, insisting that refugees make their claim for protection in the first country in which they arrive. Germany also classified some countries as "safe countries" where there is a presumption that human rights are sufficiently protected so that no one from that country is likely to have a justifiable claim for asylum. By identifying all of its bordering neighbors as safe countries the German government has in effect created a *cordon sanitaire,* thereby insulating itself against any significant refugee influx. Indeed, in 1994 the flow of refugees and asylum seekers to Germany markedly declined. Other Western European governments have followed a similar strategy, with the result that the refugee flows from Eastern Europe, the former Soviet Union, and the Third World have decreased. These policies are, in effect, the European equivalent of U.S. interdiction policies.

As European countries have sought with considerable success to reduce the number of asylum seekers and refugees, the burden for their protection and care has fallen principally upon neighboring countries within the Third World and on international agencies, especially the United Nations High Commissioner for Refugees (UNHCR).

In an effort to reduce the flow of refugees, UNHCR and other international agencies are seeking ways to protect people within countries torn by large-scale violence, where the host government is incapable or unwilling to protect many of its citizens, or indeed may be responsible for threatening their lives and safety. The goal is to create safe areas under international protection and to provide humanitarian relief so that people at risk will stay within their own country, even if it means moving to a safer region of the country. Recent reports suggest that while the numbers of refugees worldwide did not increase in recent years (prior to the Rwanda flight) the number of internally displaced persons (IDPs) has been increasing.

Wars are now predominantly internal, rather than conflicts between states. Of the eighty-two armed conflicts that took place between 1989 and 1992, seventy-nine were within borders. The increasing flight of people within or from their own country is the result of violations of human rights by autocratic regimes, ethnic and other forms of internal conflict, and the emergence of failed states whose central governments lack the authority and capacity to maintain internal order. Losses of life and brutality against specific communities and political dissenters may arouse the conscience of the international community, but it is the flight of large numbers of people that internationalizes these events and forces international agencies to take some action. For this reason, the issues of prevention and intervention—in all their many forms—have become a central concern for the United Nations and its agencies.

Prevention and intervention, laudable as these goals may be, pose three fundamental problems. The first is that governments that generate refugee flows and internally displaced persons are usually unwilling to permit outside agencies, including the UN, to intrude in what they regard as their sovereign internal affairs. Under some circumstances governments may permit, or tolerate, humanitarian assistance by outside agencies, but few governments are prepared to see outsiders mediate internal political disputes or permit outsiders to examine their human rights record. The UN was created to cope with disputes between, not within, states. But since the end of the cold war the UN General Assembly, the Security Council, and the UN specialized agencies have been increasingly intruding in the internal affairs of states, though these intrusions have been accepted only reluctantly by UN members from the Third World. Resolution 688, which forced Iraq to accept a UN military presence in northern and southern Iraq to protect Kurds and Shiites, made many UN members from the Third World uneasy, and until Iraq's recent military threats on Kuwait, some UN members were calling for an end to the embargo. As long as the UN is not empowered to work within countries over the objections of their governments, its capacity is limited to prevent conditions from arising that lead people to leave. Some 70,-000 civilian and military personnel now serve in seventeen UN peacekeeping operations at an annual cost of $3.3 billion. They function in countries where governments are weak or virtually nonexistent, often where there are no agreements with the host country, and in environments dangerous to their personnel. The UN depends upon the willingness of member countries to provide troops, and these troops can be readily withdrawn if a country finds that their presence is politically unpalatable to their own citizens. Hence the U.S. withdrew its forces from Somalia when a number of its soldiers were killed and the body of one soldier was dragged through the streets of Mogadishu. Moreover, when UN peacekeeping forces are present with the consent of the host government they are obliged to leave if such consent is withdrawn. The concept of sovereignty, however important it continues to be in recognizing the integrity of states, has thus limited the capacity of the UN to play an effective role in the management of life-threatening, refugee-producing conditions within states.

The second problem is that we know very little about how to prevent or halt the violent conflicts and human rights violations that result in a refugee flow. There is much discussion of monitoring human rights, establishing systems of early warning, offering—or withholding—economic assistance so as to improve the behavior of governments, but it is not clear what is effective. Some policy makers believe that embargoes, sanctions, and other threats can compel governments to change their behavior; others argue that an improvement in trade and investment will promote economic development that, in turn, will lead to the growth of a middle class and a government more likely to respect the rights of its citizens. Under what conditions should one either provide incentives for change, or adopt measures to compel change (what economist Thomas Schelling called compellence, as distinct from deterrence, strategies)?

The third problem is that when conflicts within states become so great that people leave their homes, countries not directly affected are reluctant to take military measures that place their soldiers at risk. It may be that governments are prepared to engage in "humanitarian" intervention, but only as long as their soldiers are reasonably safe.

Thus constrained by notions of state sovereignty, inadequate knowledge about what policies might make a difference, and an imbalance between humanitarian concerns and national interests, governments have responded to most of the post–cold war crises in a vacillating fashion. Witness the uncertain response of European governments to the break-up of Yugoslavia and the war between Serbia and Croatia; the reluctance by European states with troops on the ground in Bosnia to use coercive persuasion; the willingness of the United States to end the arms embargo on Bosnia but the unwillingness to commit any forces on the ground; the confusion over whether UN forces in Somalia are engaged in humanitarian assistance or in "nation building"; the summary withdrawal of U.S. forces from Somalia when a number of U.S. soldiers were killed; the initially confused response of UN peacekeeping forces in Rwanda and their failure to protect the threatened Tutsi minority; and U.S. policy vacillation over the political crisis in Haiti.

How to deal with the issue of illegal migration and the related question of what Europeans call "manifestly unfounded" claims for asylum is also a matter of considerable uncertainty. As we have noted, governments are adopting tighter control policies to prevent illegals and asylum claimants from entering. Many European governments are deporting those who do not qualify under immigration or asylum laws. Governments of advanced industrial countries are also giving more attention to the role that their trade, investment, and aid policies might play in influencing conditions within sending countries so as to reduce the desire to emigrate. Though it is clear that restrictive tariff policies by migrant-receiving countries affect the capacity of migrant-sending countries to expand employment opportunities, it is less clear that in the short run free trade arrangements will reduce illegal migration. Chain migrations are already in place enabling and inducing people in sending countries to join their friends and neighbors across the border. Moreover, free trade injures some sectors of the economy in the sending country and increases unemployment.

Perhaps the central question is whether we are learning to cope with the global changes that have taken place since the end of the cold war. We have moved from an era when the fundamental concern was war between the great powers to an era when conflicts within states threaten the national security of other states. What lessons for the future have we learned from Bosnia, Somalia, Rwanda, Haiti, and Cuba? How would we respond, for example, to new internal crises among successor states to the Soviet Union, or in Kosovo or Macedonia, or in Nigeria or Zaire? Are international institutions, European governments, and the U.S. government better prepared to deal with the next crisis?

Foreign Policy Options for the United States

American policy makers and the public remain uncertain as to how best to respond to the pressures for entry of asylum claimants and illegal migrants without undermining the U.S. commitment to provide protection to those who need it. One policy option is to put in place a more effective system of border controls, work authorization rules, and off-shore asylum adjudication procedures. Several European countries have significantly reduced the number of illegal entries and unfounded asylum claims through such controls. Many human rights and migrant advocates have strongly opposed these measures, but in their absence public sentiment for restricting access to public services by illegal migrants has been growing. There may be a political trade-off between perceived control over entry and our continued willingness and capacity to provide social benefits to all who live within our borders. Each of these alternative policies, it should be noted, has consequences for U.S. relations with the countries of origin.

Another policy option for more effectively controlling migration is to end the present policy of providing permanent immigrant status to refugees, and permanent status to asylum seekers and others initially provided with temporary protected status. Most countries assume that refugees and asylum seekers should return to their country of origin if conditions enable them to return safely; they provide permanent immigration status only to those who clearly cannot return home. Present U.S. asylum and refugee laws, however, are embedded in a national ethos that presumes immigration permanence to those who flee autocratic regimes, and a political system in which ethnic groups, migration lawyers, and civil libertarians can marshal support against a policy of repatriation. The outcome is a perverse one: as the number of asylum seekers has grown, the country has adopted an alternative policy of preventing initial entry by interdicting boats and pressing governments of authoritarian regimes to stop the exit of their citizens who lack entry visas to the United States. If the number of claimants continues to increase, the United States may need to choose between a policy of providing temporary protection and repatriation and a policy that is restrictive toward asylum claimants.

If illegal migrants continue to enter the United States in significant numbers, the demand for asylum does not decline, and the public continues to be concerned, then hard and often controversial political choices will have to be made.

The United States is also likely to find itself under increasing pressure to consider how it might best respond to conditions within countries that threaten to unleash large-scale population movements. At first glance it may not matter to a realpolitik view of U.S. national interests that a particular country is mistreating its minorities, or that an autocratic regime is repressing its political dissidents. But it will often matter if one country threatens or takes military measures against another whose citizens are fleeing. For this and other reasons, especially humanitarian ones, the United States cannot be indifferent to how minorities are treated in the successor states of the Soviet Union, whether Islamic political movements succeed in forcing large numbers of North Africans to flee to Western Europe, or whether conditions in Cuba, Haiti, the Dominican Republic, or Central America lead to a migrant influx to the United States. To none of these potential crises is there a clear set of policy options for the United States. What is clear, however, is that U.S. policy makers must be increasingly vigilant in monitoring internal conditions within states to see if minimum humanitarian standards are observed. When they are not, the United States must consider what steps it can take, sometimes unilaterally, sometimes with states potentially affected by a refugee influx, and sometimes with regional or international organizations.

A variety of proposals have been put on the table for expanding the capacity of the United Nations and its agencies to take on the threats created by internal wars and by refugee flows that individual countries are not prepared to undertake because their own national interests are not directly at risk. These policy options include creating an independent United Nations peacekeeping and peacemaking force so that the UN is not dependent upon the willingness of individual countries to provide troops who can readily withdraw them when they are at risk. Another policy option is to provide annual UN appropriations to UNHCR so that it can cope with refugees and internally displaced persons without having to seek financial assistance from individual UN members. Still another is to create a permanent international tribunal that can try individuals accused of initiating mass killings and "ethnic cleansings," with authority to impose penalties that will prevent those found guilty from ever leaving their country and that, therefore, may serve as a deterrent. Other options are possible, all aimed at enhancing the independent deterrence and intervention capabilities of the United Nations. The central question is whether the United States is prepared to play a leadership role in placing these and related options on the agenda of the United Nations? Will U.S. policy makers and the American public accept the argument that an expanded investment in the United Nations may result in a reduction in U.S. costs (human and materials) if otherwise the United States is pressed to deploy its own forces abroad?

The chapters in this volume consider how these flows of refugees, asylum seekers, and other international migrants have become major issues for U.S. foreign policy. The chapter by Sharon Russell provides data on population flows to the United States and other countries and considers the relevance of these movements to United States policy. Warren Zimmermann describes the threats that these flows pose to the United States and to other population-receiving countries. Aristide Zolberg considers how U.S. foreign policies and refugee policies since World War II contributed to migration to the U.S. either intentionally or inadvertently. Sergio Díaz-Briquets discusses the impacts of U.S. foreign economic policies upon international migration trends. Kathleen Newland argues that U.S. refugee policies have influenced broader U.S. foreign policy objectives, while Charles Keely shows how U.S. foreign policy has responded to mass population movements, frequently under the influence of ethnic lobbies. Two concluding chapters focus on the implications of international population movements on international norms and institutions. Carl Kaysen analyzes the growing number of instances of national, regional, and international interventions in the internal affairs of states to deal with the conditions that lead to an exodus. In the concluding chapter, Tom Farer examines changing international norms with respect to involuntary migration and considers whether the existing international refugee regime needs to be modified in light of present global conditions.

Note

[1] A.M. Rosenthal, "Hunt Them Down," *New York Times*, October 4, 1994.

1

Migration Patterns of U.S. Foreign Policy Interest

SHARON STANTON RUSSELL

Introduction

As a "nation of immigrants," the United States has a long tradition of admitting a variety of people into its polity, and these admissions have often been guided by foreign policy considerations or have given rise to political interests that have influenced foreign policy.since the Second World War, for instance,

SHARON STANTON RUSSELL is a research scholar at the Center for International Studies, Massachusetts Institute of Technology, where she is a member of the Inter-University Committee on International Migration. A political scientist, Dr. Russell has written extensively on international migration trends and policies and the relationship of migration to economic and social development. She also has been a consultant on population and human resource development issues with the United Nations, the Friedrich Ebert Stiftung, and the World Bank, where she was a visiting scholar in international migration in the spring of 1994. Dr. Russell served as a member of the 1990 UN Expert Group on International Migration Policies and the Status of Female Migrants and the 1993 UN Expert Group on Population Distribution and Migration in preparation for the 1994 International Conference on Population and Development, held in Cairo.

the admission of refugees has been clearly related to foreign policy aims.

In other cases, however, the links between international migration and foreign policy have not always been direct or explicit. Furthermore, as the chapters of this volume make clear, it is not only migration directed to the United States that has the potential to engage U.S. foreign policy interests, but also international population movements directed to other countries or regions of strategic significance.

International migration can interact with U.S. foreign policy interests in various ways. The most direct one is when U.S. foreign policy is an explicit determinant of migration flows to the United States, as in the case of migration originating in the Soviet Union during the cold war era. In other cases, U.S. foreign policy may cause or foster international migration directed to other countries, as, for instance, that of Indochinese refugees to neighboring countries. In addition, given its long tradition as a country of immigration, the United States contains certain population groups, described as "transnational" communities, with strong linkages to other countries and capable of exerting pressure on U.S. policy makers regarding both foreign policy and migration.

U.S. foreign policy can also be affected by international migration when the latter is directed to U.S. allies and is perceived as detrimental to their interests. Thus the movement of Iraqi Kurds to Turkey during the aftermath of the 1991 Gulf War triggered a collective international response that was to a large extent orchestrated by the United States, and responded to both Turkish and U.S. foreign policy concerns. Similarly, international migration may pose a security challenge in cases where it is the result of destabilization in areas of strategic interest, or when it results from the illegal activities of international criminal groups.

Given the variety of potential interactions between international migration and U.S. foreign policy and the indirect nature of many of them, the issue is to what extent they involve sizable population movements. That is, in cases in which U.S. foreign policy affects migration, does it lead to large or small migrant intakes by the United States or its allies? In cases where migration flows trigger a foreign policy response, does the size of those flows matter? These are the main questions to be addressed in the rest of this chapter.[1]

The Place of the United States in Global International Migration

The Global Picture

The United Nations estimates that by early 1985 there were nearly 106 million international migrants in the world, 45 percent of whom were in developed countries (i.e., Australia, Canada, Japan, New Zealand, the United States, the former USSR, and the whole of Europe).[2] In 1985 the United States alone was hosting nearly 16 percent of all international migrants and had the largest migrant stock of any single country. One migrant of every three in the developed world resided in the United States.

At the regional level, only the whole of Europe, with 22 percent of all international migrants, and South Asia, with 18 percent, surpassed the United States in numbers of migrants. Even the region comprising western Asia and North Africa, which includes the oil-rich countries of the Gulf that have been major importers of foreign labor, accounted for at most 13 percent of all international migrants. Sub-Saharan Africa followed, with 11 percent, a share that included all the refugees present in the region as of 1985; Latin America and the Caribbean accounted for a further 6 percent. Clearly, therefore, just as in many other spheres, the United States occupies a dominant position with respect to international migration.

Such estimates of the international migrant *stock*, although useful in providing a sense of the relative importance of migration to the United States, do not indicate the variety of movements involved. The estimates cited above include immigrants, migrant workers, undocumented migrants, and refugees, among others, but their comprehensive nature is not conducive to a better understanding of the forces shaping migration nor of the role of U.S. foreign policy in doing so. One must turn to more detailed information, particularly that pertaining to *flows* of migrants and their

changes over time, to glean the possible interactions of foreign
policy and actual migration trends.

Migration Trends

Relatively few countries in the world gather and regularly pub-
lish data on international migration flows. Table 1 presents a time
series of the information available for a selected group of developed countries and Israel.[3] Because Canada, France, and the
United States lack data on emigration, their net migration cannot
be calculated. In the case of Israel, emigration data for 1960 to
1990 could not be obtained.

Generally, net migration is a better indicator of the impact of
migration on a country than gross migrant inflows, particularly if
the receiving state does not foster immigration for permanent settlement. Thus for Germany or the United Kingdom, among others, the levels of gross immigration are considerably higher than
net migration. Indeed, in the case of the United Kingdom, annual
gross immigration fluctuated around 200,000 during 1965–84, but
net migration was consistently negative, meaning that the country
was losing population through international migration. Despite
the lack of information on emigration, a similar reversal is most
unlikely in the case of the United States, since the data presented
for that country reflect only persons granted permanent residence
rights, among whom emigration rates are low.

In general, the data in Table 1 confirm the preeminence of the
United States as a country of immigration: during 1960–90, its
annual immigrant intake has been higher than that of other immigration countries (i.e., Australia, Canada, Israel, and New Zealand), and it has also tended to surpass the net migration registered
by European countries, including those that actively fostered labor
migration during the 1960s and early 1970s. Note that the trend in
immigrant admissions by the United States has been adjusted to
reflect the timing of the arrival of undocumented migrants whose
status was regularized as a result of the Immigration Reform and
Control Act of 1986 (IRCA).

The United States has been unique among countries of immigration and other major migrant-receiving countries in the devel-

TABLE 1. Average Annual Number of Legal Immigrants and Average Annual Net Migration by Country of Destination and Period, 1960 to 1991

Destination	1960-1964	1965-1969	1970-1974	1975-1979	1980-1984	1985-1989	1990-1991
Immigrants to:							
Canada	88,008	181,976	158,857	130,127	114,056	137,910	—
United States	283,803	358,947	422,206	628,397	801,189	692,250	680,058
Israel	57,012	28,260	31,373	33,448	16,727	14,039	199,516
Subtotal	428,822	569,184	612,436	791,971	931,972	844,199	879,574
Australia	115,021	147,213	141,588	70,635	94,258	114,485	121,458
New Zealand	31,292	31,002	31,713	13,673	11,434	—	—
Belgium	69,056	65,583	64,688	58,271	47,862	48,559	—
France	174,285	203,735	192,585	70,398	78,889	36,660	—
Germany	576,211	706,144	873,051	527,483	502,179	817,754	—
Netherlands	57,746	71,009	115,425	103,571	79,419	90,567	—
Sweden	26,140	42,221	38,938	36,114	27,069	40,488	—
United Kingdom	—	215,540	205,340	186,580	186,340	232,120	—
Subtotal	1,049,752	1,482,447	1,663,329	1,066,724	1,027,449	1,380,634	121,458
Net migration to:							
Australia	106,824	128,387	112,532	54,525	81,351	103,865	115,408
New Zealand	16,281	5,439	16,921	-2,777	-4,340	—	—
Belgium	33,785	24,080	17,073	5,281	-10,801	-4,783	—
Germany	212,104	197,449	306,211	6,352	3,040	377,695	—

TABLE 1. *(Continued)*

Destination	1960–1964	1965–1969	1970–1974	1975–1979	1980–1984	1985–1989	1990–1991
Netherlands	6,528	10,679	38,952	43,833	17,457	35,079	—
Sweden	15,321	27,821	11,874	18,929	8,126	27,291	—
United Kingdom	—	-77,520	-50,400	-21,100	-27,580	24,160	—
Subtotal	390,844	316,335	453,163	105,042	67,254	563,307	115,408
Total immigrants	1,478,574	2,051,631	2,275,765	1,858,695	1,959,421	2,224,833	1,001,032
Maximum net gain	993,951	1,089,254	1,258,183	967,411	1,078,115	1,444,166	994,982

Source: Zlotnik (1994), table 2, panel 9.
NOTE: The data for Canada, the United States, Australia, New Zealand, and Israel are classified by place of birth; the data for Belgium and the Netherlands are classified by country of citizenship; and those for Germany, Sweden, and the United Kingdom are classified by place of last or next residence.

oped world in having experienced a markedly increasing trend in immigrant admissions, particularly since 1975. Excluding aliens regularizing their status under the provisions of IRCA, the average annual immigrant intake of the United States rose from 459,000 during 1975–79 to 565,000 in 1980–84, and to 606,000 during 1985–89. During the 1990s, after passage of the 1990 Immigration Act, the average annual number of legal immigrants has grown further, to reach 724,000 during 1990–92. The 1990 Immigration Act established an overall flexible cap for immigrant admissions of 675,000 starting in Fiscal Year 1995, preceded by a 700,000 level during Fiscal Years 1992 to 1994. Consequently, the high immigration levels reached so far are not expected to decline significantly in the near future.[4]

As Table 1 indicates, a number of developed countries experienced significant increases in migration levels during the late 1980s, especially in terms of net migration gains. Such changes were most marked in Western European countries, which had been experiencing very low or even negative levels of net migration during the late 1970s and early 1980s. Furthermore, the increases recorded were largely unwanted and have generally been characterized as resulting more from push factors in the countries of origin than by the desire of receiving countries to attract greater numbers of migrants.

Underlying and giving rise to such migration trends are the collapse of Communist rule in the former Eastern bloc countries and the exacerbation of conflicts in developing countries that ensued from the end of the bipolar era. The generally poor economic performance of developing countries during the 1980s and the increasing accessibility of international transport, both in terms of lower costs and expanded networks, are also important factors in the observed migration trends. As liberalization took hold in Eastern Europe, constraints on international travel were relaxed and more people were able to make their way to Western European countries where, according to policies adopted during the cold war era, asylum had generally been granted to citizens of Eastern bloc countries.

In addition, citizens of developing countries affected by conflict or internal strife also began making their way to European countries, particularly to those having generous asylum provisions. Consequently, the number of asylum seekers in Western Europe grew rapidly, passing from 68,000 in 1983 to 684,700 in 1992, before declining to 542,800 in 1993.[5] West Germany, in particular, experienced a dramatic rise in the number of asylum seekers (from 20,000 in 1983 to 438,000 in 1992) attracted to the country by the constitutional provision guaranteeing the right to seek asylum. Germany also received high numbers of "ethnic" Germans who have the right to German citizenship. Those coming from Eastern European countries other than the German Democratic Republic and from the former Soviet Union amounted to 984,000 during 1980–89, and to a further 850,000 during 1990–92.

Such rapid increases in the number of asylum seekers and other migrants whose entry and stay are allowed by existing laws but who are nevertheless not quite so welcome in large numbers were a cause of serious concern among Western European countries and prompted a number of measures to reduce migrant inflows. In general, Western European countries do not consider themselves as countries of immigration, and are reluctant hosts to the significant proportions of foreigners in their midst.

That attitude contrasts with the generally positive approach toward immigration that has characterized U.S. policy, and that is reflected in the 1990 Immigration Act. Yet the United States has not been immune to the migration consequences of the end of the cold war, and shares with its Western allies a concern about controlling unauthorized and "massive" inflows of migrants. U.S. foreign policy has therefore been instrumental in both fostering the admission of certain types of migrants and preventing other flows from reaching U.S. territory. The means to do so and their relation to foreign policy will be discussed below.

U.S. Foreign Policy as a Determinant of Migration to the United States

Admissions of Refugees and Asylees

The Post–World War II Period. Historically, the clearest link between immigration to the United States and foreign policy has been in refugee admissions. It was during the aftermath of the Second World War that the United States engaged for the first time in the massive resettlement of refugees. The 1948 Displaced Persons Act was the first expression of U.S. policy for admitting persons fleeing persecution, and it permitted the entry of up to 205,000 displaced persons during the two-year period beginning on July 1, 1948. The act was distinctive in tying refugee resettlement to immigration by stipulating that the 205,000 places used should be charged against the immigration quotas of future years.

In the event, the limit set by the Displaced Persons Act was insufficient and was increased to 415,744 on June 30, 1950. It was later complemented by the issuance of a special allotment of non-quota visas allowing the resettlement of a further 214,000 persons (Refugee Relief Act of 1953). In 1957 the Refugee-Escapee Act removed the "mortgaging" of immigrant quotas imposed under the Displaced Persons Act of 1948 and other subsequent acts, thus in effect validating the admission of refugees outside the limits on immigration set by law.

The resettlement of European refugees was part of the U.S. policy to stabilize and promote the economic reconstruction of Europe after the Second World War, but as the cold war developed, it became also a key instrument in the fight against communism. As early as 1946–50, among the 212,000 European refugees admitted, nearly 79 percent originated in Eastern bloc countries, excluding the German Democratic Republic. The largest contingents were persons born in Poland (79,000), Latvia (21,000), Lithuania (19,000), and the Soviet Union (14,000).

During 1951–60, 54 percent of the 456,000 European refugees granted permanent resident status were from Eastern Europe (excluding East Germany), with large numbers originating in Poland

(81,000), Hungary (56,000), Yugoslavia (45,000), and the Soviet Union (30,000). In 1956, after Soviet troops suppressed the anti-Stalinist revolution in Hungary, Hungarians fleeing their country were admitted by the United States as parolees, that is, as aliens granted temporary admission status under emergency (humanitarian) conditions. In 1958 an act was passed to grant Hungarian parolees the possibility of becoming immigrants.[6]

Just after the Second World War, and until the late 1950s, the vast majority of refugees admitted by the United States originated in Europe (95 percent), but the 1960s were to witness a major change in that respect. The fall of the Batista dictatorship in 1959 and the triumph of Castro's revolution in Cuba led to an outflow of persons fleeing the new regime. The attorney general of the United States admitted them as parolees, and in 1966 the U.S. Congress authorized the attorney general to adjust their status to that of permanent resident alien chargeable to the established immigration quota for the Western Hemisphere. (Subsequently, it was provided that those present on or before 1976 were no longer chargeable to the hemispheric quota.) In total, during 1961–70, nearly 132,000 Cubans were granted immigrant status after being admitted as parolees. As a consequence, refugees from developing countries accounted for 73 percent of the 213,000 refugees granted permanent resident status during the 1960s.

During the 1970s there was yet another sharp increase in the number of refugees from developing countries admitted by the United States. Not only did Cuban refugees keep appearing in the statistics as they adjusted their status or as more managed to leave Cuba, but, in addition, the end of the Vietnam War led to the eventual resettlement of nearly 837,000 Indochinese refugees: 529,000 Vietnamese, 182,000 Laotians, and 126,000 Cambodians. Consequently, during 1971–80, 87 percent of the 539,000 refugees granted permanent resident status by the United States originated in developing countries, and during 1981–90, the equivalent proportion was 85 percent out of a total of just over a million.

Since the Refugee Act of 1980. The 1980s were expected to mark a new period in terms of refugee admissions, given the passage of the 1980 Refugee Act. This act amended and supplemented the Immigration and Nationality Act of 1952 so as to provide the first permanent and systematic procedure for the admission and effective resettlement of refugees of special humanitarian concern to the United States. The act established a definition of the term "refugee" that conformed to the 1967 United Nations Protocol Relating to the Status of Refugees, and made clear the distinction between refugee and asylee status.

Thus refugees were defined as persons outside their country of nationality who were unable or unwilling to return to that country because of persecution or well-founded fear of persecution for reasons of race, religion, nationality, membership in a particular social group, or political opinion. In addition, refugees had to be outside U.S. territory to be granted refugee status. Asylees were persons who satisfied the definition of refugee but were already present in the United States. To be granted asylee status, they had to undergo an asylum adjudication procedure. Both refugees and asylees were eligible to adjust to permanent resident status after a year of continuous presence in the United States. However, at most, 5,000 asylees could do so within a given fiscal year, although this limit was later raised to 10,000 by the Immigration Act of 1990.

It was expected that the passage of the 1980 Refugee Act would change the composition of refugee admissions to the United States. In particular, before passage of the act, migrants had been considered refugees if they originated in Communist countries or in the Middle East. During 1971–80, 96.8 percent of the refugees granted permanent resident status had those origins, and although there was a slight reduction of their share during 1981–90 (it dropped to 94.6 percent), the change was minor. In fact, full implementation of the 1980 Refugee Act did not occur until 1991 when the regulations accompanying the act, which were completed in July 1990, began to be followed. In the interim, both refugee resettlement and asylum adjudication largely continued to operate according to the rules in force before passage of the act.

Nowhere was the weak implementation of the 1980 Refugee Act more evident than in the results of asylum adjudications during the 1980s. In the United States, as in other developed countries, the number of persons filing asylum claims within the coun-

Figure I. Asylum applications received, adjudicated and approved by
United States authorities, 1980–1990

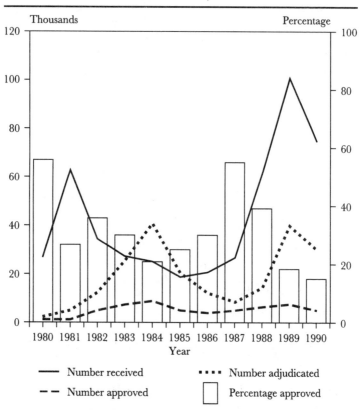

Source: *World Population Monitoring, 1993* (United Nations publication, preliminary unedited version), figure I.8.

try tended to rise during the late 1980s, although fluctuations were common. As may be seen in Figure 1, the number of asylum cases filed reached a peak in 1981 and a higher peak in 1989, and, after declining in 1991, an even higher peak of 104,000 was reached in 1992. The number of cases adjudicated, however, remained considerably lower, reaching peaks in 1984 and again in 1989. Variations were also noticeable in the proportion of cases approved among those adjudicated, which fluctuated between 20 and 40 percent. Overall, during 1980–92, the United States received 629,000 asylum applications, 218,000 of which were adjudicated. Among the latter, only about a quarter were approved. It is not known how many of those whose asylum claims were rejected ultimately left the United States.

Most of those applying for asylum in the United States during this period originated in Central America. Thus during 1984–90, asylum seekers from El Salvador, Guatemala, and Nicaragua accounted for 64 percent of the cases adjudicated. Although the majority of asylum applications from all three countries were rejected, there were significant differences in recognition rates among the three, suggesting that U.S. involvement in the conflicts affecting those countries conditioned the outcome of the adjudication procedure. Nicaraguan asylum seekers, whose country was under Communist rule, were far more likely than their Guatemalan or Salvadoran counterparts to obtain an asylum approval, regardless of the number of applications considered. During 1984–90, 26 percent of some 48,000 adjudicated asylum claims by Nicaraguans were approved, in contrast with 2.6 percent of 45,-000 comparable claims by Salvadorans and 1.8 percent of 9,500 claims by Guatemalans.

So blatant was the differential treatment to which Guatemalans and Salvadorans were subject that a lawsuit was brought against Attorney General Dick Thornburgh by the American Baptist Churches—the so-called ABC case. As a result of the lawsuit, the government agreed to grant new asylum hearings to all Salvadoran asylum seekers present in the United States as of September 19, 1990, and to all Guatemalan asylum seekers present as of October 1, 1990. Pending the reexamination of their asylum requests, the asylum seekers concerned were granted permission to stay in the country and work. Yet the differentials in asylum claims granted remained: in 1992, when Nicaraguan applications were only 2,075, some 16.4 percent were granted, whereas only 1.6 percent of the 6,781 Salvadoran applications and 1.8 percent of the 43,915 Guatemalan applications filed that year were approved.

In 1990 a new Immigration Act was signed into law. Among its provisions, the act established that the attorney general could extend "temporary protected status" (TPS) to citizens of countries experiencing armed conflict or natural disasters or other extraordinary and temporary conditions. In a number of cases, the use of the temporary protected status provision of the Immigration Act has been congruent with U.S. foreign policy interests, and in most, the United States has had an active involvement in trying to solve the conflicts raging in the countries of origin. As of mid-1994, a total of about 203,000 nationals of six countries had been granted temporary protected status for specified periods ranging initially from six to eighteen months.

By far the largest numbers granted temporary protected status originated in El Salvador. The 1990 act itself granted TPS to an estimated 187,000 undocumented Salvadorans who could remain for the period January 1, 1991, to June 30, 1992, and had the right to work. When that period expired, those who registered were granted "deferred enforced departure" status (discussed below) through December 31, 1994, largely because of the intercession of the government of El Salvador, which was concerned about the detrimental effect that the return of so many Salvadorans could have on the fragile peace process taking shape in the country. The potential loss of remittances sent home by Salvadorans abroad was also a matter of concern. The precise number of Salvadorans remaining in the United States as of mid-1994 was not known, in part because the United States does not maintain data on emigration. Only 83,000 Salvadorans had registered for deferred enforced departure status as of early 1993, and some may have repatriated following the peace agreement reached in early 1992; however, many of the original 187,000 were thought to be still in the United States pending adjudication of their asylum claims under the ABC settlement.

On March 27, 1991, the attorney general also granted temporary protected status to nationals of Kuwait, Lebanon, and Liberia. Only 343 Kuwaitis registered in the year during which the TPS program was in effect for them. Following the liberation of Kuwait the program was not extended, and by mid-1994 most Kuwaitis were thought to have repatriated. Lebanese were initially granted TPS for eighteen months, until September 28, 1992, and some 9,214 registered with the Immigration and Naturalization Service (INS). The Lebanese program was subsequently extended through December 9, 1993, and 4,018 renewed their registration. As with the Kuwaitis, most Lebanese participants in the TPS program were thought to have repatriated by mid-1994. Liberians were also granted TPS for an initial period of eighteen months, during which some 5,800 registered. About half this number registered again for the extension granted through March 28, 1994, which was subsequently extended through March 1995.

On September 16, 1991, a one-year TPS program was initiated for Somalians and 347 registered; later, their program was extended to September 17, 1994. Similarly, on August 10, 1992, TPS was granted to Bosnians; only 219 registered under the initial one-year program, which was extended to August 10, 1994.

In other cases, supplements or alternatives to temporary protected status have been instituted. "Deferred enforced departure" (DED) refers to permission granted to groups of people to remain in the United States because of conditions in their home countries. It is based upon administrative discretion not to deport them rather than on legislation, and does not necessarily require registration or specification of what conditions prevent their return. In the past, such administrative discretion was exercised in the granting of "extended voluntary departure" (EVD), which could be conferred on individuals or groups.

Apart from the use of DED for Salvadorans, the largest group to have been granted EVD or DED status as of mid-1994 was Chinese nationals. Initially, following the events of Tiananmen Square in 1989, they were permitted to remain in the United States through June 1990 under extended voluntary departure. In April 1990 an executive order was issued permitting them to live and work under deferred enforced departure status. The numbers of people covered by these provisions were not known, but during the first three months after passage of the Chinese Student Protection Act in October 1992, some 52,000 applied for adjustment of their status.

Other groups have also been granted EVD or DED status. Extended voluntary departure status was made available to Liberians in 1990, eight months before they were granted TPS. A November 1991 executive order granted deferred enforced departure until January 1, 1996, to some 2,230 Palestinian residents of Kuwait who had been airlifted to the United States after the Iraqi invasion, and who were unable to return there after the cessation of hostilities.

In still other cases, other categories of temporary status apply. For example, some Cubans, citizens of the former Soviet Union, and Vietnamese remain in the United States under "humanitarian parole," and existing law enables Cuban "visa overstayers" to be treated more like refugees than like illegal aliens. With the exception of Vietnamese parolees, who numbered 25,000 in mid-1992, the numbers in these statuses are not known with precision, since there is a certain amount of overlap among the categories.

In the face of some large-scale population movements, alternatives to all these approaches have been sought. For example, the 1992 coup in Haiti marked the beginning of a new upsurge in asylum seekers from Haiti, which was to continue episodically for some time. Large numbers of Haitians embarked for the United States, only to be interdicted at sea and taken to Guantanamo Bay for prescreening. Of the 37,000 interviewed in 1992, 10,300 were allowed to enter the United States to file formal applications.

The Impact of Refugee and Asylee Admissions. Having detailed how the law and practice of granting asylum have evolved in the United States in response to foreign policy objectives, it remains to assess the overall impact of refugee and asylee admissions on immigration to the country. Table 2 presents the overall number of persons granted asylum by Immigration and Naturalization Service district directors and asylum officers during 1984–92. They amount to 56,626 persons, 60.6 percent of whom originated in just two countries, Nicaragua and Iran, both of which were at the core of major foreign policy initiatives by the United States during the 1980s.

In the case of Nicaragua, the explicit engagement of the United States in supporting the "freedom fighters," whose aim was to depose the Communist government of Nicaragua, served both to trigger refugee flows and to provide a rationale for admitting Nicaraguans as asylees. In the case of Iran, the lingering antagonism of

TABLE 2. Number of Asylum Claims Granted by the United States
During 1984–1992 by Country or Region of Citizenship

Region or Country of Citizenship	Number	Percentage
Total	56,626	100.0
Eastern Europe	7,418	13.1
Caribbean	1,031	1.8
Central America	20,258	35.8
South America	187	0.3
Eastern Asia	1,837	3.2
Southern Asia	18,066	31.9
West Asia and North Africa	1,457	2.6
Sub-Saharan Africa	4,374	7.7
Main source countries		
Nicaragua	17,345	30.6
Iran	16,992	30.0
Poland	3,380	6.0
Ethiopia	3,214	5.7
Romania	2,052	3.6
El Salvador	1,908	3.4
China	1,683	3.0
Soviet Union	1,143	2.0
Cuba	883	1.6
Somalia	737	1.3
Afghanistan	708	1.3
Panama	622	1.1

Source: United States (1993), table 29.

the United States toward the Khomeini regime served to validate
the granting of asylum to Iranians already present in the United
States. Among the other important sources of asylees, Communist
countries predominated together with a few, such as El Salvador
or Panama, whose regimes were friendly to the United States and
depended on its assistance to maintain power.

Overall, however, the number of asylees was low and represented scarcely 1 percent of all immigrants admitted during

1984–92 (excluding those regularized under IRCA). Thus the effect of U.S. foreign policy in terms of persons actually granted asylum was minimal. There were, however, over 150,000 asylum applicants whose claims were adjudicated but rejected, and more than 400,000 whose applications were received but not adjudicated. Many of them ended up staying in the United States as undocumented migrants or, as in the case of Salvadorans and others discussed above, were granted the permission to stay only temporarily. Thus foreign policy resulted in a substantial increase in the number of migrants whose legal status in the United States remains precarious until final disposition of their cases.

With respect to overall refugee migration, Table 3 summarizes the trend in the number of refugees and asylees granted permanent residence status during 1946–92 by region of birth. As already noted, three regions have been the main sources of refugees admitted by the United States: Eastern Europe, the Caribbean and Central America, and East Asia.

Within each region, certain source countries have tended to dominate refugee flows during particular periods (see Table 4). On the whole, the total number of refugees granted immigrant status has been low in comparison to general immigration: the 2.7 million refugees account for only 14.6 percent of the 18.7 million permanent immigrants admitted during 1946–92 (a number that excludes persons legalized under IRCA). Indeed, the total number of refugees granted immigrant status over a span of forty-six years is comparable to the 2.6 million persons who regularized their status during 1989–92 as a result of IRCA. From that perspective, it can be argued that the direct immigration burden imposed on the United States by its foreign policy has been modest.

Because of their selectivity, however, refugee admissions have had implications that go beyond the mere numbers admitted. The half-million Vietnamese or Cuban refugees who have become immigrants as a result of refugee admissions constitute the core of transnational communities capable of exerting both direct and indirect pressure on further immigration from their countries of origin. Given that family reunification is the cornerstone of immigration policy in the United States, it can be and has been used to expand such communities further. That is, through the "immigra-

TABLE 3. Refugees and Asylees Granted Lawful Permanent Resident Status by the United States, 1946–1992

Region of Birth	Total	1946–1950	1951–1960	1961–1970	1971–1980	1981–1990	1991–1992
Total	2,727,744	213,347	492,371	212,843	539,447	1,013,620	256,116
Europe	1,056,401	211,983	456,146	55,235	71,858	155,512	105,667
Western Europe	246,933	42,342	181,804	11,291	6,498	3,848	1,150
Eastern Europe	798,880	168,559	266,655	43,166	64,978	151,123	104,399
Asia	1,080,382	1,106	33,422	19,895	210,683	712,092	103,184
Eastern Asia	951,854	322	28,273	16,984	198,507	623,199	84,569
Southern Asia	86,784	118	193	58	906	69,719	15,790
Western Asia and North Africa	34,993	615	3,030	7,387	10,853	12,007	1,101
Sub-Saharan Africa	32,898	12	414	90	1,518	21,723	9,141
Caribbean and Central America	544,814	163	831	132,068	252,633	121,840	37,279
South America	4,211	32	74	123	1,244	1,976	762
Oceania	172	7	75	21	37	22	10
Not stated	139	36	55	15	1	29	3

TABLE 3. *(Continued)*
Percentage

Region of Birth	Total	1946-1950	1951-1960	1961-1970	1971-1980	1981-1990	1991-1992
Western Europe	9.1	19.8	36.9	5.3	1.2	0.4	0.4
Eastern Europe	29.3	79.0	54.2	20.3	12.0	14.9	40.8
Caribbean and Central America	20.0	0.1	0.2	62.0	46.8	12.0	14.6
Eastern Asia	34.9	0.2	5.7	8.0	36.8	61.5	33.0
Southern Asia	3.2	0.1	0.0	0.0	0.2	6.9	6.2
Western Asia and North Africa	1.3	0.3	0.6	3.5	2.0	1.2	0.4
Sub-Saharan Africa	1.2	0.0	0.1	0.0	0.3	2.1	3.6

Source: United States (1993), table 33.

TABLE 4. Main Countries of Origin of Refugees and Asylees in the United States, 1946–1992

Country of Birth	Total	1946–1950	1951–1960	1961–1970	1971–1980	1981–1990	1991–1992
Total	2,727,744	213,347	492,371	212,843	539,447	1,013,620	256,116
Vietnam	528,426	—	2	7	150,266	324,453	53,698
Cuba	514,319	3	6	131,557	251,514	113,367	17,872
Soviet Union	233,672	14,072	30,059	871	31,309	72,306	85,055
Poland	208,537	78,529	81,323	3,197	5,882	33,889	5,717
Laos	181,807	—	—	—	21,690	142,964	17,153
Cambodia	126,048	—	—	—	7,739	114,064	4,245
Germany	101,460	36,633	62,860	665	143	851	308
Yugoslavia	84,615	9,816	44,755	18,299	11,297	324	124
Hungary	76,216	6,086	55,740	4,044	4,358	4,942	1,046
Romania	69,252	4,180	12,057	7,158	6,812	29,798	9,247
Italy	63,548	642	60,657	1,198	346	394	311
Iran	59,113	118	192	58	364	46,773	11,608
China[a]	40,842	319	12,008	5,308	13,760	7,928	1,519
Thailand	39,179	—	15	13	1,241	30,259	7,651
Latvia	38,667	21,422	16,783	49	16	48	349
Czechoslovakia	37,705	8,449	10,719	5,709	3,646	8,204	978
Greece	31,319	124	28,568	586	478	1,408	155
Afghanistan	27,671	—	1	—	542	22,946	4,182
Lithuania	27,627	18,694	8,569	72	23	37	232
Ethiopia	26,762	—	61	2	1,307	18,542	6,850

TABLE 4. (*Continued*)

Percentages

Country of Birth	Total	1946–1950	1951–1960	1961–1970	1971–1980	1981–1990	1991–1992
Vietnam	19.4	0.0	0.0	0.0	27.9	32.0	21.0
Cuba	18.9	0.0	0.0	61.8	46.6	11.2	7.0
Soviet Union	8.6	6.6	6.1	0.4	5.8	7.1	33.2
Poland	7.6	36.8	16.5	1.5	1.1	3.3	2.2
Laos	6.7	0.0	0.0	0.0	4.0	14.1	6.7
Cambodia	4.6	0.0	0.0	0.0	1.4	11.3	1.7
Germany	3.7	17.2	12.8	0.3	0.0	0.1	0.1
Yugoslavia	3.1	4.6	9.1	8.6	2.1	0.0	0.0
Hungary	2.8	2.9	11.3	1.9	0.8	0.5	0.4
Romania	2.5	2.0	2.4	3.4	1.3	2.9	3.6
Italy	2.3	0.3	12.3	0.6	0.1	0.0	0.1
Iran	2.2	0.1	0.0	0.0	0.1	4.6	4.5
China[a]	1.5	0.1	2.4	2.5	2.6	0.8	0.6
Thailand	1.4	0.0	0.0	0.0	0.2	3.0	3.0
Latvia	1.4	10.0	3.4	0.0	0.0	0.0	0.1
Czechoslovakia	1.4	4.0	2.2	2.7	0.7	0.8	0.4
Greece	1.1	0.1	5.8	0.3	0.1	0.1	0.1
Afghanistan	1.0	0.0	0.0	0.0	0.1	2.3	1.6
Lithuania	1.0	8.8	1.7	0.0	0.0	0.0	0.1
Ethiopia	1.0	0.0	0.0	0.0	0.2	1.8	2.7

Source: United States (1993), table 33.
[a] Includes Mainland China and Taiwan

tion multiplier factor," refugee admissions have led to the diversification of immigration in ways that might not have materialized in the absence of particular U.S. foreign policy interests.

Foreign Policy and General Immigration

Historical Experience. Despite being a "nation of immigrants," the United States has exercised considerable selectivity in determining who can be admitted as a future citizen.[7] Thus, although during the nineteenth century there was no comprehensive federal legislation to control immigration directly, the desire to maintain the homogeneity of American society led to a series of federal laws that excluded certain groups from immigration. Perhaps the most important was the Chinese Exclusion Act of 1882 that suspended the immigration of Chinese laborers, provided for the deportation of Chinese citizens who were illegally present in the United States, and barred the Chinese from naturalization. The Chinese exclusion laws were repealed only in 1943 when the United States had an interest in fostering cordial relations with China, a major ally during the Second World War.

The exclusionary sentiments reflected in the 1882 act increased during the following decades, culminating with the Immigration Act of 1917 that restricted the immigration of Asian persons, thus creating the "barred zone," known as the Asia-Pacific triangle, natives of which were declared inadmissible. The Quota Law of 1921 further restricted the admission of certain nationalities by limiting the number of aliens entering the United States to 3 percent of the foreign-born persons of that nationality present in the United States as of 1910.

However, the Quota Law exempted from limitation aliens who were residents of the independent countries of the Western Hemisphere, which comprised the Americas. The special treatment accorded to the Western Hemisphere derived both from its role as source of cheap and easily accessible labor for the United States, and from the U.S. foreign policy aim of maintaining "good neighbor" relations with the countries in its vicinity. Such policy was congruent with the view that the United States had first claim on the Americas as a focus of capitalist expansion and an area of strategic importance.

After the Second World War, opposition to the quota system mounted, but it was not sufficient to eliminate quotas from the act of 1952. However, the 1952 act abandoned the Asian barred zone and provided a limited number of immigrant slots for persons of Asian descent. Although racist considerations prevented the further expansion of immigration quotas for Asia, the indirect effects of foreign policy made more people from that region eligible for immigration.

In particular, a series of acts allowing the immigration of the foreign wives of U.S. servicemen as well as the Chinese wives of U.S. citizens opened the door for the admission of women from Asian countries where American troops were stationed. As Table 5 indicates, the changes introduced by the 1952 Immigration Act and other legislation adopted before 1965 led to a significant increase in immigration from China, Japan, and the Philippines, so that all three countries began appearing among the major sources of immigrants to the United States during the late 1950s and early 1960s. American troops were stationed in Japan as a result of the 1951 Treaty of Peace, and the U.S. government signed in 1947 a ninety-nine-year arrangement for the use of military bases in the Philippines that led to the long-term presence of American troops in that former colony. The strategic interests of the United States were consistent with maintaining close ties with certain Asian countries, most of which became major sources of immigrants.

Legislatively, it was the Immigration and Nationality Act of 1965 that, by abolishing the national origins quota system, opened the door for increased immigration from Asian countries. By establishing preference categories as the basis of immigrant admission and making family reunification a cornerstone of the selection process, the act allowed the development of immigrant "networks"—ties of kin and other relations that promoted continuing and often growing migratory movements. The communities of Chinese and Filipinos that had become established in the United States before 1965 expanded rapidly. During 1965–69, China and the Philippines became the seventh and eighth major sources of immigrants to the United States. Between 1970 and 1991 the

TABLE 5. Main Countries of Birth of the Average Annual Number of Immigrants Admitted by the United States by Period of Admission and Main Countries of Birth of Immigrants Legalized through IRCA

Country of Birth	1946–1955	Cumulative Percentage	Country of Birth	1956–1960	Cumulative Percentage
Germany	26,161	13.4	Mexico	39,332	13.8
Canada	23,087	25.2	Germany	35,791	26.3
United Kingdom	20,560	35.8	Canada	29,373	36.6
Poland	18,303	45.1	United Kingdom	24,472	45.2
Mexico	16,078	53.4	Italy	22,903	53.2
Italy	12,872	60.0	Cuba	11,114	57.1
U.S.S.R.	5,095	62.6	Hungary	9,981	60.6
Ireland	4,997	65.1	Poland	8,507	63.5
Yugoslavia	4,427	67.4	Ireland	8,210	66.4
France	3,969	69.5	Netherlands	6,067	68.5
Latvia	3,838	71.4	Japan	5,961	70.6
Czechoslovakia	3,376	73.1	Yugoslavia	5,583	72.6
Netherlands	3,016	74.7	Greece	5,373	74.5
Greece	2,917	76.2	China, People's Republic of	4,498	76.0
Total	195,173	100	Total	285,568	100

TABLE 5. *(Continued)*

Country of Birth	1961–1964	Cumulative Percentage	Country of Birth	1965–1969	Cumulative Percentage
Mexico	46,286	16.0	Mexico	42,738	11.9
Canada	34,123	27.9	Cuba	36,700	22.1
Germany	26,691	37.1	Canada	27,274	29.7
United Kingdom	24,733	45.7	United Kingdom	23,473	36.3
Italy	17,982	51.9	Italy	21,950	42.4
Cuba	14,234	56.9	Germany	16,707	47.0
Poland	8,952	60.0	China, People's Republic of	13,142	50.7
Dominican Republic	6,467	62.2	Philippines	11,513	53.9
Ireland	6,128	64.4	Dominican Republic	11,488	57.1
Colombia	6,032	66.4	Greece	11,389	60.3
Argentina	4,579	68.0	Portugal	10,677	63.3
China, People's Republic of	4,224	69.5	Jamaica	9,896	66.0
Greece	4,207	71.0	Colombia	7,895	68.2
Japan	3,987	72.3	Poland	6,778	70.1
France	3,936	73.7	Yugoslavia	5,615	71.7
Netherlands	3,858	75.0	Haiti	4,865	73.0
Philippines	3,200	76.1	Argentina	4,076	74.2
			Ecuador	3,994	75.3
			Hong Kong	3,818	76.3
Total	288,404	100	Total	358,947	100

TABLE 5. *(Continued)*

Country of Birth	1970–1974	Cumulative Percentage	Country of Birth	1975–1979	Cumulative Percentage
Mexico	60,068	15.6	Mexico	61,831	13.5
Philippines	30,541	23.6	Philippines	37,409	21.6
Italy	21,314	29.1	Cuba	33,714	28.9
Cuba	20,213	34.3	Korea, Republic of	29,620	35.4
Korea, Republic of	18,689	39.2	Vietnam	23,426	40.5
China, People's Republic of	16,240	43.4	China, People's Republic of	20,521	44.9
India	13,451	46.9	India	18,458	49.0
Jamaica	13,080	50.3	Dominican Republic	14,816	52.2
Greece	13,000	53.7	Jamaica	13,839	55.2
Dominican Republic	12,758	57.0	United Kingdom	12,542	57.9
Portugal	11,457	60.0	Canada	11,567	60.4
United Kingdom	11,274	62.9	Portugal	9,994	62.6
Canada	10,863	65.8	Colombia	8,302	64.4
Germany	7,394	67.7	Italy	8,203	66.2
Trinidad and Tobago	6,929	69.5	Greece	7,716	67.9
Yugoslavia	6,792	71.2	Germany	6,116	69.2
Colombia	5,881	72.8	Haiti	5,749	70.4
Haiti	5,783	74.3	Trinidad and Tobago	5,586	71.7
Japan	4,804	75.5	U.S.S.R.	5,455	72.8
Ecuador	4,532	76.7	Guyana	5,333	74.0
			Hong Kong	5,154	75.1
			Ecuador	4,910	76.2
Total	384,683	100	Total	459,541	100

TABLE 5. *(Continued)*

Country of Birth	1980–1984	Cumulative Percentage	Country of Birth	1985–1989	Cumulative Percentage
Mexico	66,138	11.7	Mexico	72,289	11.9
Vietnam	49,293	20.4	Philippines	50,208	20.2
Philippines	43,101	28.1	Korea, Republic of	34,760	26.0
Korea, Republic of	32,618	33.8	Vietnam	29,896	30.9
China, People's Republic of	25,939	38.4	India	26,968	35.4
India	23,256	42.5	China, People's Republic of	26,388	39.7
Lao People's Republic	20,449	46.2	Dominican Republic	25,526	43.9
Jamaica	20,121	49.7	Cuba	21,977	47.6
Dominican Republic	19,624	53.2	Jamaica	20,925	51.0
United Kingdom	14,760	55.8	Haiti	16,431	53.7
Cambodia	11,793	57.9	Iran	15,881	56.3
Canada	11,553	59.9	United Kingdom	13,336	58.5
Iran	11,360	61.9	Taiwan	12,478	60.6
Cuba	10,740	63.8	El Salvador	11,482	62.5
Colombia	10,182	65.6	Canada	11,340	64.4
U.S.S.R.	9,306	67.3	Colombia	11,198	66.2
Guyana	8,515	68.8	Cambodia	11,044	68.0
Haiti	8,053	70.2	Guyana	9,801	69.7
Taiwan	7,812	71.6	Lao People's Republic	9,387	71.2
El Salvador	7,760	73.0	Poland	8,916	72.7
Germany, Fed. Rep. of	6,617	74.2	Germany, Fed. Rep. of	6,893	73.8

TABLE 5. (Continued)

Country of Birth	1980–1984	Cumulative Percentage	Country of Birth	1985–1989	Cumulative Percentage
Poland	6,301	75.3	Thailand	6,524	74.9
Portugal	5,195	76.2	Hong Kong	6,421	76.0
Total	565,007	100	Total	605,674	100

Country of Birth	1990–1991	Cumulative Percentage	Country of Birth	IRCA	Cumulative Percentage
Philippines	55,142	8.1	Mexico	1,854,547	74.7
Mexico	54,708	16.2	El Salvador	146,383	80.6
Vietnam	51,970	23.8	Guatemala	59,863	83.0
U.S.S.R.	41,095	29.8	Haiti	47,611	84.9
Dominican Republic	31,121	34.4	Colombia	29,020	86.1
China, People's Republic of	30,223	38.9	Philippines	24,354	87.1
India	29,922	43.3	Dominican Republic	22,460	88.0
Korea, Republic of	25,588	47.0	India	18,545	88.7
Jamaica	18,427	49.7	Peru	16,564	89.4
Iran	18,025	52.4	Pakistan	15,774	90.0
Poland	14,973	54.6	Poland	15,282	90.7
United Kingdom	13,269	56.5	Honduras	15,053	91.3
Taiwan	13,194	58.5	Nicaragua	14,722	91.9
Canada	12,959	60.4	Jamaica	14,520	92.4
El Salvador	12,717	62.2	Ecuador	14,118	93.0
Haiti	12,099	64.0	Nigeria	13,593	93.6
Cuba	10,334	65.5	Iran	12,584	94.1
Guyana	10,184	67.0	Korea, Republic of	9,647	94.5

TABLE 5. *(Continued)*

Country of Birth	1990–1991	Cumulative Percentage	Country of Birth	IRCA	Cumulative Percentage
Lao People's Republic	10,152	68.5	China, People's Republic of	9,178	94.8
Nicaragua	9,829	70.0	Ghana	6,087	95.1
Colombia	9,754	71.4	Canada	5,932	95.3
Hong Kong	9,342	72.8			
Peru	8,908	74.1	Total	2,482,348	100
Pakistan	8,027	75.3			
Ireland	6,993	76.3			
Total	680,058	100			

Source: Zlotnik (forthcoming), table 3.

Philippines consistently ranked among the first three sources of immigrants, and China occupied fourth or fifth place. Both countries have major strategic importance for the United States. Similarly, immigration from the Republic of Korea to the United States intensified during the 1970s and contributed to strengthening the ties between the two countries, which have important economic and security interests in common.

Immigration from the Western Hemisphere. Among the developing countries that have been major sources of immigrants to the United States, those in the Western Hemisphere deserve attention, since the United States has traditionally had special foreign policy interests regarding that region of the world. As already noted, the exclusion of the Western Hemisphere from the quota system led to the early expansion of migration from the region, especially that originating in Canada and Mexico. Indeed, after the passage of the 1952 act, Mexico became the major source of immigrants to the United States, a position that it maintained until the late 1980s. Although the introduction of per-country limits on Western Hemisphere migration established by the act of 1976 effectively slowed down the expansion of Mexican immigration, it did not stop its growth. Furthermore, the push of Mexico's prolonged period of economic recession, which started in the late 1970s, combined with the pull exerted by its northern neighbor, resulted in high levels of undocumented migration.

The 1986 legislation that was eventually passed to control undocumented migration was not advocated on the basis of foreign policy interests, but it was clear to those discussing the bill that regularizing the status of Mexican undocumented migrants would contribute to maintaining the stability of their southern neighbor. Taking into account the results of the regularization of undocumented migrants, Mexico has been the source of nearly 4.3 million immigrants to the United States during 1946–92. That number surpasses by about 1.5 million the total number of refugees admitted during the period; it is four times the number of immigrants from Indochina and five times that of immigrants from Cuba. Thus while immigration from Mexico may not be explicitly linked to foreign policy considerations, it has major implications for the relations between Mexico and the United States that, despite the reluctance of the parties involved, may at some point engage foreign policy interests in a more direct manner.

This is not to suggest that the numbers of regular immigrants to the United States alone determine the foreign policy significance of population movements in the Western Hemisphere. In the cases of Cuba and Haiti, proximity, coupled with volatile outflows of people, has put these countries front and center among direct U.S. foreign policy concerns, although (as may be seen in Table 5) the levels of immigrant admissions from these countries have been relatively modest compared with those from Mexico.

Transnational Communities and Their Effect on Immigration

Immigration has led to the creation of transnational communities, a number of which have been successful in maintaining a distinct identity and in organizing to pursue what are perceived to be the community's interests. Since the passage of the 1965 Immigration and Nationality Act, family reunification has been a means of expanding transnational communities and developing migration networks. When the number of family groups straddling two countries is large, the likelihood that those abroad may exert influence in the home country increases. Modern communications facilitate exchanges and coordinated action.

The influence exerted by transnational communities in shaping the foreign policy aspects of immigration has a long history.[8] Thus after the Second World War, American Jews formed the Citizens' Committee on Displaced Persons to pressure the U.S. Congress for legislation allowing the resettlement of Holocaust survivors in the United States. Since then, Jewish groups have consistently lobbied for the admission of Jews leaving Communist countries, particularly those originating in the Soviet Union. Because the emigration of minorities from the Soviet Union was used as a bargaining chip between the superpowers during the cold war, Jewish groups favoring increased Jewish emigration from the USSR necessarily had to grapple with other foreign policy issues. In particular, the interests of Israel as a potential receiver of Soviet Jews had to be accommodated.

During the 1970s the number of Jews emigrating from the Soviet Union reached nearly 250,000 as a result of the detente then reigning between the superpowers. Of those emigrants, about 150,000 settled in Israel and 64,000 in the United States. During the 1980s Jewish emigration decreased to 117,000, with 29,000 settling in Israel and 79,000 in the United States. Then, as restrictions on emigration were dropped by the disintegrating Soviet Union, the number of Jewish emigrants soared to reach nearly 400,000 in 1990–91. Although the U.S. Jewish community was successful in its efforts to have the number of slots for Soviet refugees increased over the previous levels, the sheer numbers of Jews permitted to emigrate, coupled with the relative ease of obtaining a visa for Israel, and the institution of more direct air and land transport routes resulted in most Jewish emigrants—333,000— going to Israel; 66,000 went to the United States. The increase in numbers going to Israel had long been urged by the Israeli government and was supported by at least part of the U.S. Jewish community.

The Cuban community has also been fairly successful in influencing U.S. foreign policy. Although the number of persons of Cuban origin in the United States is relatively small, amounting to about 1 million in 1990, their influence has been disproportionate because of the particular circumstances in which the community was formed. Indeed, the first waves of Cuban refugees consisted largely of elements strongly opposed to the Castro regime. That stance suited U.S. interests well, since the establishment of a Communist regime in the immediate vicinity of the United States was seen as a major threat. During the 1960s overthrow of the Castro government was a major U.S. foreign policy preoccupation. As of 1994 U.S. policy still considered the Cuban government as an enemy whose isolation must be maintained—a view largely shared by the Cuban-American community. Nevertheless, because many Cubans in the United States still have relatives in Cuba, they have generally supported the admission of those who, over the years, have managed to leave the island.

Until the Cuban government began allowing large numbers of people to flee the country by boat in 1994, both the U.S. government and the Cuban-American community tended to regard the emigration of Cubans as an indictment of the Cuban government that deserved to be supported. In 1994, however, faced with increasing numbers of boat people, the Clinton administration decided to change the longstanding policy of admitting Cubans to the United States with virtually automatic adjustment to permanent resident alien status. It was expected that by interdicting Cubans at sea and keeping them away from U.S. territory, the outflow might be stemmed and either repatriation or admission by third countries might be possible for those held in the U.S. base at Guantanamo Bay. In the event, the outflow of "boat people" was stemmed only after the U.S. government negotiated with Cuban authorities and succeeded in obtaining their cooperation in stopping people from leaving Cuba in unsafe craft in exchange for an assured number of immigration slots.

Persons reporting some Irish ancestry constitute one of the largest groups in the United States, numbering nearly 23 million in 1990. However, only 270,000 of them were immigrants. Given that Ireland is still a country where economic opportunities are in short supply and where the population is growing, the Irish community in the United States has successfully lobbied for an increase in the immigration slots allotted to Irish citizens. The fact that a prestigious politician of Irish descent played a key role in putting together the Immigration Act of 1990 helped the cause; Senator Kennedy supported the creation of 55,000 slots for "diversity immigrants," and it was understood that a substantial proportion of these would be reserved for Irish citizens. Although Irish immigration to the United States does not have the same foreign policy relevance as that of Soviet Jews or Cubans, it nevertheless has been a factor in the U.S. stance toward the ongoing conflict in Northern Ireland.

These examples indicate that, especially when migrant communities originate in countries of strategic interest to the United States, they may eventually play a role in shaping the policy adopted by the latter, be it with respect to further immigration or with respect to general relations with the country concerned. The size of the community is not the main factor determining its influence. If its interests are congruent with general U.S. policy, it is likely to be effective even if it does not command a large population.

U.S. Foreign Policy as a Determinant of Migration to Other Countries

Until relatively recently, the analysis of U.S. foreign policy in relation to international migration usually focused on the number of refugees admitted by the United States and the reasons for their admission. There was less emphasis on the degree to which U.S. foreign policy itself contributed to outflows of refugees around the world. While there is a wider acceptance today of the notion that U.S. foreign policy can itself be the cause of refugee flows or contribute to them, the analysis of the elements of foreign policy most likely to produce refugees remains in its infancy.[9]

There was a high correlation between refugee-producing situations and superpower involvement during the cold war era, but it cannot therefore be assumed that there would have been no refugee flows had the superpowers remained on the sidelines. Indeed, since the end of the cold war, multiple conflicts have produced large numbers of refugees without the benefit of superpower involvement, and in some cases the resolution of the conflicts concerned seems less tractable precisely because of the vacuum left by the end of cold war competition between traditional power brokers.

Indochina

At the peak of superpower confrontation, U.S. actions were clearly crucial in eliciting or even maintaining refugee outflows. The best example is probably the case of Vietnam and, more generally, that of Indochina. After the fall of Saigon in 1975, U.S. policy was to isolate Vietnam from the world community. Although the Carter administration made attempts to normalize relations with Vietnam, these failed because of the issue of war reparations. After an initial outflow of about 130,000 Vietnamese refugees during 1975, 1976 witnessed the departure of only 5,000.

However, tensions between China and Vietnam led to further outflows in 1977 that kept on growing as Vietnam declared war on the Khmer Rouge governing in neighboring Cambodia in 1978. By then, the United States was pursuing a rapprochement with China, Vietnam's enemy. In an effort to further isolate Vietnam, the United States supported non-Communist guerrilla forces in Cambodia that were allied to the Khmer Rouge. War and dire economic conditions fueled further refugee outflows.

Refugees from Cambodia, Laos, and Vietnam fled to neighboring countries that, in turn, exerted pressure on the United States to "solve" the refugee problem. Until 1989 resettlement outside the region was the solution of choice. Between 1975 and 1988 nearly 1.5 million Indochinese refugees were resettled abroad, 1.15 million in developed countries, 700,000 in the United States. The United States was fairly successful in eliciting the support of other Western countries in the resettlement effort, although such support was officially orchestrated by the international community through the activities of the United Nations High Commissioner for Refugees (UNHCR).

The subsequent large outflows of Indochinese "boat people" that began in 1988, and their dramatic "pushback" from the shores of Malaysia and Thailand, prompted a new international response. With institution of the Comprehensive Plan of Action (CPA) in 1989, resettlement of bona fide refugees continued, but the new asylum seekers, many of whom were believed to be economically motivated, were no longer granted blanket admission to asylum countries in the region, or nearly automatic resettlement in third countries. Those "screened out" through newly introduced individual asylum determination procedures were to be repatriated—voluntarily or forcibly if necessary. By the end of 1993, new outflows had virtually ceased.

Central America

Another clearcut case where U.S. involvement led to population displacement and refugee outflows was that of Central America. Under the Reagan doctrine, the United States openly supported freedom fighters attempting to overthrow Marxist-Leninist regimes in developing countries. Support was especially strong for the Contras who opposed the Sandinista regime in Nicaragua. As a result, between 500,000 and 1 million people were uprooted, and Nicaraguans fled their country in substantial numbers, although many were not officially recognized as refugees.

The United States further supported the repressive regimes of El Salvador and Guatemala, whose gross violations of human rights and pursuit of low-intensity conflict, together with continued poor economic conditions, resulted in the further displacement of large populations—in the case of El Salvador, more than 1 million people, or nearly one-quarter of the country's total population. While the majority fleeing these conflicts went to the United States, as of early 1990 there were an estimated 1.2 million refugees and displaced persons in Central America and Mexico. With the change of government in Nicaragua and the successful unfolding of the peace process in the region, that number tended to decline during subsequent years (see Table 6). However, refugee statistics fail to reflect the many people who were displaced within their own countries, as well as those who became undocumented migrants, especially in Mexico and the United States.

Indirect Effects of U.S. Policies

In other cases, the United States was not the first power to intervene, and its actions, although fostering refugee outflows, were not the principal cause of those flows. That was the case in Afghanistan, where the government was overthrown by a successful Communist coup in 1978. In 1979, to protect the newly established regime, the Soviet Union occupied the country, thus triggering the largest outflow of refugees from a single country in recent times. By early 1985 there were 4.3 million Afghan refugees in Iran and Pakistan.

Although the United States did not intervene directly in Afghanistan, it provided aid to Pakistan and helped arm the mujahedeen rebel groups operating from that country. Between 1982 and 1991 the United States provided $2 billion in military and other aid to the Afghan fighters. The Soviet Union withdrew its troops from Afghanistan late in 1988 and early in 1989 following the

TABLE 6. Refugees in Central America and Mexico by Country of Asylum, 1982–1993

Country of Asylum	Early 1982	Early 1985	Early 1990		Early 1991		Early 1993
			Refugees and Displaced Persons	Refugees Receiving UNHCR Assistance	Refugees and Displaced Persons	Refugees Receiving UNHCR Assistance	
Belize	7,000	3,000	30,100	4,863		5,450	20,400
Costa Rica	15,000	16,800	278,600	32,000	278,000	42,334	114,400
El Salvador			20,300	201		560	19,900
Guatemala	50,000	70,000	223,000	4,948		5,400	222,900
Honduras	29,000	47,800	237,000	34,666		2,069	100,100
Mexico	146,000	175,000	356,400	47,000	340,000	48,626	361,000
Nicaragua	22,500	18,500	16,230	1,000	16,000	7,392	14,500
Panama	1,500	1,100	1,400	1,138		342	1,000
Total	271,000	332,200	1,163,030	125,816	634,000	112,173	854,200

Sources: Office of the United Nations High Commissioner for Refugees, Refugee Map 30, June 1982; Office of the United Nations High Commissioner for Refugees, "Report on UNHCR assistance activities in 1984–1985 and proposed voluntary fund programmes and budget for 1985" (A/AC.96.657); Office of the United Nations High Commissioner for Refugees, "UNHCR activities financed by voluntary funds: report for 1989–1990 and proposed programmes and budget for 1991" (A/AC.96/751, part IV); Office of the United Nations High Commissioner for Refugees, "UNHCR activities financed by voluntary funds: report for 1990–1991 and proposed programmes and budget for 1992" (A/AC.96/774, part IV); United Nations High Commissioner for Refugees, *The State of the World's Refugees,* 1993, pp. 152–153.
NOTE: According to sources at the Office of the United Nations High Commissioner for Refugees, the figures presented here are provided mainly by governments of asylum countries based on their own records and methods of estimation.

1988 Geneva Accords, but fighting between the mujahedeen and forces of the Najibullah regime continued. The United States failed in its efforts to bring about a negotiated settlement and continued arming the mujahedeen until Najibullah's overthrow in 1992. Although the repatriation of nearly 1.8 million Afghan refugees took place in that year, continued fighting between rival mujahedeen groups within Afghanistan has led to further refugee outflows.

These cases illustrate the variety of ways in which U.S. foreign policy can lead to refugee flows to other countries or exacerbate them. Although far from comprehensive, they nevertheless show that U.S. foreign policy is far more likely to have affected in major ways the international migration flows directed to other countries than those to the United States itself. Not only have these consequences of foreign policy been ignored for too long, but the fact that they are largely considered as the inevitable costs of maintaining power reveals a large gap in international law: it does not address the standards that ought to guide the relations between one nation-state and the citizens of another.

International Migration Flows that Trigger a U.S. Foreign Policy Response

As already noted, the end of the cold war has brought about an inflow of asylum seekers to Western European countries that has prompted the search for a unified response to such developments. In addition, the end of the bipolar confrontation in the developing world has in some instances led to the resolution of longstanding conflicts and to important refugee repatriations. In others, however, the vacuum left by the withdrawal of superpower involvement has led to serious internal conflicts that have tended to produce major refugee outflows. In this context, the United States has been confronted with the necessity of developing appropriate responses to emerging conflicts and of forging new relationships with its allies and with the United Nations, a process that may significantly change the context of U.S. foreign policy.

The Gulf Crisis and Iraq

The first test of the changing United States role in the new international context was its involvement in the 1990–91 Gulf War. The war itself caused significant population displacement and prompted changes in the policies of countries in the region toward the admission of certain migrant workers, as well as the forced repatriation of many.[10] In addition, the defeat of Iraq prompted the Kurdish uprising and Shiite revolt within that country, which led to major population displacements.

Indeed, immediately following the liberation of Kuwait in February 1991, the locus of armed hostilities shifted to Iraq itself; as a result, some 1.4 million Iraqi Kurds and Shiites moved into Iran and another 350,000 to 400,000 Iraqi Kurds moved toward the border with Turkey. Most of the Iraqis in Iran returned home during July and August 1991, but those intending to reach Turkey were stopped at the border and triggered an unprecedented response by the international community led by the United States. Having problems with its own Kurdish minority, Turkey was loathe to provide safe haven to Iraqi refugees. Instead it closed its border and called upon the United States to provide protection to Iraqi Kurds within Iraq.

Largely in response to a U.S. initiative, on April 5, 1991, the United Nations Security Council took an unprecedented step by adopting Resolution 688 in which it demanded that Iraq end the suppression of its civilian population and permit international assistance to those in need within its territory. U.S. forces were then called upon to lead a coalition of forces in an operation that would create a "safe area" in northern Iraq and thus ensure the delivery of emergency assistance to the affected population. This was the first instance in which refugee flows had been averted by the "internationalization" of population displacement. Although on April 18 the United Nations and the government of Iraq signed a Memorandum of Understanding permitting the United Nations to provide humanitarian assistance inside Iraq, the creation of safe havens with military aid from abroad had been carried out without acquiescence of the government of Iraq.

These developments launched a new era in which state sovereignty would no longer be supreme. Through Resolution 688, the international community validated the need to intervene when a state takes concerted action against its own citizens. "Humanitarian intervention" was justified not only on grounds of the threat posed to a country's own citizens, but also because of the destabilizing effects that mass population movements might have in neighboring countries.

New Contexts of U.S. Response

International efforts to "internalize" refugee movements—that is, to contain affected populations in safe areas within or near their countries of origin—continued with the dissolution of former Yugoslavia. So too did the pattern of "relief under conflict" and military involvement in humanitarian assistance that emerged in Iraq and continued with U.S. involvement in Somalia, where the breakdown of civil society in 1992 displaced at least 3 million Somalis, nearly 1 million of whom sought refuge in other countries, including Ethiopia, Kenya, Djibouti, and Yemen.

The population movements resulting from conflicts in the former Yugoslavia have been significant.[11] As of mid-1993, over two-thirds of the Bosnian population had been displaced; 1.3 million had fled the country, and the vast majority had taken refuge in the other republics of the former Yugoslavia. The largest number (390,000) were in Croatia, itself the source of some 350,000 refugees, roughly a third of whom were outside the former Yugoslavia. In addition, ethnic Albanians from Kosovo and elsewhere sought refugee abroad. Although West European governments were publicly resistant to sharing the burden of these flows, it was estimated that altogether more than 530,000 refugees from the former Yugoslavia were in European countries outside the former Yugoslavia as of mid-1992. Most of these were permitted to enter or remain under mechanisms for "temporary protection," rather than as individuals seeking asylum as "convention refugees."

As in Iraq, the situation in the former Yugoslavia presented the United States with a new set of foreign policy complexities. U.S. options, ranging from participation in airdrops of food and medical supplies (which began in March 1993) to the possibility of U.S. military intervention, had to be coordinated—both bilaterally and multilaterally—with the positions of European allies, as well as with the various United Nations bodies involved. At the same time, in the wake of the less-than-successful experience in Somalia, U.S. public enthusiasm for such measures waned.

Less dramatic population movements have also resulted in new forms of coordination between the United States and its allies, drawing the United States into ongoing discussions with European countries, along with Canada and Australia, about ways to mitigate international migration pressures. Most notably, the rapid rise in the number of asylum seekers during the late 1980s and early 1990s and the prospects of large-scale movements from the East and the South have prompted U.S. participation in a variety of fora such as the Inter-governmental Consultations on Asylum, Refugee and Migration Policies (the IGC), the Vienna Process on East-West Population Movements, and topical meetings sponsored by the Organization for Economic Cooperation and Development (OECD) and the International Organization for Migration (IOM), among others. In addition, migration has emerged as a topic on the agenda of the Conference on Security and Cooperation in Europe (CSCE). Dialogue in such arenas has focused not only on control mechanisms but on the uses of aid, trade, and foreign policies to help stem future migratory flows to industrial countries.

As noted earlier, new legislation and policy changes in a number of European countries contributed to the decline in the number of asylum seekers in Western Europe in 1993, with the largest decreases being recorded by Germany and Sweden. Significant declines continued in the majority of European countries (with the exception of the Netherlands) during the first quarter of 1994, leading to perhaps premature and overly optimistic speculation that Europe's "asylum crisis" was over.

As the asylum crisis subsided, concerns mounted over irregular and illegal migration into Central and Eastern Europe, and the topic became a renewed focus of cooperation among industrial countries. An IOM study of these flows in 1993 reported at least 100,000 "transit migrants" in Poland, notably from the former

Soviet Union, Romania, and Bulgaria; between 100,000 and 140,000 in the Czech Republic; between 30,000 and 50,000 in Bulgaria; and 42,000 in Romania.

International Migration as a Security Issue

As Myron Weiner has argued in his 1993 volume, *International Migration and Security,* international population movements can be a perceived or actual security threat in a number of circumstances: when refugees or migrants actively oppose the regime of their home country; when they pose a security risk to the regime of the host country; when they are seen as a cultural threat or a social and economic problem for the host country; or when the host country holds migrants hostage in order to threaten their country of origin.

A number of the population movements already discussed fall into these categories. In addition, there are new or emerging international flows that have the potential to pose security threats. The former Soviet Union and China are two cases in point.

The Former Soviet Union

Emigration from the former Soviet Union—or the lack of it—was a major concern of U.S. foreign policy during the cold war era. For most of this century, the USSR imposed exit restrictions that effectively limited the emigration of its citizens, and most of these were from selected ethnic or religious groups (Jews, Germans, Armenians, Greeks, Evangelicals, and Pentacostals) with external "homelands" ready to receive them or powerful states ready to intercede on their behalf. Emigration levels have fluctuated with the tenor of East-West relations. Between 1948 and 1970, only about 60,000 people emigrated. Detente led to average annual outflows of some 35,000 during the 1970s, before revival of the cold war reduced these levels to roughly 7,300 annually between 1981 and 1986. With *perestroika* and *glasnost,* emigration again rose to an annual average of 100,000 in 1987–89. Relaxation of exit restrictions in 1989 led to significant outflows in 1990, estimated at between 377,000 and 452,000.[12]

The dissolution of the former Soviet Union has brought to the fore significant sources of potential and actual instability that are of central interest to U.S. foreign policy. In these, population movements—formerly "internal," now international—figure as both causes and consequences. According to an April 1994 study by the Inter-governmental Consultations, all but three of the twenty-three borders dividing the republics of the Newly Independent States (NIS) have a history of being contested; there were already at least eighty reported ethnically related territorial disputes, and possibly more to come, among ethnic groups officially recorded to number at least 128 and estimated by ethnographers to be several hundred. Military confrontation between Armenia and Azerbaijan displaced more than 1 million persons, while fighting in Georgia, Tajikistan, and Moldova created both refugees and returnees. More than 22 million people reside in areas of Belarus, the Russian Federation, and the Ukraine, where threats of nuclear blackmail, contamination, smuggling, or proliferation persist.

Despite its own economic and political crises, roughly 2.5 million Russians (or nearly 10 percent of the 25.3 million Russians recorded in non-Russian republics by the 1989 census) have returned to the Russian Federation since 1991. In addition, a July 1994 study by the International Organization for Migration reports there were between 300,000 and 500,000 persons in Russia from outside the former Soviet Union. The Russian Federal Migration Service estimates that 10 million people will have migrated to Russia by the year 2000. The Russian Federation experienced a net in-migration of almost 440,000 people in 1993, the largest annual increase since the Second World War, with net flows significantly larger between July and December than in the preceding six months. Nearly half of the net in-migration was from the Central Asian Republics and Kazakhstan, although every former Soviet republic except Belarus contributed to it. During the second half of 1993, Ukraine, which had been gaining population from Russia, became a country of net emigration.

There have also been sizable outflows of Russian-speaking populations (Russians, Ukrainians, and Belarussians) from Tajikistan, whose numbers were reduced from roughly 560,000 in 1989 to between 70,000 and 80,000 in early 1994. Economic transformations, political and ethnic tensions, and outright wars have all played a role in these international population movements. In 1993 nearly a quarter of all immigrants to the Russian Federation reportedly qualified under Russian law as refugees or "forcibly displaced persons" fleeing violence or persecution. The potentially destabilizing effects of these flows make international migration in the region a cause for watchful U.S. foreign policy concern.

China

The United States has longstanding foreign policy interests in China. As in relations with the former Soviet Union, restrictions on emigration have constituted a frequent topic of policy dialogue, and the reception of dissidents has been a means of registering U.S. views. With one-fifth of the world's population, China is also already a major source of migrants to the United States and other countries, and potentially an even greater source in years to come. In addition, the Chinese constitute an important transnational community in the United States.

China is on the move in more ways than one. As of mid-1994 there were an estimated 100 million internal migrants, 20 million of whom were employed in China's booming coastal cities. These numbers, fueled by high but geographically disparate rates of economic growth, were expected by the Chinese Ministry of Labor to increase by 10 million in 1994 with the loosening of decades-old restrictions on internal movement introduced in June of that year. The rising numbers of internal migrants have been accompanied by increasing international mobility, especially from Guangdong Province, a magnet for some 8 million internal migrants and the historical source of many Chinese emigrants to the United States, and from Fujian Province, the source of the majority of Chinese in Southeast Asia.

China is also a major source of organized illegal migration, and human smuggling, facilitated by criminal syndicates, has become big business—on a global basis rivaling if not overtaking illegal drug trafficking in dollar volume—and a major international security concern. Indeed, in response to human smuggling incidents in the summer of 1993, President Clinton declared the problem to be a threat to national security and put the U.S. response in the hands of the National Security Council. The complex air, sea, and land routes used for human smuggling operations are reported to involve at least thirty countries. It is estimated that roughly half a million illegal Chinese migrants entered Europe, the former Soviet Union, and North America during the early 1990s. In Asia 100,000 are thought to have entered Thailand, with lesser numbers going to Hong Kong, Japan, and Taiwan. The number of predominantly Chinese (but also other Asian and African) migrants waiting in Moscow and St. Petersburg for "trans-shipment" to Western Europe and the United States is reported to range between 20,000 and 50,000. In Central Europe, the Czech and Slovak Republics, Hungary, and Poland are favored way stations, while in the Western Hemisphere the more popular routes involve Belize, the Dominican Republic, Guatemala, and Mexico.

The rapid and uneven pace of economic, social, and political changes in China explains only part of the recent and potential future international population flows. Thomas Homer-Dixon, reporting on findings of the Project on Environmental Change and Violent Conflict, has noted that growing scarcities of renewable resources and associated environmental pressures in China have already contributed to the accelerated internal population movements noted above; in the worst-case scenario, he has cautioned that environmental scarcity may lead to the country's political fragmentation and mass population movements beyond its borders.[13]

Conclusion

This chapter has focused on only some of the major international population movements of most clearcut relevance to U.S. foreign policy interests. Of necessity, many others have been neglected. These include the complex migrations that have occurred and will occur within and among the areas of Israel, Gaza, and the West Bank; the potentially destabilizing movements by illegal migrants from other African countries into South Africa and existing or potential refugee situations elsewhere in Africa (Burundi, Liberia, Mozambique, Rwanda); the dynamic labor migrations within East and Southeast Asia that affect the economic competitiveness of these countries and, indirectly, of the United States; and movements associated with the formation of regional trading blocs, as in the Southern Cone of South America. Also neglected are many small-scale movements. Migrations by only small numbers of people may be of foreign policy and security concern if they involve people bent on terrorist activities (such as the bombing of the World Trade Center) or the movement of strategic materials (such as plutonium) or arms.

The chapter has explored the historical and continuing role of U.S. foreign policy as a determinant of migration to the United States. While the causal links have been most evident in the case of refugee admissions, the total numbers of refugees admitted have per se been relatively modest. More significant has been the effect of refugee admissions on the diversification of immigration streams, and the expansion through family reunification of the transnational communities generated by those admissions. However, general immigration to the United States has not been without its foreign policy influences and consequences. Large numbers of immigrants originate from countries of strategic interest to the United States, and the transnational communities that have developed through immigration exert influence on U.S. foreign and immigration policies.

U.S. foreign policy has also been shown to be a determinant of international migratory movements to other countries either directly, as in the cases of Indochina and Central America, or indirectly, as in the case of Afghanistan. Conversely and especially in the post–cold war era, volatile and large-scale international population flows (or the prospect of them) have challenged U.S. foreign policy makers to find new forms of response to conflicts, to develop new and complex relationships with old allies and international organizations, and to participate in reshaping the basic tenets of the global refugee regime.

The security aspects of international migration are multiple, and this chapter has focused on only two of central concern to U.S. foreign policy: the former Soviet Union and China. In both cases, longstanding restraints on migration have been eased. Underlying ethnic tensions, disparate rates of economic growth and the transition toward democracy, resource scarcities, and political instabilities are likely to be both causes and consequences of international population movements in the decades to come.

Notes

[1] Hania Zlotnik, chief, Mortality and Migration Section, Populations Division, United Nations, provided the migration data on which this chapter is based.
[2] United Nations (1994a) provides the full estimates for each country of the world.
[3] See Zlotnik (1994) for full details on the nature of the data used.
[4] All data relative to migration to the United States were derived from official Immigration and Naturalization Service (INS) statistics as published in the annual Statistical Yearbooks of the INS. The 1992 Statistical Yearbook, in particular, was used to derive information on the 1980s and 1990s.
[5] Data on the number of refugees and asylum seekers in the world were generally obtained from publications of the United Nations High Commissioner for Refugees (UNHCR). See, in particular, UNHCR (1993) and UNHCR (1994). In addition, reference was also made to the special chapter on refugees in United Nations (1994b) and to Gordon (1993a, 1993b, and 1993c).
[6] For a comprehensive description of the acts relating to immigration see United States, Department of Justice (1993).
[7] This section draws upon Reimers (1982), Keely (1993), Zlotnik (forthcoming), and United States (1993).
[8] See Reimers (1982).
[9] This section is based on Gibney (1991), Zolberg, Suhrke, and Aguayo (1989), United Nations (1994b), and U.S. Committee for Refugees (1993).
[10] These included some 750,000 Yemenis expelled from Saudi Arabia in October 1990 and roughly 300,000 to 350,000 Palestinians who returned to Jordan. These movements, while not the direct result of U.S. policy, have altered the context of U.S. foreign policy. In the case of Yemen, the massive return of migrants was arguably a factor contributing to the 1994 outbreak of civil war in that country. In the case of Jordan, returning migrants swelled that country's population by about 8 percent and its labor force by about 10 percent in the space of a few months. The financial consequences were felt not only by Jordan, which had to provide expanded services for returnees at the same time that it experienced a sudden drop in remittances and the loss of foreign assistance from Kuwait and Saudi Arabia, but also by the PLO, which lost budgetary resources derived from taxes on the incomes of Palestinians abroad. Ultimately, the financial constraints provided strong impetus for renewed Arab participation in the Middle East peace process. For a fuller discussion of the Gulf War, see Russell (1992).
[11] See U.S. Committee for Refugees (1993) and Rogers and Copeland (1993). On new forms of coordination between the U.S. and its allies concerning interna-

tional migration, see Keely and Russell (1994) and Russell and Keely (forthcoming).

[12] See United Nations (1994b) and United Nations Economic Commission for Europe (1994) for a fuller discussion of historical and recent flows.

[13] Homer-Dixon (1994).

2

Migrants and Refugees: A Threat to Security?

WARREN ZIMMERMANN

Introduction

Migrants have always been seen as a threat. The people of Jericho were rightly intimidated by the arrival of a motley band of Israelites at the end of their forty-year migration. Today Jericho is on the verge of a new—and perhaps equally destabilizing—migration. Americans have always been of two minds about migrants. In the nineteenth century Chinese were welcomed as

WARREN ZIMMERMANN is a senior fellow at RAND and a distinguished fellow at the New School for Social Research. He was a Carnegie teaching fellow in history at Yale and a journalist in Washington before joining the Foreign Service in 1961. Ambassador Zimmermann served two tours totaling five years in the Soviet Union, the second tour as deputy chief of mission. He has been a U.S. ambassador three times, including as chair of the U.S. Delegation to the Vienna CSCE Follow-Up Meeting (1986–89), a major East-West negotiation that produced significant human rights advances in the Soviet Union and Eastern Europe, and as the last U.S. ambassador to Yugoslavia (1989–92). He was director of the Bureau for Refugee Programs, an assistant-secretary-of-state–level position, until March 1994.

laborers, but, when no longer considered useful, were expelled and excluded for sixty-one years. In the 1920s immigrants who had their own (sometimes bizarre) political views came under suspicion. Two of them—Sacco and Vanzetti—were executed for a crime most modern scholars believe they did not commit. In the 1950s the shadow of communism put many immigrants under a cloud of suspicion.

In 1975, right after the fall of Saigon, Americans polled opted by 54 to 36 percent against taking Vietnamese refugees. The then-governor of California, Jerry Brown, preceded Pete Wilson by two decades in charging that immigrants take jobs from Californians. The Los Angeles riots of 1992 recapitulated a black antipathy to Asians that first manifested itself a century ago. And Californians have sometimes been inclined to blame Mexicans for their problems—from border raids in the 1870s, to taking jobs from Californians in the 1930s, to Communist subversion in the 1950s, to drugs and environmental damage in the last two decades.

Today there is a new wave of perceived threats in the United States. It takes various forms. California feels the force of immigration, legal and illegal, from Mexico and Asia. Florida is concerned about ethnic swamping from Haiti and (potentially) Cuba. Many Americans worry that newcomers are a source of terrorism, crime, or narcotics trafficking. And there are fears that immigrants are eroding our economic and cultural welfare.

Similar fears pervade Western Europe. A migration challenge is anticipated from the East, from which nearly half a million Bosnians have reached Western Europe and—many Europeans fear—even more Russians are poised to move. An even larger challenge is perceived to come from the south, where North Africans have traditionally sought work in Europe and where an unsettled Algeria troubles the sleep of the French. Countries that have never considered themselves consumers of immigration are now compelled to define their approach to intending immigrants and asylum seekers, as the United States, Canada, and Australia have had to do.

Finally, refugees and migrants are increasingly seen as a threat to global stability and security. "Spillover" of the Bosnian conflict could drive Kosovo Albanians into Macedonia and Albania, destabilizing both. Genocide in Rwanda and perhaps again in Cambodia, the restless nature of Kurdish ambitions, the tendency of Middle Eastern countries to use migrants as shields—all threaten a world order in which human and economic contacts can go forward in tranquility.

There are various ways security can be threatened by migratory movements. Myron Weiner has identified five broad categories.[1] The first is when refugees and migrants are working against the regime of their home country, as the Ayatollah Khomeini did during his stay in France. The second is when migrants pose a risk to their host country; the bombing of the World Trade Center in New York by Middle Eastern immigrants is an example. The third is when immigrants are seen as a cultural threat, prompting countries, for example, to pass laws restricting the right of immigrants to acquire citizenship. The fourth is a perceived social or economic threat, e.g., taking jobs from host country workers. And the fifth is when the host country uses immigrants as instruments to threaten the country of origin, as, for example, when Saddam Hussein used foreigners as hostages during the Gulf War. In this chapter I shall concentrate on the second, third, and fourth categories, since they represent the majority of real or imagined threats.

I should explain what I mean by security. I will use the word in its broadest dictionary sense: not only freedom from danger but also freedom from fear or anxiety. Migration can threaten the lives of individuals, as we have seen in Rwanda, but no wave of migration is likely to threaten a whole receiving nation, as the danger of nuclear war threatened the people of the United States and the Soviet Union. Migrations can, however, weaken governments, create economic strains for host country citizens as well as for migrants themselves, and disrupt the psychological well-being and happiness of large numbers of people. Migrations can also create a perception of threat where no threat exists, even in the broadest sense of the word. In analyzing the degree of threat posed by migrants and refugees in the world today, I will try to be as precise as I can about when the threat is real and when it is imagined. Even perceptions must be taken seriously, but to treat them as real is to overreact.

A final introductory word. This chapter deals with the dark side of migrations—the negative aspects they embody or imply. It needs to be stressed that migration in general is largely a positive factor. People migrate to seek a better job or a better life, or they migrate because they are in danger and migration provides a safety valve, or they migrate to join family members. International law guarantees people the right to leave their country as well as to return to it. While no country has a legal obligation to receive refugees or migrants, most developed countries have recognized a moral obligation to do so. The most experienced refugee-receiving countries—the United States, Canada, and Australia—rightly see their policies as in an enlightened humanitarian tradition. The dynamic that runs through this chapter pits the obligations of law and humanity against the requirements of security and the fears of danger.

How Threatened Is America?

Three general "threats" by migrants to the security and well-being of Americans have been adduced. One is the economic and/or cultural damage to a state perceived by the accretion of immigrant and refugee groups. The second is the crisis created when a sudden exodus explodes large masses of migrants onto American shores. The third is a more classical security threat—migrants bringing crime, terrorism, or drug trafficking.

"California, Here We Come"

The strongest case for the damage done by large numbers of immigrants and refugees has been made by the state of California. Pete Wilson, the governor, has claimed that illegal immigrants and their families total nearly a million people in Los Angeles alone—making it a city of illegal immigrants the size of San Diego—that two-thirds of all babies born in Los Angeles public hospitals are born to parents who have entered the United States illegally, and that California devotes nearly 10 percent of its budget to federally mandated services for illegal immigrants and their families. Wilson has argued that the government's immigration policy is perverse—

the Border Patrol is supposed to keep illegal immigrants out, while the federal government insists that, once they're in, the states must provide free health care, education, and other benefits. California has sued to compel the federal government to pay the cost of federally mandated services to illegal immigrants.

Independent studies, while rejecting Wilson's figures as exaggerated, confirm the serious nature of California's problem. An Urban Institute study on undocumented aliens estimates that California has the highest concentration of the national total of undocumented aliens—about 43 percent—and the highest percentage of them in any state's population—about 4.6 percent.[2] The study calculates California's costs for educating the children of undocumented aliens at $1.3 billion—40 percent less than the state's own estimate but still considerable. The study reckons California's incarceration costs for undocumented aliens at $368 million and its Medicaid cost in a range between $113 and $165 million. On the other hand, California receives annual tax revenues of $732 million from these aliens.

While California has always had immigration problems, and has often complained about them, there is a new volume and intensity to the current situation. More immigrants have entered California over the last decade than in the five previous decades. The foreign born accounted for over 50 percent of California's population growth during the 1980s and for 95 percent of its growth between July 1, 1992, and July 1, 1993. It should be noted, however, that during that last year California's population grew less than that of the nation as a whole.

Florida, second to California in migrant arrivals, has made similar arguments, adding that—because of massive arrivals of Cubans—Miami is the site of the largest homogeneous refugee population in the United States. Texas, while joining California and Florida in the suit to recover costs, has not so far shown as frenetic an attitude as the other two states. In 1994 illegal immigration was not a major election issue in Texas, whereas in California it was a dominant issue. Then-Governor Ann Richards balanced her criticism of the federal government with efforts to maintain close ties with Mexico. The reason for the difference between Texas and California seems to be economic. Texas exports about three times

as much to Mexico as California does. California also feels the
weight of the illegal problem more than Texas, which has only a
third or a quarter the volume of illegal immigrants. New York,
third in illegal immigration, has chosen to explain away any problems; both state and local officials have gone out of their way to
stress the value of foreigners.

Many experts believe that the perceived threat derives more
from cultural than from economic factors. There is a feeling, often
expressed subliminally, that a treasured way of life will be upset by
a large influx of people who speak a different language and have
different habits. Typically, the fear is that they will move to highly
populated areas, the tax base will erode, and services will become
more difficult to provide. Latinos, who by the year 2020 are expected to outnumber African-Americans as the largest minority in
the country, seem to provoke the most concern, which is often
focused on the place of Spanish in the schools. The fear is enlarged
for native Americans by the fact that, unlike some migrants, they
have no second home to return to.

There is a major dispute over whether California's claims are
justified and, in a larger sense, whether immigrants add to or
detract from American economic and cultural values. Professor
George Borjas has written that immigrants will consume $20 bil-
lion more in welfare benefits over their lifetimes than they will
contribute.[3] Professor Don Huddle contends that immigrants are
extremely costly to the U.S. taxpayer.[4] He estimates that public
school education in 1992 for legal immigrants cost $8.15 billion
and for illegal immigrants $4.25 billion and that health care cost
$13.34 billion for legal immigrants and $2.5 billion for illegal immigrants.

Another Urban Institute study takes sharp exception to these
claims.[5] The Urban Institute argues that immigrants pay more
taxes than they receive in public services; immigrants generate
more jobs than they take; in the past decade immigrants have
received less public assistance than native-born Americans; and
immigration has no negative effect on African-American workers.
A U.S. Labor Department study in 1989 reached similar conclusions, asserting that immigrants do not have a pronounced effect
on the earnings and employment of the native born.

Many of the concerns expressed currently turn out to be less disturbing when viewed in a broad national context. While times, of course, have changed, the foreign born today represent only half the percentage of U.S. residents that they represented in the early twentieth century. Canada, Australia, New Zealand, and Israel all have a larger percentage of foreign born than we do. Moreover, immigrants do not become an underclass; in fact, within ten years of arrival, legal immigrants have a higher household income than native-born Americans. Even the pictures of a Mexican crossing the border illegally, while frequent, are not typical—most illegal immigrants came in legally but then overstayed their visas. Latinos, about whom most of the concern is expressed, constitute only 9 percent of the U.S. population.

What seems clear is that the United States, a country of immigrants, continues to have an enormous absorptive capacity. The very fact that we have been able to accept over a million Southeast Asians since 1975, 130,000 Cuban boat people in 1980, 300,000 illegal immigrants a year, as well as nearly a million legal immigrants and refugees annually attests to the extraordinary resilience of America. The problem or "threat" is, in fact, limited to a few heavily impacted states. Three-fourths of all immigrants settle in California, Texas, New York, Florida, Illinois, and New Jersey, and, as noted, not all of those have complained of difficulties. Of the estimated 3.4 million undocumented aliens in the United States in October 1992, 87 percent were in those states plus Arizona.

Mexican illegal immigration is special for two reasons. The first is that Mexico and the United States lie along one of the two most volatile fault lines for major migration in the world. That line divides different cultures, different religions, different languages, and—most important—different standards of living. This complex of differences makes mass migrations virtually inevitable. (The other major fault line, with similar migration consequences, is the Mediterranean Sea, dividing Europe from North Africa.)

The Mexican propensity to migrate is compounded by a tradition of U.S. labor recruitment in Mexico, formalized from 1941 to 1964 in the Bracero Program for Mexican farmworkers. The North American Free Trade Agreement (NAFTA) is not expected to have any short-term effect in diminishing migration, though the hoped-for improvement in the Mexican economy from NAFTA may reduce immigration in a matter of decades. Until then, the stimulation to Mexican migration will almost certainly continue. Thus it needs to be recognized that there are problems, even though they are not of the disastrous dimensions that doomsayers think. The waves of illegal immigration are clearly the place to begin. They demonstrate that the United States has lost (if it ever had) an important aspect of sovereignty—control of its borders. They burden the welfare and education systems of some large states. And they contribute to hiring practices that may be illegal and often injurious to the migrant. Illegal immigrants undoubtedly perform services that Americans want. But that is not to say that the same services cannot be performed in other ways.

A major general problem has been the near-breakdown of the U.S. asylum system. As of the summer of 1994 there was a backlog of over 400,000 asylum applications before the Immigration and Naturalization Service (INS), with new cases running at about 10,000 a month. The system creates its own abuse. Any alien in the United States, legal or illegal, can apply for asylum. Largely because of the backlog, the case is not heard for months or years. Meanwhile the asylum seeker is issued a work permit that permits application for a Social Security card. The ability to work is a powerful incentive for an asylum seeker not to show up at his or her hearing and risk a turndown of the asylum application. Even if an alien is ordered deported, the INS will be unable to deport him or her in three cases out of four.

On July 27, 1993, President Clinton announced a comprehensive program to deal with illegal immigration. It involves adding additional agents to the Border Patrol and enlisting new technologies in border operations, improving the technology for deportation of criminal aliens, streamlining the asylum process and doubling the number of INS officers and immigration judges, tightening sanctions against employers who hire unauthorized workers, and encouraging aliens to become U.S. citizens. The crime bill signed by the president on September 13, 1994, provided for some of the necessary resources, including funding for the updating of information systems and for the doubling of asylum personnel. The bill also gave the attorney general authority over the issuance of work authorizations to asylum applicants. The intention of the INS in the new regulations is to compel asylum applicants to wait six months for work permits so as to make the prospect of work less an incentive for application for asylum. Legislation has also been proposed to provide for the expedited exclusion at U.S. airports and other ports of entry of unauthorized aliens—an effort to limit the numbers who enter the overloaded domestic asylum system.

Another reform under consideration is the establishment of some form of national identity system. Many experts believe that this would greatly assist enforcement. The trade in fraudulent driver's licenses, Social Security cards, and other documents is widespread and highly successful. As it is, very few illegal aliens are caught and even fewer deported. But a national identification card is not a panacea. First, it is difficult to make a "smart" card that the forger's art cannot duplicate. Second, there remains a strong civil libertarian opposition to national IDs. This may dissipate somewhat with the advent of a U.S. health care system, which is likely to use national IDs. Moreover, the widespread belief that most Americans' vital statistics are already in somebody's data base could also attenuate the opposition.

The Commission on Immigration Reform, a presidential advisory body headed by former Representative Barbara Jordan, proposed on August 3, 1994, a computerized registry of names and Social Security numbers of all citizens and aliens authorized to work. The aim is to screen out those without valid work authorization and thus create a disincentive to illegal immigration. The proposal, which stops short of advocating a national identity card, was welcomed by many immigration experts. It is sure to be controversial, however, and has already drawn fire from the American Civil Liberties Union and ethnic groups.

The success of such reforms, modest as they are, could well dissipate much of the fear about immigration. Economic redress to the impacted states would also help. The economic imperative is perhaps the most important factor in determining whether people will remain nervous; if the U.S. economy turns up, tensions should be allayed. California, however, has undergone something more than a cyclical downturn. As the top state for defense-connected industries, it has felt the cutbacks in the defense budget more than most. Defense industries, military bases, and jobs in manufacturing all declined in the early 1990s. Even though job creation in California seemed to have increased as of late 1994, and there was still a market for low-skilled jobs that Californians will not take and immigrants will, the geopolitical changes in California's fate may extend its antiforeigner hostility beyond whatever negative views exist in the rest of the country. The three to two victory on November 8, 1994 of Proposition 187, which would deprive illegal immigrants in California of education, health, and other benefits, reinforces this conclusion.

In the final analysis, the question of whether massive immigration will be seen as a threat by Americans will depend on the value system of Americans themselves. The numbers, large as they may seem, are not impressive historically. The decade of the 1980s is the highest ever for immigration, but America is a much more populous country than it was in 1910. While the debate rages over the relative contribution of migrants, the anecdotal evidence also conflicts. Two Laotian refugees were arrested for murdering two German tourists in the same month that two immigrants (one from Nigeria, one from Jamaica) squared off at center in the National Basketball Association final of 1994. Congress, for all its criticism of the immigration snafus, seems to remain wedded to substantial immigration and refugee programs; the cooperation between the liberal Senator Edward Kennedy and the conservative Senator Alan Simpson seems as close and as productive as ever.

In short, the American people seem disposed to consult hopes rather than fears—that is, if their government doesn't blunder. That is a big "if," however, and the offshore situations in Haiti and Cuba remain a high-visibility challenge to America's tolerance of a liberal immigration policy.

The Threat of Swamping: Haiti and Cuba

The policy problem connected with Haiti resembles one of those children's puzzles in which a ball can be maneuvered into a hole only by dislodging the other balls from their holes. No U.S.

government has wanted to assume the responsibility of accepting massive numbers of Haitians. Nor since the Reagan administration has it been palatable simply to pick up Haitian boat people and send them home. The puzzle has been to operate between these poles.

The Bush administration elected a tough policy toward Haitians who took to boats. On May 24, 1992, it instituted a policy of interdicting the migrants on the high seas and returning them to Haiti. A refugee processing center was established in Port-au-Prince in the fall of 1992; returned boat people, as well as other Haitians, were encouraged to apply for refugee status there. The U.S. government argued that this arrangement offered refugee processing to virtually all Haitians who wanted it, excepting only those who were too frightened to apply in Haiti itself.

The Bush policies came under heavy criticism, from presidential candidate Bill Clinton, among others. Human rights advocates, immigration lawyers, and the UN High Commissioner for Refugees (UNHCR) all argued that it was a violation of international law to return Haitians before they had been given a refugee hearing. The problem for the government was that, as experience had shown, if Haitians were interviewed on the Coast Guard cutters that picked them up or at Guantanamo Bay, the inevitable result would be more Haitians taking to boats. This magnetic effect would quickly result in an overwhelming of the processing capabilities. Various efforts were made to enlist Caribbean countries in the processing or provision of safe haven for Haitians. No significant interest was shown, either by host countries or by the Haitians themselves. They wanted to go to the United States and to nowhere else, period.

Even before his inauguration President-elect Clinton was compelled to deal with the puzzle of one ball dislodging the others. He was told that if he implemented his pledge to revoke the interdiction-and-return policy, thousands of boats were likely to set sail as soon as he was sworn in. Clinton decided to maintain the Bush approach but to make a concerted effort at a political solution that would get rid of the oppressive military regime and restore elected President Aristide to power. The failure of the so-called Governors Island Agreement and an upsurge in police violence in Haiti persuaded Clinton on May 8, 1994, to announce the resumption of processing outside Haiti. The predictable result of the processing that was initiated off Jamaica was the revival of the magnet and the swamping of the processing facilities with boat people.

These problems might not have arisen if the United States had been prepared to receive a hundred thousand or more Haitians. Virtually nobody has argued for that, partly because nobody is sure how many Haitians would actually come, and partly because of the fear of "ethnic swamping" of the sort that had come from Cuba over a decade before. Moreover, the United States has no effective way to welcome Haitians temporarily, pending improvement in the political situation in Haiti, without letting them disappear permanently into the population. Thus the Clinton administration has been faced with a very small range of options.

The administration decided against going back to the interdiction-and-return policy; human rights in Haiti had deteriorated to the point where that would simply be inhumane. Moreover, the volume of Haitians who set sail following the introduction of offshore processing made this alternative nonviable as well. The administration responded to the flood by announcing that successful applicants for entry to the United States would go not to the United States, but to a safe area in a Caribbean country and, later, to Guantanamo. Of the 21,627 Haitian interdicted between June 15 and mid-September 1994, 585 were admitted to the United States (before the doors closed), 6,921 were voluntarily repatriated to Haiti, and about 14,000 remained at Guantanamo.

This minimigration crisis coalesced with the worsening political cimate in Haiti to move the president toward a policy of getting to the root of the problem—the military dictatorship that had overthrown the elected president, reversed the trend toward democracy, and committed egregious human rights abuses, including some 3,000 political murders. The U.S. military intervention in Haiti and the restoration of President Aristide, whatever their other consequences, should reduce emigration, at least in the short run. If the country is not pacified, however, boat traffic may resume (it continued even while Aristide was in office in Haiti the first time). Emigration from Haiti stems from a combination of political instability and economic distress. Dealing successfully with both these endemic Haitian problems remains unfinished business for President Clinton.

Cuba represents another facet of the Caribbean migration problem. The southern United States had already weathered the influx of 130,000 Cubans within a five-month period in 1980. With the Cuban economy in a shambles and with Castro possibly near the end of his reign, a series of crises seemed possible.

The first of these hit in the summer of 1994 when over 30,000 Cubans fled the island, most taking to rafts, some finding their way directly to Guantanamo. The rafters were sent to Guantanamo, which at peak held 32,000 Cubans in September 1994. Hastily arranged negotiations between the United States and Cuban governments produced an agreement on September 9, 1994. The Cuban government pledged to take "effective measures in every way it possibly can to prevent unsafe departures using mainly persuasive methods." The United States agreed to admit a minimum of 20,000 Cubans yearly (previous annual admissions had run at the rate of 3,000). During the first year of the new program, about 26,000 Cubans are expected, adding in the backlog of those with petitions currently on file.

There are troubling aspects to this agreement, even apart from its continuing to favor Cubans over other ethnic groups. For the first time, the United States has colluded with a foreign government, a dictatorship at that, in preventing people from leaving their own country—a right long sanctioned in international human rights law. Moreover, the agreement is only as good as Castro's word or his ability to keep it. The closing days of his regime could reshuffle the cards. As a parting shot Castro could re-open the gates to a migration exodus, or his mismanagement of the Cuban economy could provoke an outflow, or his departure from the scene could trigger a chaotic situation leading to a mass emigration. The United States is not ready for any of these eventualities.

The Criminal Side of Migration

It is difficult to distinguish crimes committed by immigrants from crimes committed by native Americans. Are there special "immigrant" crimes that native Americans normally do not commit? Are immigrants a special source of crime? Do they bring criminal tendencies with them?

The tentative answer is that immigrants bring no special criminal propensities but no special law-abiding propensities either. The foreign born account for 25 percent of the federal prison population—a high figure since they are only 9 percent of the population. In state prisons, however, the foreign born account for less than their percentage of the overall population. Drug trafficking, because of its international nature, relies to a large extent on mobility across borders. Immigrants can supply this, but so can native-born Americans and foreigners.

International terrorism is an area in which immigrants have already played a significant role and may play a larger one. Two events in the fall of 1992 brought this home: the slaying of several Central Intelligence Agency (CIA) employees, apparently by a Pakistani asylum seeker (who left the country as easily as he entered it), and the bombing of the World Trade Center in New York City by immigrants from Middle Eastern countries. Migrants have often used foreign countries as staging areas for terrorist assaults on their own countries. Less often have they attacked the host country itself. These two incidents are so far relatively isolated, and there is no reason for any Draconian measures that would affect immigrants as a whole. What *is* needed is more scrupulous monitoring of data bases in consulates abroad so as to prevent the entry of people who have already been identified as involved in terrorism, as well as more effective mechanisms for keeping them out of the country.

A final category, impressive in its volume, is the Chinese population smuggled into the United States illegally. Estimates run as high as several hundred thousand illegal immigrants a year. Typically, the Chinese arrive by boat, but overland and air arrivals are not uncommon. Alien smuggling of Chinese is inherently a criminal activity, not only because it produces illegal aliens, but also because those smuggled usually become engaged in criminal activity in the United States. This is not because they are criminals when they begin. It is because, to pay for their passage, they indenture themselves to criminal gangs in the United States. While the rights of possible refugees need to be protected—and have been, during the interception of Chinese boats—these operations are essentially criminal, not refugee, activities. They should be treated primarily as law enforcement problems.

While there are some disturbing trends involving migrants in the areas of drug trafficking, terrorism, and alien smuggling, none has reached a dimension to affect overall immigration and refugee policy. The tightening up of consular monitoring abroad, as well as the INS's requested authority to exclude asylum seekers before they enter the United States, should help reduce the entry of criminals into a U.S. asylum system where it remains difficult to keep track of them.

Why Is Europe Panicking?

Unlike the United States, Europe has come to the problems of migration quite late. In the East, the collapse of the Soviet Union has left some 65 million people outside areas of their own ethnicity. In Central Europe, the crisis in Bosnia has uprooted 4 million people and sent nearly a quarter of them into refuge in countries to the west. In Western Europe, the unaccustomed flow of migrants from the East, as well as continuing flows from the South, has caused many Europeans to push the panic button. Immigration, according to German Chancellor Helmut Kohl, will be Europe's "central challenge" in the coming years.

Disruptions attributable to the demise of communism, the break-up of the Soviet Union and Yugoslavia, and the outbreak of nationalist conflicts have wreaked havoc throughout the former Soviet empire. Western Europeans have clamored loudly for protection against the hordes of Russians and others who seemed poised to flee west. In fact, the flood from Russia has not taken place and probably will not. Refugees from the East have tended to move no farther than neighboring countries.

Over 2 million Russians from non-Russian countries of the former Soviet Union have settled in Russia, and more seem to be on the way, since 25 million Russians live outside the borders of the Russian state. It remains to be seen whether these immigrants—who may constitute the greatest immigration volume in Russian history—will prove a threat to stability or not. Georgy Arbatov, the venerable chairman of the Institute of the USA and Canada, is clearly worried. He wrote recently: "The fate of Russians in the Near Abroad . . . creates very dangerous problems. If . . . they begin a mass exodus to Russia, we will see an explosion of the most militant chauvinism in Russia, which will smash all the modest democratic achievements we have made." Arbatov undoubtedly knows that the Russian extreme nationalist Vladimir Zhirinovsky comes from Kazakhstan.

Other parts of the former Soviet Union have felt the brunt of violence and forced migration. Virtually all Azeris living in Armenia have fled to Azerbaijan or to parts of Turkey and Iran. About 300,000 Armenians living in Azerbaijan have found refuge in Armenia and Russia. South Ossetians have fled Georgia, and Turks have left Uzbekistan for nearby states. For those remaining, life is grim and often dangerous. Russians, for example, are discriminated against in Estonia, Latvia, and a number of southern republics.

To the west the Bosnian problem has overshadowed the earlier issues of migration (e.g., Romanians, gypsies) with which Western Europe had been preoccupied. Sadako Ogata, the energetic UN High Commissioner for Refugees, reached a tacit understanding with West European governments. They would give temporary protection to Bosnian refugees on the understanding that the refugees would ultimately go home. (Critics of the U.S. decision not to accept a massive number of Bosnian refugees sometimes overlook the fact that when the United States accepts refugees, it is for good. Few if any European countries have made such a commitment.) The West Europeans' desire to unburden themselves of their refugee load helps to explain the energy with which Europe has pressed a peace agreement on the Bosnian side.

For Europe, the Bosnian refugee crisis is the functional equivalent of the Haitian crisis for the United States, and the European fear of a Russian onslaught is the functional equivalent of the U.S. fear of a mass migration from Cuba. Instead of boat people, Western Europe has been confronted by asylum seekers. From under 20,000 asylum seekers in 1980, the figure rose to 550,000 in 1992, not counting the Bosnians. Germany received two-thirds of these, with France a distant second. The reason for this extraordinary pressure on the European asylum system is that it is the only avenue for political refugees or economic migrants to be legally admitted. Doris Meissner, U.S. commissioner of immigration and naturalization, has called it an "ersatz immigration system" because it allows the candidates to self-select. While the pressure slackened somewhat in 1993 because Germany and other countries tightened their rules, in the seven years before that European immigration had tripled.

The central problem for migration in Europe (except for France) is that Europe has had no tradition of, no vocation for, and no longstanding experience with immigration. The European practice was to bring in guest workers—most recently Turks, Eastern Europeans, and North Africans—to deal with Europe's chronic labor shortage. There is irony in the fact that both Europe and the United States owe a major source of immigration to guest worker agreements—with the United States it was the Bracero Program, which stoked immigration to California and Texas. In both the European and American cases, it was reasonable that immigrant aliens should be allowed to bring in their families, and that they should make a claim on the same social services available to citizens.

Until recently, Europe was insulated from immigration to the east by the cold war and to the south by the existence of colonial regimes. With the collapse of both communism and colonialism the pool of potential immigrants has widened considerably. Professor Aristide Zolberg believes that the break-up of empires is a far greater cause of refugees than the end of the cold war. In any case, European migration has been transformed. In fact, every country in Western Europe except Ireland is now a receiver of immigrants. Moreover, as noted earlier, Western Europe lies astride one of the major migration fault lines. The Mediterranean Sea divides a European from a North African culture that differs dramatically in fertility (North Africa's is four times Europe's), in economic development, in religion, and in political freedoms. What demographers call "push" and "pull" factors operate at their maximum in such an environment.

The factors that seem to concern Western Europeans most are

economic, cultural, and security related. For a decade now unemployment in Europe has been in double digits; immigrants are seen as a job threat. There is, moreover, the fear of Islamic fundamentalism; two-thirds of Europe's foreigners from outside the European Union are Muslim. Immigrants in Germany—many of them young, poor males—are also perceived as increasing the crime rate.

All these fears seem greatly exaggerated. In the European country with the most foreigners—Germany—there is no correlation between the unemployment rate and immigration. As for the fear of Muslims, it is the fact that they are different rather than dangerous that appears to motivate the sense of threat. Although there may be some evidence of a connection in Germany between migrants and crime—the percentage of non-Germans arrested in 1992 was four times their percentage of the German population— the more dramatic increase has been in violence committed by the radical right against foreigners.

Western Europe has not handled its migration transformation with notable grace. It is prepared to accept workers but not assimilate them (France does a better job at this than Germany or the United Kingdom). The tragic murder of an ethnically Turkish child by a neo-Nazi in Germany exposed the fact that it is possible for three generations of Turks to live in Germany with none of the attributes of German citizenship. European countries have not always accorded immigrants equal access to social benefits deriving from work, to education and vocational training, and to employment assistance. The European Union has dealt with migration on an all-European level, but for the most part in an effort to devise better ways to exclude migrants or to return them to countries they came from or passed through—thus shifting the burden to fragile Eastern European countries much less able to handle it. Many European countries tightened their asylum rules in 1993.

While migration has understandably become a major issue in Western Europe, there is little to suggest that mass migration is a serious threat. This is not to say that the future is necessarily unclouded. The Bosnian war could continue, leaving half a million Bosnian refugees stranded in Western Europe. Algeria could be taken over by a militantly fundamentalist regime, causing thousands of middle-class Algerians to flee to France. Still, as of now the European fears are greatly overblown.

Fortunately, there seem to be some stirrings of debate in Europe over its approach to migrants. It started in Germany over the murders and assaults on families of foreign born. Former President Weizsacker, not for the first time the conscience of his country, led the protest against citizenship laws that make it difficult for a non-ethnic German to become a citizen. In fact, one out of fourteen residents of Germany is not a citizen (a much larger proportion than in the United States, even though many U.S. resident aliens choose not to become citizens). Recently, the official in charge of foreigners in Germany lashed out at her own government for its failure to naturalize foreigners. Since 1991, however, it has become easier for foreigners to become German citizens, though there are long residence requirements. The UK, one of the more restrictive countries in Europe, has been taken to task by *The Economist,* which cited a think-tank conclusion that Britain may be losing out on skills that immigrants can bring.[6]

The short-term prognosis for Europe's receptivity to foreigners is not favorable. In the 1980s the rise of right-wing parties in Germany coincided with the jump in asylum applications and the influx of ethnic German immigrants. With the 1993 legal restrictions on asylum, there will be little stomach for a return to the more liberal approach exploited by the extremists. The same dynamic applies in France, where the powerful Interior Minister Charles Pasqua, who favors zero immigration, has weakened the right by tightening immigration laws. On the positive side, the speed of recovery from the recession will dissipate some of the fears of foreigners, who tend to be treated better when economies flourish. Logically, Western Europe should be more willing to accept migrants transiting Eastern Europe since it has a stake in fostering stability there; its current restrictions put strains on countries unable to handle migrants whose preferred destination is the West. Finally, Europeans will have to consult their own liberal traditions, remembering—whether they like it or not—that they are multiethnic societies and that their receptivity to different ethnic groups distinguishes them from the virulently nationalist attitudes of Serbia and some other countries to their east.

The Threat to World Security

One of the major paradoxes of the subject of this chapter is that migration issues that present the greatest danger to the people in their region are often seen by others as much less threatening than issues of much less magnitude. There has been no more serious refugee crisis in the last decade, in terms of human suffering, than the Rwanda crisis. Nevertheless, in France people are much more worried about the potential threat of a mass migration from Algeria, while in the United States principal worries concern Haitian and Cuban rafters and Mexicans spilling illegally over the southern border.

The embarrassing reason for this selective perception of threat is that most of the bloodiest refugee crises occur in less developed areas, far from the living rooms of citizens of North America and Western Europe. Moreover, the receiving states for the mass of refugees generated by these cataclysms also tend to be poor. A million refugees fled the Mozambican civil war for Malawi, one of the poorest countries in the world. Rwandan and Burundian refugees washed back and forth between those two equally poverty stricken countries and hardly better off Zaire and Tanzania. Bosnia has become such an important issue in the West in large part because so many Bosnian refugees have fled to Western countries. The most direct threats to global security ended with the disappearance of the cold war. There is little perception today of the existence of migration threats that do not impinge directly on one's values or livelihood.

There are, nevertheless, significant threats—or at least challenges—posed by migration to a stable and productive world order. They can be grouped in several categories.

Spillover. Refugee crises, if not resolved or at least calmed down, can spread. The greatest current fear of spillover probably comes from Bosnia. If, by accident or design, violence broke out in Kosovo, the historic area of Serbia 90 percent populated by Albanians, spillover could become a reality. Albanians could flee to Albania, already militantly anti-Serb, and to Macedonia, whose population is about 30 percent disgruntled Albanians. The moderate government of Macedonia could easily become destabilized, leaving the field to a match-up between the Albanians and the Macedonian nationalists who form a major political force in Macedonia. Interested neighbors could come into play: Serbia, which ruled Macedonia between the wars; Bulgaria, which has traditionally claimed that Macedonians are really Bulgarians; Greece, which has been waging a fierce economic war against Macedonia on the absurd assumption that Macedonia was threatening it; and Turkey, whose interest would derive from the involvement of its traditional enemy, Greece.

Such an outcome in the Yugoslav crisis would certainly erode Europe's stability and put the question even more starkly than Bosnia did as to whether military intervention should be tried.

Severe Persecution of Minorities. For moral if for no other reasons international society ought to feel threatened by the employment of genocide or other means of persecuting minorities. Even though Rwanda is in the heart of Africa, with very few ties outside, genocidal conduct there cannot go unnoticed and should not go unresponded to. Saddam Hussein's treatment of Iraq's Kurdish and Shiite minorities did produce a strong Western effort to protect them. This category of issues opens the strongest case for moral equivalence, e.g., the life of a Rwandan is worth the same as the life of a Bosnian Muslim.

The Destabilization of States. For the moment this is largely a potential rather than a real category. Can migrants really destabilize states? Whatever the fears of Americans and Europeans about mass immigration, it can hardly be seriously argued that the stability of the United States and European states is threatened by it. There may be a stronger case for arguing that the hostilities in Rwanda, which tore the country apart, were touched off by refugees. In the realm of the potential, one wonders if Saudi Arabia's enormous immigrant population might play a political role in the event that the regime begins to crumble. (It is interesting that the Saudis, who maintain one of the most expensive refugee camps in the world for Iraqis, are adamantly opposed to resettling any Iraqis, their traditional enemies, on Saudi territory.)

Failed States. Failed states like Somalia, Rwanda, and (perhaps soon) Zaire tend to be copious refugee producers—a threat to their neighbors and, as in the Somali case, a challenge to the world. The Somali crisis drove one-sixth of the Somali population into Kenya and other neighboring states, while the rest faced famine inside the borders of Somalia. With no functioning government to deal with (or against), international rescue operations had to assume a political as well as a humanitarian role. This is what happened in Somalia, where the UN made the capture of one of the warlords its primary objective. When nobody is really in charge, the capricious nature of agreements, deals, and temporary arrangements dominates. UN peacekeepers and humanitarian agencies in Bosnia discovered that no agreement, from cease-fires to laissez-passer for relief convoys, was worth the breath it was pronounced with. The consequences of failed or failing states come high on the list of threats to neighbors and, for moral reasons, the world at large.

Technological Scourges: Land Mines. Land mines have become the weapon of choice for ethnic conflicts. They are used all over the world—in Afghanistan, in Cambodia, in Mozambique, in Angola. According to one estimate there are over 100 million of them planted in sixty-two countries. They are indiscriminate in their targets; in fact, they kill or maim many more civilians than soldiers. Because of the difficulty in removing them, they remain lethal for years, and even decades, beyond the time of the conflict during which they were planted. By anybody's definition of threat, they will be a major menace for a long time to come. In fact, it is hard to imagine any other weapons system that even approaches the threat they pose to individual human beings. Here is an issue that cries out for priority international treatment, both in outlawing these atrocious weapons and in developing the technology and will to remove those that exist.

Root Causes. Population pressures, environmental deterioration, poverty, and human rights abuses all play a major role in increasing refugee flows. The connection among these "root causes" is complex. For the most part, one factor (e.g., a steep increase in population) is not usually enough to touch off a migration crisis, but it can contribute significantly. The Rwanda debacle was due primarily to the tribal enmity between Hutus and Tutsis, but it is also relevant that Rwanda is one of the poorest countries in Africa and has one of the highest birth rates. Root causes are not susceptible to short-term solutions, but there are many reasons for getting at them beyond the refugee crises they help to generate. Clearly they will need to command a growing part of the world's attention.

These issues, most of them capable of a significant threat level, are already provoking some remedial action on the part of international organizations and governments. A landmark advance was Security Council Resolution 688, passed during the Gulf War in 1991. It was a response to the massive flight of 1.7 million Kurds into the mountains of northern Iraq. In the face of neighboring Turkey's refusal to give them asylum, a mechanism for taking care of them in Iraq was born. Resolution 688 stated that Iraq's repressive actions "threaten international peace and security"—a breathtaking assault on the traditional protections of sovereignty—and it insisted that Iraq allow immediate access by international humanitarian organizations to all those in need of assistance, thus legitimating a foreign humanitarian intrusion into Iraq regardless of Saddam's views.

Resolution 688 established a precedent of conducting refugee operations before people became classic refugees, that is, before they fled their country. The UN built on this precedent in Bosnia. In a bold and necessary move, Sadako Ogata decided to project UNHCR relief into the heart of Bosnia. Beyond this, she was prepared to provide relief while a war was going on—the first time UNHCR had involved itself in a combat situation. The UN peacekeeping apparatus also had to adjust to the need to protect the humanitarian convoys; the protection it provided was also unprecedented.

From these new approaches to humanitarian relief came a new concept—the "right to stay." If refugees have the right to leave their country, they should also have the right to stay there. Whether by design or accident, the right to stay was a convenient idea for countries that felt threatened, or at least burdened, by the weight of refugees—over 20 million outside their country, at last count. The haven provided to Afghanis, Ethiopians, Somalis, and Bosnians by neighboring countries was never meant to be permanent. Moreover, in Bosnia the UNHCR faced the painful dilemma of whether to help Muslims reach Croatia at the cost of abetting Serbian ethnic cleansing, or whether to treat them in

Bosnia where they were in constant danger. No clear choice was made, though the tendency was to provide relief within Bosnia.

Ogata also reemphasized the UNHCR's priority on repatriation—helping refugees return home after the conflict was over. Successful repatriation operations were in fact mounted to return 370,000 Cambodians in time for them to vote in the 1993 election. An even more massive return of Mozambicans is now underway following the end of the civil war there, and Afghanis have braved continuing conflict and land mines to return in large numbers. Repatriation is obviously the right way to close the refugee circle; it also has the effect of diminishing whatever threat neighboring countries may feel from the presence of refugees on their soil. Surprisingly, however, the international community does not respond as readily to financial appeals for repatriation as it does for appeals to deal with a mass refugee outflow. Repatriation is, of course, less crisis-driven. But it provides the firmest assurance that refugee policy is actually working and that its inherent threats have been contained.

Dealing with the Threats

This chapter has dealt with a range of threats and perceived threats posed by migration to the security of the United States, Europe, and the world as a whole. In many cases the threats are more apparent than real. Nevertheless, even exaggerated concerns need to be faced, because they affect people's attitudes and actions and can affect public policy. In this final section I suggest some remedies that could reduce the threat level in each of the categories examined.

Threats to the United States

Immigration problems, though concentrated in a few states, are real and must be dealt with. Not for the first time, there is a strong public perception that the United States has lost control of its borders and that its policies are inconsistent and riddled with exceptions. Americans have a right to expect a higher degree of predictability in immigration policy than they are seeing. The INS will need to follow through on its reform of asylum policy, its improvement in border policing, and its plans for expedited exclusion of inadmissible aliens. Employer sanctions, which can be an effective way to cut down on illegal immigration, should be strictly enforced. Some form of nationwide ID card should be introduced, perhaps in the less contentious variant suggested by the Commission on Immigration Reform. Finally, states impacted by massive immigration should receive some reimbursement from the federal government.

In its immigration and refugee policies, the United States should move away from the special treatment accorded to certain ethnic groups. The Cuban Adjustment Act of 1966, described below, should be repealed. The Morrison-Lautenberg Amendment effectively awards refugee status to all Jews in the former Soviet Union—a designation that was appropriate before the Yeltsin government but is now seen as a mask for an immigration program. Some Latin American groups can qualify for temporary protected status in the United States; others cannot. In fairness to the real meaning of "refugee," family reunification—essentially an immigration rather than a refugee principle—should be limited to close family members. Clear refugee qualifications should take precedence over a desire to reward countries with which the United States has had a tradition of acceptance. Our refugee program is increasingly seen as a collection of exceptions to recognized standards. It will be difficult to maintain it unless it can capture a basic consistency rooted in genuine need.

Nowhere is the need for predictability and consistency clearer than in the way the United States deals with potential mass migration from Haiti and Cuba. The Clinton administration should use the breathing space—and that is all it is—provided by its success in Haiti and Cuba to design a policy that treats future Haitian and Cuban migrants more equitably, while protecting the borders of the United States. An early step, as noted, should be to seek repeal of the Cuban Adjustment Act of 1966, which gives preferential treatment to Cubans over any other migrants, including Haitians. Cubans picked up on the high seas may be taken to the United States, where they can qualify for permanent resident status in one year. While this provision is not mandatory—it was ignored during the boat crisis of 1994—it is discriminatory, and can even provide an incentive for Cubans to leave.

The Haitian problem has called forth considerable hemispheric cooperation. This can now be built on to create a potential safe haven regime in future Cuban or Haitian emergencies. A key principle must be that boat people will not be repatriated involuntarily. On the other hand, given the magnet effect created by the initial American decision to process Haitian boat people for possible admission to the United States, no variant that includes refugee processing for the United States seems viable. A solution must therefore be found in inter-American cooperation to provide enough safe areas to maintain fleeing migrants until the political situation at home allows them to go back. These could be supplemented by the use of Guantanamo and by the construction of a facility on an uninhabited Caribbean island. UNHCR might be persuaded to take the lead in leasing and running such a facility.

With regard to migration issues involving Haiti and Cuba, the Clinton administration would do well to move quickly with the momentum achieved before new crises in these highly volatile countries overwhelm the progress made so far. Migration policy should be closely integrated with U.S. political policy. It should neither dominate, as it did with Haiti, nor be subordinate, as it was with Cuba. In the Cuban case, in fact, there are compelling reasons, generated by migration episodes, to pursue a gradual improvement of bilateral relations, in the interest of providing a smooth transition to democracy following the Castro era.

Threats to Europe

A key problem for Western European countries is that they do not consider themselves immigration countries, even though all but Ireland are. They have plenty of organizations seized with migration issues, but none takes a particularly receptive view of migrants. Europe needs to adjust its focus; international organizations transcending Europe can help here. A new international organization, with a mandate to encourage liberal immigration policies as far as practicably possible, is one possibility. One approach would be to give the Conference on Security and Cooperation in Europe (CSCE) a larger migration mandate. A big advantage of CSCE is that it includes not only Western European countries, but also the states of Eastern Europe and the former Soviet Union (which view migration with a very different optic from Western Europe), plus the United States and Canada (which have always taken a more positive view of immigration than Europe). CSCE already has some migration experience. The November 1993 CSCE Rome ministerial meeting put mass migration on the CSCE agenda. High-level follow-up will be needed.

Western Europeans have a long way to go in making their mindsets more positive. They will have to understand that Islam can be benign and cooperative as well as disruptive. They will also have to change the discriminatory practice of denying citizenship even to those whose families have been resident for generations. It is fortunate that this debate has started in Germany, whose approach to naturalization has been the most retrograde. In sum, the Europeans need to draw the correct conclusions from the fact that, willy nilly, they are now multiethnic societies.

Eastern and East Central Europe, as well as the former Soviet Union, have become grounds for ethnic conflict. For the United States, political policies must take precedence over migration policies in these areas. In Bosnia, for example, a large and successful American humanitarian relief effort was used by both the Bush and Clinton administrations to disguise the lack of a forceful political approach. The reality is, however, that migration and refugee policies will not work in a place like Bosnia, where Europe has been ineffectual, unless the United States is prepared to play a large political role itself. This is not necessarily true of the former Soviet Union, where Russia is anxious to take the lead. The objective here is to moderate Russian actions, not to compete with them.

The Global Threat

There are several levels of remedy necessary for dealing with threats to world security. With 20 million refugees outside their countries and another 20 million persons displaced within them, the problem has reached unprecedented proportions. On the technical, ground level there are new requirements stemming from this enormous challenge. The concept of safe havens needs to be used more; in Bosnia it failed because the safe havens for Muslims were, for the most part, in Serb-controlled territory. A better precedent exists in Sri Lanka, where the belligerents allowed UNHCR to open relief centers for civilians affected by the war. Ethnic conflicts provide unpromising terrain for the establishment of safe havens, because the combatants have no scruples about barbaric treatment of civilians. Still, if the concept can gain momentum from successful use, it could save lives.

The worldwide explosion of refugees and displaced persons suffering from war, ethnic violence, or human rights abuse has led to a new emphasis on protection of refugees abroad. Two-thirds of the budget of the State Department's Bureau of Population, Refugees, and Migration goes for assistance abroad as opposed to admissions to the United States (though the proportion changes if the budgets of domestic agencies are included). The UNHCR budget is at record levels but still underfunded. It is clear that resettlement of refugees in developed countries is not the main answer, though it should continue in the United States and increase in Western Europe. It is more cost-effective to care for refugees near their homes. It may be more humane as well, since their repatriation will be easier if the political situation at home improves.

In a broader time frame, the international community needs to focus on ways to prevent migration forced by either political or economic pressures. Population increase, environmental degradation, and poverty should all be attacked for migration and other reasons. So should human rights abuses, a major direct cause of migration. Sovereignty has been for too long a sacred cow in international affairs; it has protected dictators from scrutiny and action from abroad. Resolution 688 on Iraq was a welcome challenge to unlimited sovereignty. It needs to be built on, so that intrusive human rights policies can be deployed in time to prevent the human tragedies that lead to flight.

Preventive approaches are not likely to succeed without strong multilateral mechanisms. The UN as currently structured is not up to these tasks, but there is no substitute for it. A major overhaul is called for—for example, to improve peacekeeping through tougher rules of engagement, a standing peacekeeping force, and a more effective conflict resolution system. The United States has been a notable foot-dragger on these issues, hesitating even to contribute troops to UN peacekeeping forces. The UN will never improve unless the United States is prepared to contribute financial resources and personnel to its reform.

Most important of all is to change the way people look at the world. Ethnic conflicts that spawn most of the world's refugees derive from a view of the nation and the nation-state that is as pernicious as it is outmoded. In reality there are few existing nation-states—that is, states comprised of a single nationality. What does exist is an exclusivist concept that elevates Serbs, or Hutus, or Russians above all other nationalities, that despises ethnic minorities, and that is prepared to use force to deal with them. When such a concept takes power in the armory of an ethnic hegemon, the result is war, ethnic cleansing, and severe persecution.

The world needs to get away from the nation-state as an operating concept and as a value system. All the most successful countries in the world, excepting Japan, are multiethnic states. The United States, of course, is the most successful of all of them. This alone gives us a mandate to lead the effort to eliminate the global threat to security that comes from the migration forced on people by their ethnic enemies.

Notes

[1] Weiner (1992/93), pp. 91–126.
[2] Clark, Passel, Zimmermann, and Fix (1994), p. 8.
[3] Borjas (1993).
[4] Huddle (1993).
[5] Fix and Passel (1994).
[6] *The Economist*, April 30, 1994, pp. 65–67.

3

From Invitation to Interdiction: U.S. Foreign Policy and Immigration since 1945

ARISTIDE R. ZOLBERG

Introduction

B y way of its central role in international affairs, its weight in the world economy, and its prominence as a fountainhead of global cultural change, the United States influences world conditions more than any other country: and since these in turn shape international migrations, it thereby also contributes to the determination of population movements.For self-evident reasons, this is especially true for the neighboring region. Hence if we adopt a broad definition of "foreign policy," encompassing the disparate activities generated by the United States that, intentionally or not,

ARISTIDE R. ZOLBERG is University-in-Exile Professor of Political Science and director of the International Center for Migration, Ethnicity, and Citizenship at the Graduate Faculty of the New School for Social Research. He is also cochair of the MacArthur Program on Globalization and Liberalism. His research encompasses African and European politics, as well as international migrations and immigration and refugee policy in advanced industrial societies. He is coauthor of *Escape from Violence: Conflict and the Refugee Crisis in the Developing World*.

have an impact on the world at large, we are led to conclude that it plays a major role in stimulating immigration, albeit a somewhat diffuse one. If we abide instead by a more conventional definition, focusing principally on security and possibly also foreign trade, then the impact of U.S. foreign policy appears more limited, but also much more tangible with regard to specific flows.

Although the second approach is more appropriate for present purposes, it is nevertheless useful to keep in mind that foreign policy in the narrower sense takes place within the broader context provided by externally oriented American activities as a whole. In this regard, it might be noted that U.S. immigration policy is itself a major immigration-generating factor. From the perspective of a world steeped in mercantilism, the decision of the founders of the American republic to nationalize the land and sell it cheaply to immigrants from any European state constituted an aggressively acquisitive act. This was compounded by easy naturalization, which encouraged them to relinquish attachments to their community of origin on behalf of an entirely new national identity, and thereby established a radically subversive "Lockean" norm regarding relations between individuals and the state. In keeping with this, after the Civil War the United States undertook a diplomatic campaign on behalf of the right of expatriation, whereby individuals who emigrated obtained the possibility of freeing themselves of obligations to their original state. Throughout, American agents scoured Europe for passengers, land buyers, and workers; operating with the active support of the diplomatic establishment, they steadily enlarged the domain of emigration. From the 1850s onward, American employers also turned to Asia, and toward the end of the nineteenth century, to Mexico and neighboring islands of the Caribbean.

Notwithstanding the restrictions imposed in the 1920s, the maintenance by the United States—together with a few other "overseas settlement countries"—of a *positive* immigration policy, providing for a substantial number of annual admissions for permanent settlement, institutionalized the possibility of changing one's membership from one state to another as a norm of international society. Its standing is nowhere better demonstrated than when it is defensively rejected—Germany (or Japan, or Italy) is not an immigration country. Although the total number of annual admissions provided by the immigration countries is small in relation to world population, it is quite large in relation to total international migration. Moreover, the existence of these policies has contributed to the formation of a worldwide "emigration culture" that fosters aspirations to relocate and probably lowers the threshold of individual decisions to leave.

Considered in its narrower sense, U.S. foreign policy can affect immigration both directly and indirectly; directly, by intervening in the determination of the level and composition of admissions to the United States; indirectly, by altering conditions in some foreign country so as to increase or decrease the movement of its nationals toward the United States. This can be done intentionally, or it might occur as an unintended consequence of U.S. action. Historically America's wars have been a major source of immigration, both directly—as in the case of Vietnam, discussed later on—and indirectly. For example, the fact that the Philippines ranks today among the leading sources of immigrants—in sharp contrast with its broadly comparable neighbor, Indonesia—can be traced to late nineteenth century American imperialism and its associated decision, in keeping with Kipling's admonition, to shoulder the "white man's burden." Because Filipinos were U.S. nationals—albeit not citizens—while their country was a U.S. colony, they were allowed to migrate to the United States, even after the adoption of a policy of Asian exclusion in 1924. Although the 1934 settlement guaranteeing independence set a limit of fifty admissions per year, economic and strategic linkages between the two countries were strengthened after independence in 1946, fostering networks that facilitated the rapid expansion of migration to the United States after racial barriers and nationality quotas were removed in 1965.

However, the fact that some element of foreign policy contributes to immigration does not necessarily mean that it is a "cause," since the policy in question may itself have been devised primarily to serve domestic objectives. This was generally the case until the end of World War II. For example, in 1863, at the initiative of Secretary of State William H. Seward, the United States imposed on a reluctant China a treaty that, among other things, allowed

nationals of each country to travel freely to the other; while this
facilitated the operations of American traders in China, the prime
objective was clearly to procure Chinese labor for railroad construction on the West Coast.

So long as immigration policy was governed largely by laissez-
faire, albeit with increasingly Draconian barriers against Asians
and accumulating qualifications designed to deter various categories of undesirables, foreign policy objectives in themselves rarely
came into play in the shaping of immigration policy. The only
instances I have been able to identify involved attempts by those
responsible for American diplomacy to mitigate restrictionist congressional initiatives, out of concern they might jeopardize relations with the states whose nationals were being targeted. The first
occurred in 1907, when to prevent Congress from enacting the
anti-Japanese bill, President Theodore Roosevelt agreed to secure
instead a "gentlemen's agreement" whereby Japan restricted the
emigration of its own nationals. In effect, diplomacy was harnessed
to the objectives of racially motivated restrictionism.

The second case pertains to Mexico in the 1920s. Although the
congressional restrictionists who gained the upper hand in the
1920s saw Mexicans as a "mixed breed" and hence even more
objectionable than Russian Jews or Greeks, contrary to their
wishes the independent countries of the Western Hemisphere
were exempted from the national origins quota system and not
subject to a numerical limitation. This was largely attributable to
the power of the agricultural interests concerned. However, the
restrictionists succeeded in establishing a militarized Border Patrol
in 1924, and subsequently renewed their efforts to subject immigration from Mexico to quota limitations. At this time, the State
Department joined agrobusiness in arguing on behalf of continued
exemption, on the grounds that the imposition of quotas would be
construed as an unfriendly act and jeopardize Ambassador
Dwight Morrow's negotiations to relieve the plight of nationalized
American businesses.[1]

Shortly after Pearl Harbor, the United States initiated an agreement with Mexico for the joint management of a massive program
of temporary workers. Although it has been suggested that "foreign policy considerations were central to this North American

initiative, which was begun as part of wartime collaboration between the two countries,"[2] there is no gainsaying that it was designed primarily to solve anticipated worker shortages, and hence
should be regarded as yet another instance of the harnessing of
diplomacy to domestically generated immigration objectives.

A much more explicit case, also during World War I, was the
enactment of a law providing for the admission of 105 Chinese per
year as ordinary immigrants. This was initiated by the Roosevelt
administration in 1943 at the request of Generalissimo Chiang
Kai Chek on the grounds that Chinese exclusion was inappropriate treatment of a wartime ally and was being exploited by the
Japanese for propaganda purposes. Although the measure had
hardly any effect on immigration, it constituted a major breach in
the Draconian anti-Asian wall erected in 1924, and was a prelude
to other minor exceptions that, over the next two decades, prepared the ground for a more general change of policy.

The situation changed markedly after World War II when, as a
by-product of the rise of the United States to global leadership,
foreign policy decision makers deemed it necessary to resolve the
problem of displaced persons in Germany by resettling some of
them in the United States. Since the existing immigration system
stood as an obstacle to the achievement of this objective and could
not be reformed because of the entrenched power of congressional
restrictionists, there arose a growing disjunction between policy
pertaining to "ordinary" immigrants and policy pertaining to
groups defined as "refugees." This differentiation led also to the
development of distinctive policy-making processes and administrative apparatuses in each of the two spheres.

Foreign Policy and Immigration
in the Postwar Period

Initiated largely in the Congress, immigration policy continued
to be driven almost exclusively by domestic considerations arising
from the putative economic, political, and cultural impact of various quantities and types of newcomers, as assessed by leading
actors in the political process. These include not only business and
labor, but also religious and ethnic groups, as well as those con-

stituted on the basis of a general orientation toward change. Because of the diversity of concerns involved, political alignments for
or against a given immigration policy do not fit neatly in the usual
"conservative-liberal" framework. For example, the imposition of
sanctions on employers of unauthorized foreign labor enacted in
1986 was supported by organized labor as well as those who think
growing Latino immigration jeopardizes national integration, but
opposed by employers dependent on cheap Mexican labor and by
Latino groups who feared it would lead to discrimination.

Meanwhile, refugee policy came to be governed largely by considerations arising from foreign and security policy; reflecting the
major institutional change induced by America's new role in world
affairs, it originated within the "imperial presidency." However, it
was shaped also by organized ethnic groups that skillfully exploited
the immigration opportunities the policy made available. After
controversial beginnings, by the 1950s a consensus emerged regarding the desirability of welcoming and even encouraging "defectors" from the European Communist countries. Subsequently,
foreign policy was used to promote emigration from these countries—most of it resulting in immigration to the United States—by
making improved relations conditional on the reduction of barriers to exit.

From the late 1950s onward the policy was applied to the Western Hemisphere as well as Southeast Asia. This resulted in much
more immigration than anticipated. Moreover, quite unexpectedly, the commitment of the United States to the maintenance of
an open door enabled its antagonists to harness the refugee outflows to their own foreign policy objectives. In the face of this, the
United States in effect reversed its stance, insisting that as a condition for improved relations the originating countries must sharply
reduce the outflow, if necessary by imposing stricter control on the
exit of their citizens. After shaky beginnings, the new policy became more effective; however, it created a human rights dilemma
that has not yet been resolved.

The Development of American Refugee Policy

At the end of World War II, Jewish organizations in the United States renewed their efforts to secure the admission of surviving victims of Nazi persecution, and in order to get around opposition founded on anti-Semitism, organized a broadly based coalition on behalf of "displaced persons" more generally.[3] Nevertheless, they made little progress, and the situation worsened at the end of 1946 with the election of the first Republican Congress since the New Deal, which enhanced the power of the stalwart restrictionists. However, after the onset of the cold war, under the leadership of Secretary of State George Marshall, the Truman administration began to treat the reconstruction of Europe as a major priority. In relation to this, the problem of displaced persons in Germany came to be viewed as a threat to the social and economic stability of a strategically crucial region. Given local conditions, the solution required some sort of international resettlement, which would necessarily involve admission to the United States. At the same time, the administration confronted the Soviet Union on the issue of forced repatriation, and led a successful effort to constitute the Western dominated International Refugee Organization as the major instrument for resettlement. "By taking these steps, the Truman administration converted the refugee issue into an aspect of the emerging cold war, and thus provided a new basis for conservative support which was only marginally related to traditional interest group politics."[4] To secure congressional approval, the administration accepted discriminatory provisions against Jews. America's first refugee act, which provided for the admission of 202,000 persons by "borrowing" entries from the future quotas of the originating countries, was signed into law in June 1948, the very month the Berlin blockade began.

The 1948 law was followed by additional ad hoc enactments responsive to the imperatives of the cold war. The Refugee Relief Act of 1953, which provided for the admission over the next three years of 209,000 persons who could not be accommodated under the low quotas for their respective countries, was identified in a 1953 National Security Council memorandum as a device to "encourage defection of all USSR nations and 'key' personnel from the satellite countries" in order to "inflict a psychological blow on communism" and, "though less important . . . material loss to the Soviet Union," as the emigration entailed a brain drain of professionals. Responding to constituency pressures as much as to foreign policy objectives, subsequent measures facilitated the immigration of Greeks as part of a strategy to defeat Communist forces in the Greek civil war, and of southern Italians, to relieve postearthquake conditions that were thought to foster communism.

In 1956 the United States seized upon Khrushchev's hint of greater freedom for the satellites to encourage oppositional initiatives in Hungary. However, the Soviet tanks rolled in on November 4, triggering the exodus of several thousand freedom fighters, as well as many others who took advantage of the temporarily open border. Some 200,000 altogether managed to cross into Austria, which welcomed them on condition of rapid resettlement in other countries. This was organized by the International Committee on European Migrations and the United Nations High Commissioner for Refugees (UNHCR), with the United States and Canada each taking about 20 percent of the total and nearly all the Western nations accepting a share of the remainder. As too few visas were available under the 1953 act, the Eisenhower administration resorted to an obscure provision of the Immigration and Nationality Act of 1952 that gave the attorney general discretionary authority to "parole" any alien into the United States for reasons of emergency or if it were "deemed strictly in the public interest." Thus did parole authority, intended to deal with medical emergencies or judicial proceedings, come to be used repeatedly from then on to admit persons from Communist countries.

Upon expiration of the 1953 law, the Refugee-Escapee Act of 1957 made additional room for existing applicants from the same groups, but also included a more general provision for admitting as refugees in the future "persons fleeing persecution in Communist countries or countries in the Middle East." In 1960 the United States adopted a Fair Share Law, whereby it admitted under parole authority refugees in European camps in the proportion of one for every four resettled by other nations. However, the immigration impact of these enactments was limited because tight restrictions on exit made for few refugees except for Germans, most of whom were absorbed by the Federal Republic; and this exodus too ground to a halt with the building of the Berlin Wall. It might be noted that the situation in the Pacific was broadly similar: the Chinese Nationalist losers settled in Taiwan, and subsequent defectors from the People's Republic of China went mostly to Hong Kong.

Altogether, from 1945 to 1965, some 700,000 persons were admitted to the United States under the various "refugee" measures, out of a total of about 5 million immigrants. It can thus be estimated that during this period foreign policy–driven admissions added between 15 and 20 percent to ordinary immigration; however, with regard to European immigration regulated by the quota system the increment amounted to one-third.[5] These additions provoked little political division at the time, not only because of the cold war consensus, but also because the policy was congruent with the dictates of a "humanitarian" perspective as well. Given the elimination of right-wing dictatorships from all of Europe except Spain and Portugal, severe political oppression was encountered almost exclusively in the Soviet Union and its satellites. Moreover, members of Congress representing urban constituencies were quick to discover that the enactments in question could be used to secure the admission of various groups disfavored by the notorious national origins quota system that, despite the Truman administration's efforts to the contrary, was reenacted in 1952 over the president's veto.

Cold War Consensus:
The International Refugee Regime

Concurrently, the United States also took the lead in developing an international refugee regime,[6] culminating in the enactment of the 1951 Geneva Convention and the creation of the office of United Nations High Commissioner for Refugees. Designed once again as an instrument of "containment," initially the regime pertained only to Europe, and to the consequences of past events. The signatories—which did not include the United States until 1980—were not obligated to participate in the resettlement of existing

refugees, but only to consider their application for asylum if they
came knocking at the door. The time and place limitations of the
1951 convention were removed in 1967 as a result of the accession
of many new Asian and African states to membership in the General Assembly.

Despite its limitations, the regime established in effect a near-
universal right to be *considered* for asylum when persecution,
broadly defined, could be credibly alleged. In the course of meeting their obligations, most participating states institutionalized
procedures for the adjudication of asylum claims and the admission of those selected as residents—permanently in the overseas
immigration countries, or for a temporary period in Europe that
commonly led to permanent residence.

The vast majority of the internationally uprooted who have
qualified as "convention refugees" since the 1967 protocol came
into effect originated in the Third World and received asylum in
neighboring countries. However, from the late 1970s on a growing
number of claimants turned to the developed world, particularly
Western Europe. This was attributable, in part, to the escalation of
refugee-generating conflicts worldwide, itself a consequence of
more aggressive direct and indirect confrontations by the superpowers in various regions of the Third World—Southeast Asia,
Afghanistan, the Horn of Africa, southern Africa, and Central
America. However, it was also a response to the narrowing of
other avenues to immigration, particularly in Europe, where the
1973–74 oil shock brought an end to labor-importing programs.
Over the next decade, as the immigration gates shut ever tighter,
pressure mounted on Europe's remaining asylum gates, and when
these in turn began to be shut down in the second half of the
1980s, part of the demand shifted to Canada and most recently to
the United States.

Cuba: The Cold War Comes to America's Backyard

Introducing a set of case studies covering the Caribbean and
Central America, Christopher Mitchell states that "since 1960,
U.S. foreign policy has exerted a major influence over U.S. immi-
gration policy" throughout the region except for Mexico, and fur-

ther, that it "often helps cause immigration as well as influencing immigration *policy.*"[7] This is, if anything, an understatement: America's impact on the economic and political life of its "backyard" has been so overwhelming that it is difficult to sort out which aspects of international migration are attributable more specifically to foreign policy in the narrower sense.[8]

Following a brief military occupation in 1898, Cuba's political and economic development was shaped more indirectly by U.S. investors and ambassadors. Its economy centered on sugar plantations, with highly concentrated ownership of land and a labor force of proletarianized peasants, held in place from the 1930s onward by the dictatorial rule of Fulgencio Batista. As will be elaborated in the discussion of Central America, this combination of elements is particularly conducive to revolutionary upheavals. In the post–World War II period, acquiescence to the rule of the Batista regime was undermined by very high unemployment. One of several challengers was a small guerrilla group organized by urban middle class radicals, with the support of peasants from the regions where it operated. Somewhat unexpectedly, Fidel Castro's July 26th movement successfully undermined the regime; after the failure of a last minute effort by the U.S. Central Intelligence Agency (CIA) to change the course of events, Batista fled, and in January 1959 Castro and his troops entered Havana without a fight. He then quickly consolidated his power base by implementing a radical agrarian reform.

The unexpected advent of a successful Socialist revolution in America's own backyard in 1959–60 constituted an unprecedented challenge to its hegemony, which demonstrated the inadequacy of traditional instruments of regional control. Not only Castro's specific policies, but the consolidation of the revolution itself and its potential effect on similarly constituted neighbors brought him inexorably into a confrontation with the United States. Washington's overriding policy became the overthrow of the regime and the containment of "other Cubas."

Cuba also constituted a major turning point with regard to the linkage between foreign policy and immigration, in that for the first time the ongoing policy of encouraging defectors required the immediate and massive provision of first asylum in the United

States itself. Overall, the case illustrates not only the prominence of foreign policy considerations in the making of refugee policy, but also the key role of refugee policy in the formation of refugee flows: "If Castro's policies created the potential for mass exodus, U.S. policies made the exodus possible."[9] But as we know from hindsight, these policies also provided an opportunity for Fidel Castro to turn emigration into a weapon of his own.

Immediately after coming to power, Castro encouraged the emigration of potential opponents; concomitantly, in keeping with established policy, Washington welcomed the massive exodus of the upper and middle class Cubans as an instrument contributing to the delegitimation and destabilization of the new regime. In the absence of numerical limitations on annual immigration from the Western Hemisphere, there were no legal obstacles to their entry, and Washington quickly opened the door wide by way of a "passive admissions policy." In this manner, some 200,000 landed between January 1959 and the end of 1962, when the missile crisis prompted Cuba to close its border.

The Cubans were initially regarded as temporary exiles who would return when the Castro regime fell or was overthrown, an objective on whose behalf they were enlisted into the Bay of Pigs operation. After its failure, however, the immediate strategic value of additional refugees sharply declined. Concurrently, the United States envisaged the exiles' permanent settlement, and in 1962 devised a Migration and Refugee Assistance Act to alleviate the costs incurred by localities. The following year, during the missile crisis, the United States imposed a blockade on Cuba and drastically reduced flights, leaving some 350,000 holders of visa waivers stranded within Cuba itself. The boycott and sanctions that isolated Cuba from 1962 on fostered severe economic difficulties, and these in turn brought about a deterioration in the material and political positions of the middle strata of Cuban society, prompting growing demands for the authorization to emigrate. By 1965, however, the Communist party had been formally established and the regime was fully in control. Fidel Castro decided it was time once again to rid Cuba of the discontented, and in September declared that all who wished to leave Cuba were free to do so. The decision also provided an opportunity to redistribute the emigrants' housing to party faithful.

In response, President Johnson declared that "those who seek refuge here will find it," and indicated that he would use his authority to massively parole those seeking family reunion and others languishing in Cuban prisons. It is noteworthy that this declaration was issued on the occasion of signing the newly enacted immigration law, according to which parole authority was to be used only for urgent individual cases. Following a short-lived boatlift, Cuba and the United States negotiated a program of orderly departures by way of "freedom flights." When the exodus turned out to be larger than expected, Castro restricted the exit of males eligible for military service, technical personnel, and persons convicted of counterrevolutionary crimes, and in August 1971 he announced that the airlift would end after those already registered left.

Altogether, some 270,000 Cubans left for the United States over the seven-year period. On the American side, although the policy initially received strong bipartisan support, as time wore on some critics suggested that the acceptance of refugees by the United States might strengthen the Cuban regime by reducing discontent. The changing class and racial composition of the refugees also triggered doubts regarding their desirability, and there were increasing congressional rumblings over the costs of the airlift and the assistance program. However, the cold war consensus still prevailed.

Indochina

As a by-product of the Vietnam War, the massive resettlement of Indochinese in the United States from 1975 on provides a dramatic example of the unanticipated immigration consequences of foreign policy.[10] Motivated by a sense of obligation, the initial program was limited to employees and former employees of the United States and their dependents. However, after this was accomplished, more refugees appeared on the scene, and concern that they might destabilize the first asylum countries prompted the launching of a new resettlement program. This may have acted as a magnet, prompting the exit of Vietnamese who seized the opportunity to improve their economic condition.

As the Khmer Rouge and the North Vietnamese neared victory, on April 3, 1975, President Ford invoked the prospect of a massive refugee crisis to justify the administration's proposed last-ditch aid package to the Thieu government. Albeit not noted as such at the time, this marked a reversal of the postwar stance, and anticipated arguments that would be voiced more explicitly at the time of the Mariel crisis five years later, as well as the rationale invoked in support of President Reagan's policy in Central America.

Although it was granted that the United States must provide a haven for its most prominent Indochinese associates, no thought appears to have been given to any sort of massive rescue operation, and the rapid pace of events caught the American authorities unprepared. In Saigon, afraid of precipitating the collapse of the Thieu government as well as a deadly stampede, as occurred in Da Nang when the South Vietnamese army retreated from the highlands in March, Ambassador Graham Martin refused to plan for an evacuation. Despite this, some of his staff, as well as officials serving in the field, felt a strong obligation to rescue their Vietnamese coworkers, and began to develop an unofficial evacuation scheme for both Americans and high-risk Vietnamese. Leaving aside the millions of military and civilian personnel serving the collapsing regime, the latter included over 100,000 employees and former employees of U.S. agencies, plus their families, totaling close to 1 million people.

On April 12 some 800 Cambodians were evacuated with the American embassy staff from Phnom Penh; however, several thousand more reached the Thailand border on foot, most of whom were subsequently relocated to the United States. A few days later, after the administration failed to obtain congressional approval for military aid, President Ford formed an Interagency Task Force to organize an evacuation plan for Vietnam. On April 17 Secretary of State Kissinger ordered the removal of Americans, and also asked Ambassador Martin to submit a plan on behalf of as many as 200,000 Vietnamese. Initially, it was thought they might be transported to neighboring countries, where some might obtain long-term asylum; the remainder would be resettled in the United States and other third countries.

However, Thailand and Malaysia made it very clear that they would accept refugees only for temporary asylum, and on condition that they be quickly resettled elsewhere. The UNHCR, which was contacted to explore the possibility of third country resettlement, treaded cautiously because it wanted to develop good relations with the incoming regime, and in any case questioned the Indochinese's qualifications as "convention" refugees. The "third country" option was largely ruled out because those contacted viewed the problem as an exclusively American one, except for France. In the face of this, the task force director decided instead to move the Indochinese to U.S. bases and Guam for processing and eventual resettlement in the United States. Given the constraints of the immigration law, which allowed for only 17,400 refugees a year, the plan would require once again a massive exercise of the president's parole authority.

The end came more quickly than anticipated. On April 21, the day the Thieu government lost its last battle, President Ford declared in a television interview that the United States had an obligation to evacuate large numbers of South Vietnamese; the following day the Senate Judiciary Committee unanimously approved parole for 150,000 Indochinese, including 50,000 "high-risk" Vietnamese; and Saigon fell a week later. By the end of the month, the United States had evacuated some 65,000 Vietnamese, and about the same number made it out on their own in commandeered planes and vessels, by sea in fishing boats and makeshift craft, or overland through Laos and Cambodia to Thailand. However, tens of thousands of American-connected Vietnamese were left behind, not to mention the over 1.5 million military and civilian personnel who served the defeated regime.

With the country in the midst of a recession and lingering prejudice against Asians, to mobilize opinion leaders on behalf of his program, President Ford appointed an Advisory Committee on Indochina Refugees and proposed federal funds for resettlement. Although the American public—as represented in polls—opposed massive Indochinese immigration, the refugee program was accepted as an obligation even by the antiwar camp, and no significant opposition surfaced. Less than a month after the final evacuation of Saigon, a grumbling Congress approved the Indochina Migration and Refugee Assistance Act, authorizing funds for a massive two-year resettlement program; concurrently, the United States provided support to first asylum countries within the region. Overall, about 130,000 refugees were resettled in the United States and a mere 6,000 in third countries, mostly in France. However, when processing was terminated in December 1975, there were still 80,000 Indochinese in camps throughout Thailand, including Cambodians and Laotians as well as Vietnamese.

Having discharged what it considered its obligation, following its defeat the United States distanced itself from the region altogether; in contrast with the past use of "defectors" as an instrument of foreign policy, little was made of the thousands who continued to flee to neighboring countries. After the emergency program expired, Indochinese were being admitted at the rate of a mere 100 a month under the seventh preference category of the immigration law. However, within the State Department a group of regional specialists advocated additional resettlement, both on grounds of continued obligation to erstwhile associates and because the new arrivals threatened to destabilize the remaining non-Communist countries in the region. Working with experienced refugee advocates within the nongovernmental organization (NGO) world, they took the lead in organizing a blue ribbon Citizens' Commission on Indochinese Refugees, modeled after the Citizens' Committee on Displaced Persons created after World War II. The group successfully mobilized widespread support on behalf of Indochinese, and, in coalition with others, contributed to the expansion of U.S. refugee admissions more generally throughout the 1980s.

In May 1976 the State Department requested and obtained authorization to parole what it insisted was a final group of 11,000 Indochinese, mostly Laotians. A UNHCR representative declared the decision catastrophic, because it would act as a magnet and contribute to the further draining of Laos. By 1977 the flow from Vietnam subsided. However, the following year, there was an unprecedented outpouring of "boat people," uprooted by Vietnam's severe economic setbacks and its decision to nationalize private trade. Many were ethnic Chinese, who were acutely affected by these developments. There were indications as well that Vietnamese officials welcomed the opportunity of an "ethnic cleansing," and that some of them, as well as Chinese entrepreneurs, profited from the exodus and contributed to its further expansion by providing vessels to those attempting to get out. China responded to reports of discrimination against the Sino-Vietnamese by cutting off aid to Vietnam, and the deterioration of relationships between the two countries in turn further jeopardized the situation of the target group.

Although an advisory panel reported to the secretary of state that many "fled primarily because of . . . economic and social conditions" rather than because of persecution, the department's regional specialists insisted that "there existed strong foreign policy reasons for developing a long-range refugee program."[11] After authorizing another 15,000 paroles, the White House formed a new interagency task force under the leadership of Philip Habib, one of the State Department's refugee advocates, which recommended massive resettlement to alleviate pressures on the Association of Southeast Asian Nations (ASEAN) countries. This was subsequently endorsed by the National Security Council as well.

Shut tight since the Khmer Rouge takeover, Cambodia now began to generate refugees as well. However, despite mounting reports of horrendous exactions, the Carter administration was more interested in supporting the government of Thailand and in wooing China to counterbalance the growing Soviet influence in Hanoi than in sounding the alarm about the situation in Cambodia. It therefore refrained from overt criticism of Khmer Rouge rule. Accordingly, in March 1978, when parole was extended to another 25,000 Indochinese, Cambodians were not included. The Citizens' Commission then took up their cause, and in the fall of 1978, Congress enacted a joint resolution directing the attorney general to modify the parole criteria to admit Khmer as "categoric" refugees.

Despite the repeated use of parole, resettlement fell further behind, and by November 1978 only 38,000 of the 94,000 recent arrivals in first asylum countries had been relocated. In the face of growing international tensions within the region, U.S. ambassador to Thailand Morton Abramowitz urged rapid expansion of resettlement on an international basis, as well as sanctions against Vietnam for its "pushout." Under pressure from the United States and the ASEAN countries, the UNHCR organized an international consultation on December 11 and 12, but this failed to produce a solution. The situation became even more dramatic after the Vietnamese launched their lightning offensive against Pol Pot, precipitating a massive flight of Cambodians toward Thailand. The Thai closed the border and treated all those trying to cross it as illegal immigrants; many were brutally pushed back by the army. Two months later, the outbreak of war between China and Vietnam produced another exodus of Sino-Vietnamese, most of whom were ruthlessly rejected by Malaysia.

Widely reported by the media, these events provoked a groundswell of support throughout the West for a major rescue effort, and the Carter administration took the lead in organizing another conference in Geneva in July 1979. This time, the industrialized nations pledged a total of 260,000 admissions for resettlement, as well as adequate aid. Also, Secretary-General Waldheim announced that under pressure from the West, Vietnam had pledged to make every effort to stop "illegal departures." Paralleling a demand the British authorities in Hong Kong had made of China some time earlier, this marked a major turning point in both foreign and refugee policy. As Loescher and Scanlan have pointed out, the Western countries faced a human rights dilemma, which was resolved at the expense of the victims: "Control over the outflow of people from Vietnam was restored by undercutting the right of people facing persecution to move out of danger and flee their country."[12] After the Vietnamese authorities clamped down, there was a dramatic decline in new arrivals; confident that the refugees would be soon removed, the first asylum countries became more cooperative as well.

However, the Cambodians along the Thai border were still in jeopardy. Given the prime objective of countering Soviet supported Vietnamese aggression, Ambassador Abramowitz refrained from criticizing the Thai government's actions; persuaded that it was imperative to stabilize the situation, since the UNHCR was ineffective, he urged the United States to take the lead in organizing local relief, providing food and clothing not only to the refugees but also to armed Cambodian resistance groups, including the Khmer Rouge; and this should be coupled with substantial resettlement in the United States. However, the Thai opposed resettlement because they believed it would encourage more people to leave Cambodia. Sharing this view, regional UNHCR officials undertook to negotiate the Cambodians' repatriation; however, their efforts failed.

The prospect of admitting a large number of Cambodians in addition to the Vietnamese to whom a commitment had already been made came up for consideration while the United States was in the midst of the Cuban-Haitian crisis. Whereas Indochinese activists within the State Department championed the program, the coordinator for refugee affairs and the State Department's Bureau of Refugee Programs opposed it on the same grounds as the Thai and the UNHCR. Once again, riding on a wave of media induced sympathy, the Citizens' Commission on Indochinese Refugees and its congressional allies gained the upper hand. Despite mounting reluctance in the country at large and within the Congress, shortly before stepping down, the Carter administration agreed to accept 30,000 Cambodian refugees, and processing began in January 1981.

Soviet Jews

Although after the death of Stalin the Soviet Union maintained a highly restrictive exit policy, in the 1960s voices arose within the Kremlin to rid the country of the politically disaffected and the Jews.[13] The situation of the latter was somewhat ambiguous. Having benefited from the elimination of the official anti-Semitism of the Tsarist regime, by the end of the 1930s they constituted the most educated group in the Soviet Union, and were especially prominent among scientific and technical elites, a position they still held in 1970 when barriers were raised to their mobility. Like all Soviet citizens, they lacked freedom of religion and were heavily dependent on the state for the maintenance of their cultural life; but as a minority, in a society still rife with anti-Semitism, Jews were especially vulnerable to harassment.

Anti-Semites within the Kremlin would be happy to see them go, but there was concern that the opening of the door to Jews would invite pressure from Germans and Armenians for exit visas as well, and that in addition to occasioning a very real brain drain, a liberal emigration policy for certain minorities would anger ordinary Russians. In the 1960s fewer than 10,000 Jews were allowed to leave; however, in the latter part of the decade, they initiated an unprecedented public campaign for exit visas, which, thanks to more open communications, evoked considerable support in the United States and in Western Europe, including from Communist parties. By virtue of their political experience, the well-organized Jewish groups in the United States persuaded foreign policy decision makers to incorporate Jewish emigration as a condition for improved relations with the Soviet Union. The Kremlin responded with a mixed strategy, granting some visas to relieve the pressure, cracking down on applicants as a deterrent to others—which had the effect of mobilizing further support abroad.

In 1971 the Nixon administration promised a liberal admissions policy for those able to leave, including the use of "parole" if necessary; eager to conclude the Salt agreement and to broaden its trade with the United States, the Kremlin relented and granted thousands of exit visas, rising to an unprecedented 2,500 a month in 1973. The move was rationalized on the basis of nationality policy, whereby Jews were allowed to leave for their designated "homeland" in Israel. The fiction was maintained, despite the fact that most of the emigrants preferred to go to the United States and did end up there, an outcome that the Soviets may have welcomed because of Arab objections to substantial immigration into Israel.

In 1972, however, Moscow began requiring educated emigrants to compensate the state for the costs of their training. The return to a more restrictive policy prompted legislative action in Congress to make trade concessions explicitly conditional on the liberalization of emigration policy. Despite their reluctance to allow human rights issues to intrude on detente, President Nixon and Secretary of State Kissinger bowed to congressional pressure. The Soviet

Union reacted by temporarily suspending the collection of the education tax and allowing emigration to rise to unprecedented levels. After the policy changed again in the wake of the Yom Kippur war, the American linkage between the right of exit and trade was formalized by enactment of the Jackson-Vanek Amendment to the Trade Act of 1974, whereby most-favored-nation treatment may not be granted to any "nonmarket economy country" that limits the rights of its nationals to emigrate.

Subsequently, Jewish emigration fluctuated widely as a function of the general state of relations between the superpowers, the short-term economic interests of the Soviet Union, and the relative clout of anti-Semites within the Kremlin; in the late 1970s about one-third of recent Jewish emigrants surveyed attributed their departure to the authorities' desire to get rid of them. It is noteworthy that a similar pattern prevailed with respect to Soviet citizens of German descent, whose exit was linked to diplomatic and trade negotiations with the Federal Republic.

The 1980 Refugee Act and Beyond

Although agreeing to the successive Indochinese programs, Congress was determined to narrow the president's parole authority, both to regain control over immigration policy and as a concomitant of its attempt in the post-Vietnam period to restrain presidential power in the sphere of foreign policy. Encompassing the expanding network of NGOs concerned with refugees, the reformers wanted the United States to sign the 1951 convention and 1967 protocol, and reorient its own refugee policy toward the international norm. The Carter administration was responsive to these objectives, in keeping with its overall commitment to the promotion of human rights as a goal of foreign policy.

The movement benefited from the pressure of events. To insure congressional approval of the Salt II agreement, during 1978 and 1979 Moscow approved over 50,000 visas to Soviet Jews. Existing provisions for the annual admission of 17,400 refugees were clearly insufficient, and the pace of resettlement also outstripped existing governmental assistance programs. In February 1979 the Carter administration therefore created a new Office of the U.S.

Coordinator for Refugee Affairs, and a year later the Congress enacted a new refugee law.

In keeping with the reformers' aspirations, the law incorporated the "convention" definition of refugees as persons with a "well-founded fear of persecution." It established a normal baseline of 50,000 entries a year, approximately three times the previous level, but the president was given authority to admit a higher number in a given year if justified on the basis of humanitarian concerns or the national interest. The level and allocation among various groups were to be determined in consultation with Congress. By requiring claimants to demonstrate that their exit was attributable to a legitimate fear of persecution, the law eliminated the presumption that all those fleeing Communist countries were de facto refugees. Given some 8 million people worldwide who met the convention definition, most of them in first asylum countries awaiting resettlement, the law specified further that preference should be given to people "of special humanitarian concern to the United States." Parole authority was to be used henceforth only for individual cases, as originally intended.

The measure also established for the first time, in keeping with international law and the established practices of other liberal states, a statutory process whereby any alien physically present in the United States—irrespective of immigration status—could claim asylum on the grounds of meeting the criteria used to define refugees. "Asylees" would be charged against annual refugee admissions, but it was anticipated that they would amount to no more than some 5,000 out of the 50,000 total. In fact, asylum subsequently emerged as one of the most perplexing and controversial aspects of refugee policy. Omitted from consideration altogether were those who feared returning because of general conditions rather than "persecution," and hence did not meet the convention criteria for asylum. Since the 1960s such persons might be granted "extended voluntary departure" (EVD), a discretionary device developed by the Immigration and Naturalization Service (INS) that could be put into effect when the State Department judged it appropriate.

Thus despite the legislators' intent, both by what it did and did not do, the law granted the executive considerable latitude in shaping refugee policy and, should it so wish, to harness it to foreign policy objectives as in the past. As interpreted by the Reagan and Bush administrations, "of special humanitarian concern" was applied to Communist countries almost exclusively, and within those, to groups that had strong advocates in the United States, notably Soviet Jews and Indochinese. The asylum process and EVD were implemented in a similar manner as well. The Mariel crisis, which erupted less than two months after the law was enacted, highlighted its inadequacy for dealing with such situations, and policy was made in effect by the White House. As will be discussed shortly, the crisis also revealed the vulnerability of the United States to the manipulation of human outflows by an antagonist. Coming on top of the Vietnamese pushout, the Mariel experience prompted a reappraisal of the longstanding foreign policy based commitment to welcome all those wishing to leave Communist countries as refugees.

The Reagan administration's approach to foreign policy sharpened the disparity between U.S. responses to different groups seeking recognition as refugees with a claim to resettlement in the United States. In keeping with its more aggressive stance toward the Communist world, the administration encouraged its citizens to "defect," and concomitantly undertook to resettle those who did; but its rejection of human rights considerations as inappropriate to the conduct of foreign policy, as well as its emphasis on law and order, fostered a more restrictive policy toward refugees and asylum seekers from other countries, and especially those seeking to escape from violence attributable in large part to U.S. policies in the Caribbean and Central America.

Arrivals from Southeast Asia reached an all-time high of 163,-797 in 1980, and by the following year, "virtually all of the domestic forces influencing policy . . . demanded a radical reduction in Indochinese admission levels";[14] however, the NGOs, which had developed an organizational stake in large-scale resettlement, remained strong advocates of an open door. Carrying out its mandate under the new law, the INS began to subject Indochinese to individual interviews for qualification as refugees, while regional specialists in the State Department and hardliners generally continued to advocate a permissive admission policy on foreign policy grounds. Their views ultimately prevailed, and in September 1981 President Reagan recommended raising the number of admissions under the 1980 Refugee Act to 173,000, of whom 119,000 were set aside for Indochinese. However, Congress limited federal reimbursement to the states for resettlement, and cut the period of assistance by half to eighteen months. This in turn prompted the states to put pressure on the federal government to reduce the intake of refugees. The legislators also induced the State Department to discontinue attributing refugee status to the Indochinese on a "categoric" basis, and to ascertain their qualifications on an individual basis instead. Consequently, the rate of acceptance of those confined in first asylum countries dropped precipitously, leaving those rejected to linger in the camps. However, foreign policy considerations prevailed once again, and in mid-1983 the Reagan administration issued a National Security Council directive restoring the more permissive categoric approach. Accordingly, by the fall INS acceptance rates in Southeast Asia rose to 83 percent.

After dipping sharply at the end of the Carter presidency, with *perestroika* and *glasnost*, emigration from the Soviet Union, including Jews, ethnic Germans, Armenians, and Christian Pentecostals, resumed and rapidly expanded. However, the very reforms that made massive exit possible also rendered the award of refugee status to the emigrants more questionable. With regard to Jews, initially the United States maintained its established policy whereby the emigrants traveled to a reception center in Vienna, and after a short stay went to await completion of the process in Rome, where those wishing to go to the United States rather than Israel were issued refugee visas by the INS. However, the growing exodus rapidly exceeded the limits of the ongoing system.

The first problem arose when the outbreak of violence in Azerbaijan in late 1987 prompted a large increase in Armenian applications. To meet the demand, the State Department reallocated some 15,000 of the slots scheduled for Southeast Asia to Soviet citizens; but Congress objected because Thailand was invoking the slow pace of resettlement as a justification for pushing boat people out to sea. The president resolved the problem by expanding the annual refugee quota by 15,000 to 83,500. However, a large number of Armenians were stranded in Moscow in July 1988 when the U.S. consulate abruptly suspended scheduled departure interviews; this was prompted by the depletion of budgetary funds as well as a determination by State Department lawyers that Armenians were being accepted as refugees without any finding of persecution, in violation of the 1980 law. The move was bitterly ironic, because it came in the wake of President Reagan's visit, in the course of which he urged Secretary Gorbachev to lift remaining restrictions on emigration. In the face of an outcry at home and abroad, the State Department appealed for private support and resumed processing; but a more demanding standard of documentation was required, leading to the rejection of some 100 Armenian applicants. In mid-September, the INS office handling Jews in Rome also began enforcing the more demanding standards. The rate of turndown rose further at the beginning of 1989.

Thanks to the effective efforts of American advocacy organizations, over the next several years, the number of refugee admissions set aside for Soviet citizens under the 1980 law rose to 50,-000; and in 1990 the ambiguity of the applicants' status was resolved by enactment of a law whereby Soviet Jews and Evangelical Christians were declared categoric refugees, which made it unnecessary for them to demonstrate individual qualification.

Foreign Policy and Migration in the Western Hemisphere in the 1980s

The Cuba-Haiti Crisis of 1980

The "freedom flights" organized in 1965 were interrupted in 1973, leaving over 100,000 approved emigrants stranded in Cuba. Their hopes soared when negotiations resumed three years later. For the first time exiles were allowed to visit their homeland, and Castro authorized the departure of some political prisoners as well as persons of dual nationality. However, relations between the antagonists deteriorated again when Cuba participated in military operations in Angola and Ethiopia. Early in 1980 the CIA predicted that Cuba might resort to large-scale emigration to reduce the discontent occasioned by deteriorating economic conditions, and Castro himself threatened to unleash a torrent of people; however, on the American side nothing was done to prepare for this eventuality.

Already bogged down in the hostage crisis and a difficult electoral campaign, the Carter administration was thus taken by surprise in April 1980 when some 10,000 Cubans invaded the Peruvian embassy and asked for political asylum. After some hesitations, including a temporary airlift to Costa Rica, Castro announced that everyone could leave and opened up Mariel harbor to those wanting to fetch their relatives. He also released some 8,000 common criminals as well as imprisoned homosexuals, mental patients, and the terminally ill. The Florida Cuban community then launched a massive boatlift.

Aware of public opposition to immigration and the growing unpopularity of the Indochinese refugee program, the Carter administration was initially reluctant to provide massive asylum; but after presidential candidate Ronald Reagan seized upon the boatlift as a campaign issue, it shifted to a more positive stance, and the INS began distributing applications for asylum. However, as the exodus grew, bringing in its wake some thousands released from prisons and mental institutions, the administration began having second thoughts. Its problems were compounded by a concurrent increase of asylum claims by Haitians, who also came by boat and landed surreptitiously along the east coast of Florida. In contrast with Cubans, however, those apprehended were generally detained as ordinary undocumented immigrants and their asylum claims massively turned down. After the African-American community charged that the differential treatment was motivated by racial discrimination, the Carter White House awarded to all arrivals the status of "entrant," a newly created ad hoc category that enabled beneficiaries to remain in the United States while their status was being resolved, but did not allow them to apply for permanent residence. Those who could not be immediately released to relatives were confined to military installations.[15]

Although Castro closed Mariel at the end of September, probably in order to secure the cooperation of the United States in dealing with renewed airplane hijackings, the episode had shattered what remained of the cold war consensus on refugee policy. The administration's indecision over Mariel contributed to President Carter's deteriorating political situation, and a riot among Cubans confined at Fort Chaffee, Arkansas, was blamed for the defeat of the incumbent governor, Bill Clinton. In December the outgoing administration began talks with Cuba to regularize migration, and an agreement was reached on most points the following month, including Cuba's willingness to take back those deemed "excludable" by virtue of their criminal status. However, Cuba delayed signing the agreement, possibly to persuade the incoming Reagan administration to engage in formal negotiations.

Instead, the United States stopped issuing visas to Cubans until the Castro government agreed to take back the excludables. In July 1981 Washington announced further that it would henceforth interdict boats across the Florida straits and turn their passengers back to Cuba (as well as Haiti). However, these were bargaining ploys, and eventually the Reagan administration did engage in negotiations, which led to the signing of a migration agreement in December 1984, whereby Cuba would take back 2,476 excludables, while the United States would accept former political prisoners as refugees, and resume the issuance of ordinary immigration visas to Cuban nationals in Cuba up to the usual per-country limit of 20,000 a year. Cuba suspended the agreement when the United States launched Radio Marti in May 1985, and the United States responded by suspending the issuance of visas. Two years later, the agreement was restored, but shortly suspended once again. As of 1991 there were only about 200 "excludables" in American prisons.

The Mariel crisis dramatically revealed the downside of America's cold war refugee policy, whereby the commitment to take in any citizens of Communist countries who might get out rendered adjoining states vulnerable to a massive self-propelled exodus, or worse, to a willful pushout. Henceforth, Cubans were no longer welcome defectors, but "bullets aimed at Miami." In line with this, the Reagan administration shortly began to invoke the threat of an invasion of "feet people" to mobilize support for its interventionist policies in Central America. With mounting opposition to immigration generally, even politically powerful defenders of the tradi-

tional open door for Cubans lost ground, making it easier for
Washington to act decisively.

As materials conditions deteriorated further after the break-up
of the Soviet Union in 1991 and the enactment of yet stiffer sanctions by the United States the following year, Cubans were ever
more desperate to get out, while the weakened apparatus of control provided more opportunities for them to do so. By mid-1994
the influx of boat people recorded in Florida had surpassed the
total for all of 1993. The possibility of another Mariel came nearer
in early August when the Cuban authorities stopped valuable vessels but allowed rafters to leave unimpeded.

Possibly in response to entreaties from Florida's Democratic
governor, Lawton Chiles, at this time the American authorities
acted promptly and firmly to dissuade Florida based Cubans from
staging a boatlift, while indicating to Castro that Washington
would consider a massive Haiti-style interception of departing vessels. Although stopping short of a blockade, Washington then expanded patrols to stop the still growing exodus, which passed the
20,000 mark at the end of August 1994, and also explored further
holding emplacements in the Caribbean region. The first contingent landed in Panama on September 6.

Concurrently, however, negotiations got underway to resolve
the crisis and regularize ordinary immigration. A deal was struck
at the end of merely one week, whereby Havana pledged to stop its
citizens from fleeing in exchange for Washington's agreement to
accept at least 20,000 new Cuban immigrants a year.

Haiti

Burdened with a long history of political instability, Haiti is the
only country in the Western Hemisphere ranked within the World
Bank's bottom-most category of "low income economies." Its links
with the United States were reinforced during the protracted period of military occupation, from 1915 to 1934, and even after-
ward, Haiti remained in effect a U.S. protectorate. In the absence
of economic development, many of the country's rural poor were
driven to seek work abroad, in the sugar cane fields of the Dominican Republic or Puerto Rico. Despite its especially brutal charac-

ter, the regime launched by Francois Duvalier in 1957 was treated benevolently by the United States as a reliable ally in the cold war against Cuba. After "Papa Doc" undertook to destroy the political opposition, mostly professionals from the mulatto upper class, many fled to the United States, where their entry was unproblematic because there were at that time no numerical restrictions on immigration from the Western Hemisphere, and the group easily met the "qualitative" requirements. In their wake came a somewhat larger stream from more modest strata, driven by deteriorating political and economic conditions; American aid designed to increase market agriculture may have contributed to uprooting poor peasants. Adding to Haiti's woes was the reinstatement of American sugar protectionism, which had a catastrophic effect on the many thousands of Haitian cane cutters in the Dominican Republic. As demand for immigrant and visitor's visas escalated, U.S. consular officers instituted more demanding procedures; however, the main effect of this policy was to increase illegal entries.

As indicated earlier, after it was accused of discrimination, the Carter administration granted Haitians the status of "entrants," on a par with Cubans; however, in mid-1981 the Reagan administration reinstated differential treatment and began incarcerating apprehended Haitians. It then secured from the Duvalier government the right to search Haitian vessels on the high seas and its agreement to stop unauthorized emigration as a condition for receiving aid. The U.S. Coast Guard stopped and boarded unflagged vessels in the Westward Passage, and returned Haitians deemed bound for the United States as undocumented aliens to their country of origin. Although the INS insisted the arrangements included procedures for the determination of refugee status, of over 20,000 interdicted from the program's inception to 1989 only six were brought to the United States to pursue their asylum applications. Interdiction was an effective deterrent to entry, as indicated by a drop in the number of Haitians apprehended in Florida; concomitantly, the number of people turned back on the high seas climbed to unprecedented levels. As the result of court challenges, eventually most of the incarcerated Haitians were released, and many qualified for "amnesty" under a special provision of the Immigration Reform and Control Act of 1986. Under the pressure of liberal activists in Congress, U.S. diplomacy shifted from unqualified support of the Haitian government to a more balanced stance, with some recognition of Haiti's democratic opposition. This helped to undermine Jean-Claude Duvalier, who was driven from power by a popular uprising in 1986. After a series of dictatorships, in 1989–90 Haiti was swept up in the worldwide wave of democratization. The country's first free elections, monitored by the United Nations, returned populist priest Jean-Bertrand Aristide as president. However, he was ousted by the military in September 1991. Although there is no evidence of direct American involvement in the coup, Aristide was deplored by the large American firms exploiting cheap Haitian labor, and the CIA sought to undermine his standing in Washington; furthermore, the United States trained and supported the Haitian police, which collaborated with the military and helped launch what became its terrorist auxiliary, according to Allan Nairn, writing in *The Nation,* October 24, 1994.

In the wake of the coup, thousands attempted to flee the country. However, President Bush used the treaty that granted U.S. ships the right to intercept Haitian vessels on the high seas to divert the Haitians, first to Guantanamo Bay and later directly back to Haiti. Over 30,000 were returned in this manner in the sixteen months following the coup.

Democratic presidential candidate Bill Clinton pledged to change the policy, but reversed himself immediately after taking office to prevent a flood of refugees that would weaken his political base in Florida. Over the next year and a half, the administration vacillated between putting pressure on President Aristide to accept a compromise, and on the military to relinquish power. In July 1993 U.S. special envoy Ambassador Lawrence Pezullo secured the agreement of Haiti's military to restore Father Aristide by October 30; however, no sanctions were provided. The Haitian leaders violated their pledge, organized a humiliating reception for the token ship sent out to mark an American presence, and further stepped up the repression. Over the next few months, the newly organized "Haitian Front for Advancement and Progress" (FRAPH) sponsored by the government killed hundreds of Aristide supporters. The exodus continued, albeit at a lower rate, with many attempting to reach the United States by way of the Bahamas.

Under pressure from the Congressional Black Caucus and its liberal allies, in late March 1994 the Clinton administration announced it would adopt a tougher negotiating stance toward the military, but still rejected the option of using American troops to oust them. The following month, the Coast Guard departed from established policy and allowed a vessel carrying some 400 Haitians to land in Florida; however, the administration denied this signaled a more permissive refugee policy, and insisted Haitians seeking refugee status must continue to apply at the U.S. embassy in Port-au-Prince, where highly restrictive procedures remained in force. Matters came to a head a few days later, following yet another massacre of Aristide supporters, including women and children. Adopting the strategy used to induce a change of U.S. policy toward South Africa a few years earlier, a number of Washington lawmakers got themselves arrested after staging a sit-in in front of the White House; concurrently, Randall Robinson, executive director of TransAfrica, a lobbying group for Africa and the Caribbean, undertook a hunger strike to induce a change in refugee policy.

In response, despite the objections of Secretary of State Warren Christopher, the administration announced that Haitians intercepted at sea would no longer be automatically sent back, but would have an opportunity to establish their refugee status. The president also fired his special envoy Lawrence Pezullo and replaced him with former Representative William Gray 3d, who had been a member of the Congressional Black Caucus. The United States further secured a new Security Council resolution imposing stiffer sanctions to back up the embargo, and the president hinted that force was no longer ruled out to restore President Aristide. Although this drew objections from most Latin American countries, preparations for an invasion got underway.

Haitians picked up by the Coast Guard were sent for processing to a U.S. hospital ship anchored off the coast of Jamaica, and the administration also planned to open an interviewing center in the Turks and Caicos Islands. In the first few weeks, nearly one-third were granted refugee status, as against one in twenty previously. By the end of June the number of boat people surged to its highest level in two years. In the face of this, the administration shifted gears once again and announced it would no longer allow Haitians fleeing by boat to be resettled in the United States, but would provide them with safe havens within the Caribbean. However, this plan went awry when Panama withdrew its earlier offer to accept refugees. On July 31 the Security Council authorized a U.S. invasion and occupation of Haiti if sanctions failed to remove the military, and subsequently Washington issued what was in effect an ultimatum. Thanks to last minute negotiations, in late September American troops landed in Haiti with the consent of the junta; soon thereafter Aristide was returned to power.

Central America

The revolutionary and counterrevolutionary conflicts that engulfed the region in the post–World War II period, climaxing in the 1970s and 1980s, were rooted in an explosive social configuration.[16] While in the 1930s the rest of Latin America started to follow an import-substitution industrialization strategy, the Central American countries remained largely plantation economies with an extremely unequal distribution of landed property, maintained by brutally authoritarian landlord dominated governments, beholden to American companies and ultimately dependent on U.S. politico-strategic force. Dramatic population increase intensified pressures on the land, producing considerable urban migration, much of it channeled into an informal sector. Given established links with the United States, once uprooted, unemployed Central American peasants easily moved there in search of work when the opportunity arose. The emigration "push" intensified in the mid-1970s when, after regional sugar production expanded to pick up the U.S. market share vacated by the exclusion of Cuba, American sugar interests engineered the adoption of a highly protective policy. The violent upheavals had an additional and more direct displacement effect.

Economic and political determinants of migration are especially difficult to disentangle, as the conditions that gave rise to the conflicts also drove people northward in response to opportunities provided by U.S. employers, and, in turn, the presence of established Central American communities in the United States facilitated a rapid expansion of the movement when violence broke out.

Nicaragua. Under Marine occupation from 1909 to 1933, Nicaragua inherited an American organized National Guard used by the Somoza family as the main instrument of its three-generation-long dictatorship. With aid from Cuba, in 1961 the opposition organized the Frente Sandinista de Liberacion National (FNSL), along the lines of Castro's original movement. In 1976 President Carter chose Nicaragua as a showcase for Washington's new human rights activism, thereby legitimizing the growing opposition. The assassination of Pedro Joaquin Chamorro, a moderate opposition figure, sparked a widely based insurrection; although Washington tried to broker a middle-of-the-road solution, the Sandinistas gained the upper hand. Some 200,000 Nicaraguans sought protection in Honduras and Costa Rica during the insurrection; most returned after Somoza's fall, but a large segment of the National Guard remained in Honduras, where they became the nucleus of the American supported contras.

The Sandinistas then undertook a program of radical structural change, including a major agrarian reform and a literacy campaign. Their close relations with Cuba, as well as the support they provided to revolutionary forces in El Salvador and Guatemala, determined the Reagan administration to step up economic and diplomatic pressure, and to enlist the contras in a covert war against the regime. Violence, economic deprivation, and the Sandinistas' attempt to draft young men into the war against the contras created about 250,000 internally displaced, and 300,000–500,000 refugees in neighboring countries and the United States. In the early 1990s the conjugated effects of U.S. directed economic and strategic pressure, of the Sandinista government's ill-conceived policies, and of the collapse of communism forced the regime to hold open elections that resulted in its peaceful relinquishment of power.

El Salvador. The smallest and most densely populated country of Latin America, El Salvador was traditionally ruled by an alliance of coffee-growing oligarchs and the army, with support from the

Catholic Church and the United States. In 1932 a Communist led peasant rebellion sparked by a drop in coffee prices was brutally repressed by the military, at the cost of between 10,000 and 20,000 lives. After the failure of reformist efforts in the 1960s, a leftist opposition gained ground among the rural and urban masses. In the face of the government's repressive violence—some 30,000 were killed by the security forces—the Frente Farabundo Marti para la Liberacion Nacional (FMLN) and the Frente Democratico Revolucionario (FDR) launched an armed struggle. Assigning a high priority to defeating the insurgency, the Reagan administration supported the center while trying to control the extreme right, and also channeled resources and support to the Salvadoran armed forces. The insurrection was contained, but at the cost of considerable violence, which produced some 500,000 internally displaced and over 1 million emigres, mainly to Mexico and the United States.

Guatemala. The biggest and most important country of Central America, with the United Fruit Company as its largest landlord, Guatemala underwent a Mexican-style revolution in 1944. In 1950 the newly elected president, Jacobo Arbenz, launched an agrarian reform that extended to uncultivated land, thereby leading to a confrontation with United Fruit. Deciding that Arbenz was unacceptable, Washington undertook a diplomatic offensive as well as a covert operation to remove him. The landed oligarchy and foreign investors established a highly repressive corporatist state, with the army as the most important political actor, which emerged as one of the worst human rights violators in the hemisphere. However, some leftist army officers rebelled; unlike in El Salvador, the movement's urban base remained weak, but they established a solid base among the mostly Indian peasant communities of the north and on the Pacific Coast. The army counterattacked with a successful counterinsurgency campaign that created massive displacements and prompted the Carter administration to suspend military aid. Between 30,000 and 100,000 persons were murdered from 1966 to 1982; and as of the latter date it was estimated that 1 million were internally displaced, and 200,000 had gone abroad. Of the latter, 46,000 were recognized as refugees in Mexico.

In 1986 Vinicio Cerezo, a Christian Democrat, was elected president; however, the army maintained control behind the scenes, and the civilian government was therefore unable to undertake the economic and political reforms required to solve the country's protracted civil war. After extended negotiations, a settlement was negotiated between the guerrillas and the government.

Although the impact of discrete developments is quite clear, assessment of the overall consequences of U.S. foreign policy toward the region on immigration to the United States is difficult because it is impossible to determine whether alternative regime outcomes would have fostered more or less movement. For example, Lars Schoultz has suggested that perhaps fewer Guatemalans would have immigrated to the U.S. if the reformist Arbenz government had been allowed to persist;[17] but would the United States not have subjected an Arbenz regime to the same treatment as Castro and the Sandinistas? Arguing from the opposite perspective, in the 1980s President Reagan sought to enlist support for his policy in El Salvador by agitating the specter of "feet people" who would run north in case of a Communist takeover. However, in reality the violence in El Salvador generated a much larger migration to the United States than did the Sandinista regime in Nicaragua, despite the conflict carried out by the contras with U.S. support.

But variation in the immigration that actually took place from different countries cannot be explained by the factors operating at the source only. For example, the limited movement of Nicaraguans to the United States is attributable in part to the fact that in contrast with Cuba, after the Sandinistas came to power Washington deliberately sought "to avoid creating a pathway to the United States for disaffected Nicaraguans."[18] The immigration authorities imposed very demanding requirements for visitor's visas, achieving a refusal rate of 70–80 percent, and allocated very few admissions to Nicaraguans under the 1980 refugee law, on the grounds that safe havens were available in neighboring countries.

Matters were further complicated by the fact that Central Americans had access to the United States overland by way of Mexico; they could ask for asylum at the border, or cross the notoriously porous border surreptitiously, and either initiate the asylum process inside the country or settle in unobtrusively within Latino communities. As noted, the asylum process provides considerable latitude to the executive, and foreign policy entered into play by way of the advisory opinions supplied by the State Department. Anticipating a favorable outcome, Nicaraguans tended to initiate contact with the INS to file a claim as "positive" applicants; most of them were then released on their own recognizance. In contrast, Guatemalans and Salvadorans were largely "defensive" applicants, requesting asylum after being apprehended as illegal aliens; most of them were detained, and initially many Salvadorans were deported. As expected, the rate of favorable rulings was higher for Nicaraguans than for the others.

Nevertheless, U.S. policy was not very effective, since despite the attempt to deter Salvadorans, they grew into by far the largest Central American community in the country. Since most of them entered after 1982, they were not eligible for regularization under the Immigration Reform and Control Act of 1986. In April 1987 President Duarte pleaded that they not be deported because this would exacerbate unemployment and deprive many families of much-needed remittances. The Reagan administration was divided, with the State Department endorsing the recommendation and the INS arguing against it. However, the administration's policy toward Salvadorans came under increasing fire in the courts, and at the end of the year deportations ground to a halt anyway. Meanwhile, opponents of the administration's Central American policy mounted an effort to secure temporary protected status (TPS) on behalf of Salvadorans, and succeeded in incorporating provisions to that effect in the 1990 immigration law.

The Dominican Republic

Given the overriding objective of minimizing radical regimes in America's backyard, the Dominican Republic can be reckoned as a foreign policy success that was achieved without the violence that engulfed many other countries in the region and generated massive flows of displaced persons, many of whom sought havens in the United States. However, since the early 1980s masses of

Dominicans have been driven by economic necessity to move to the United States, a development induced in large part by the nefarious impact of American agricultural protectionism.

In 1961–62, in the face of unfolding events in Cuba, the Kennedy administration adopted a strategy of "conservative preemption" by helping to eliminate Raphael Trujillo, the dictator who had ruled since 1930. Elected president in early 1963, left-of-center Juan Bosch was then overthrown by the military in September of that year, and when the officers appeared incapable of containing a popular movement to reinstate Bosch, the United States landed troops and in effect took over the government for seventeen months. The occupation ended in 1966, when Dominican voters elected rightist Joaquin Balaguer as president. After a centrist interlude, Balaguer returned to power in 1986 and was renewed in 1990. As the leading sugar producer in the region after Cuba, the Dominican Republic derived considerable benefits from the exclusion of Cuba from the U.S. market, and further expanded its production in the early 1970s in response to high world prices and the elimination of U.S. trade barriers; concomitantly, it was the hardest hit by the return of American protectionism in the latter part of the decade. Although it received the largest quota allocation, which amounted to approximately half the regional total, its export tonnage to the United States dropped from an average of 815,335 tons in 1975–81 to about one-fourth that level at the end of the 1980s.

After Trujillo's downfall, to reduce urban unemployment that was thought to be a source of political radicalization, the United States implemented a liberal immigration policy for Dominicans. Additional consulates were provided, which issued not only immigrant but also visitor's visas, despite common knowledge that many of the recipients would stay on. Thus by the time Western Hemisphere immigration was subjected to the preference system in the late 1970s, there was a critical mass of Dominicans in the United States who could pass on family reunion priorities. After U.S. sugar policy wreaked havoc with the Dominican economy, the demand for visitor's visas more than doubled; although consular procedures were tightened, little was done to deter Dominican overstayers, and the migration continued to expand. As of 1986 remittances from Dominicans in the United States approximately equaled the annual budget of the Dominican government; they amounted to one-tenth of the country's GNP, and nearly one-fourth of its foreign exchange.

Conclusion

As the United States assumed its mantle as the leading Western power, some aspects of the existing immigration system emerged as obstacles to the pursuit of foreign policy objectives. Accordingly, as early as 1943 the Roosevelt administration undertook to breach the wall erected against Chinese immigration. After the war, decision makers concerned with Europe—at the time the most important strategic theater—became persuaded that the presence of several hundred thousand displaced persons constituted an economic and political liability. Although some might be welcomed in other overseas immigration countries—Palestine was hardly available, because of British opposition to Jewish immigration—in effect, there was no alternative but to resettle most of them in the United States. Since this could not be accomplished within the established immigration framework, they resorted to a series of ad hoc measures, which benefited from the support of proimmigration groups.

Whereas this was a finite objective that would be achieved when remaining displaced persons were disposed of, with the onset of the cold war, the United States also encouraged "defection" from Communist countries and committed itself to welcome those who did. This unprecedented policy arose from the fact that during their consolidation, Communist regimes tended to impose Draconian barriers to the exit of their citizens, for a combination of economic, strategic, and political reasons. On the economic side, it was largely a matter of avoiding brain drain; strategically, in a period of international confrontation, any emigrant might be enlisted in the security apparatus of the enemy. On the political side, however, the situation was more ambiguous: on the one hand, exit afforded the possibility of removing opponents or potential opponents, but on the other, it delegitimized the regime by demonstrating what people would do if allowed to "vote with their feet."

In practice, the immigration impact of this policy was quite limited because very few people could get out, with the exception of those under Russian occupation in Germany prior to the building of the Berlin Wall, who tended to settle in the allied zones. Similarly, while a large number of Cubans were allowed out and perhaps even encouraged to leave when Castro first came to power, during the period of consolidation exit was severely tightened up. Consequently, it can be estimated that the intrusion of identifiable foreign policy objectives had the effect of increasing legal immigration for the period as a whole by only 15 to 20 percent. It might be noted as well that during this period, U.S. economic policies toward the developed world—notably the Marshall Plan and the Bretton Woods system as a whole—had the effect of reducing the emigration "push" as country after country joined the privileged group of affluent industrial democracies.

Responsive to the demands of urban constituencies, the Kennedy administration undertook to reform the immigration system as a whole, a project that was completed by its successor in 1965. While there is no gainsaying that the discriminatory national origin quotas constituted an easy target for anti-American propaganda abroad, and hence that their elimination served the national interest, these considerations hardly came into play. Moreover, while the law was justifiably hailed as a "liberal" reform, it also imposed for the first time a quantitative limit on immigration from the independent countries of the Western Hemisphere, and its legislative history indicates very clearly that the objective was to deter the growth of brown and black immigration. Again, domestic considerations were clearly at the forefront, as indicated also by the fact that only 7 percent of total immigration under the "preference" system (initially applicable only to the world outside the Western Hemisphere) was set aside for refugees.

Thus while, contrary to expectations, the framework established in 1965 fostered a considerable increase in immigration and a major shift in its composition from Europe and Latin America to Latin America and Asia, this outcome is definitely not attributable to foreign policy in the narrow sense. However, as in the previous period, diplomatic and strategic considerations contributed to an increase in immigration by way of ad hoc measures to welcome various groups as refugees, but much more directly than in the past, U.S. policies played a major role in bringing about the conditions that produced the flows, notably in Cuba and Indochina, and later on in Central America as well. The successive waves of refugees whose admission was governed by ad hoc measures, mostly initiated by the executive branch, included the second wave of Cubans, Soviet Jews, and Indochinese, amounting altogether to some 2 million additional entries to date.

After 1980 the Indochinese and Soviet Jews were accommodated within the framework of a new refugee law, which itself reflected the efforts of post-Vietnam reformers to shift U.S. foreign policy from a purely "realpolitik" stance focused on the struggle against communism toward a more "humanitarian" orientation, concerned with the promotion of democracy. However, in the hands of the Reagan and Bush administrations, the procedures provided by the law, including the allocation of annual quotas and the granting of asylum, were harnessed quite explicitly to foreign policy objectives, albeit also responsive to pressures from well-organized American ethnic communities. Although it is difficult to provide quantitative estimates for the increment in immigration attributable to foreign policy during the period from 1965 to date, it is evident that the special programs noted, the expansion of the quota provided under the 1980 law, the granting of asylum requests, the award of temporary protected status—much of which appears to lead to permanent settlement—and the availability of legalization under the 1986 law for some of those uprooted by U.S. induced violence, add up to several million—perhaps as much as one-third above total ordinary immigration.

The historical perspective provided here highlights the radical evolution of the relationship between foreign policy and immigration in the last two decades—from invitation to interdiction, from diplomatic pressure on antagonists to let their people go to insistence that they keep them in, or at least regularize the flow within limits established by the United States. When and why did this come about? Although Mariel was obviously a major turning point, there are indications that it functioned as the proverbial straw that broke the camel's back. Already during the period of the Cultural Revolution, the British authorities in Hong Kong demanded that the People's Republic enhance its border controls to contain the flood of refugees, and around the same time there were suggestions in Washington that the post-1965 "freedom flights" were of greater benefit to Castro than to the United States. In the same vein, a few years later there were suspicions that Vietnam was engaging in a "pushout" to rid itself of its population of Chinese ancestry, as well as to destabilize the remaining non-Communist countries of Southeast Asia; consequently, in 1979 the West demanded Hanoi's cooperation in regularizing departures as a condition for the normalization of relations.

Viewed in global perspective, Mariel occurred at a time when issues related to immigration and its sequels had begun to move to the fore throughout the world of capitalist democracies. Everywhere these issues were driven by an inextricable combination of economic, social, and political concerns, reflecting growing awareness that the period of rapid economic growth had ended, but exacerbated by the fact that both foreign workers and refugees originated mostly in the Third World, and that many of them were people of color.

While domestic opposition to immigration did not produce a reversal of foreign policy, there is little doubt that after Mariel, U.S. decision makers gave increasing weight to the immigration consequences of their politico-strategic options, particularly with regard to neighboring countries whose nationals might turn to the United States for first asylum. Despite its adamant stance on Cuba generally, the Reagan administration negotiated an immigration agreement in 1984; and while its invocation of the danger of "feet people" from Central America may have been a ploy to mobilize support on behalf of its foreign policies, it did in fact seek to deter asylum seekers, including Nicaraguans who in an earlier era might have been welcome. The remnants of the old policy of encouraging defectors and of putting pressure on Communist countries to adopt more liberal exit policies were swept away with the collapse of the world to which it was applicable, and as developments in 1994 indicated, even Cuba is no longer an exception. In this regard the United States is clearly on a convergent path with its European associates, and it is unlikely to reverse course in the foreseeable future.

Although there is also considerable discussion of the worldwide uprooting effects of the developed world's economic policies, this has received little more than token consideration in the formulation of alternatives. In any case, it is extremely difficult to ascertain the validity of various hypotheses that are put forward in this regard. For example, both advocates and opponents of the North American Free Trade Agreement (NAFTA) invoked its immigration consequences, the former arguing that by fostering more rapid growth in Mexico it would reduce unwanted migration toward the United States, the latter that by eliminating marginal units of agricultural production, it would have uprooting effects in rural areas. While the truth is likely to entail a combination of the two—uprooting effects in the short run, but stabilization over the long term—in reality immigration considerations played a marginal role in determining the outcome. Since the struggle over trade policy, broadly speaking, is structured by a longstanding confrontation between sectors oriented to the global economy and domestic production respectively, this too is unlikely to change in the foreseeable future.

Notes

1. Divine (1957).
2. Rico (1992), p. 222.
3. This section is based on Zolberg (1990).
4. Loescher and Scanlan (1986), pp. 14–15.
5. Kraly (1990), pp. 77–78.
6. For a general overview of the subject, see Gordenker (1987).
7. Mitchell (1992b), pp. 5, 9.
8. This section is based mostly on Loescher and Scanlan (1986), Zucker and Zucker (1987), and Dominguez (1992).
9. Fagen, Brody, and O'Leary (1968), p. 102.
10. This section is based on Loescher and Scanlan (1986).
11. Loescher and Scanlan (1986), p. 128.
12. Loescher and Scanlan (1986), pp. 145–146.
13. The principal sources for this section are Dowty (1987) and Loescher and Scanlan (1986).
14. Loescher and Scanlan (1986), p. 198.
15. However, in 1984 the Justice Department ruled that by virtue of a 1966 law,

Cubans *could* become permanent residents, thus restoring the invidious distinction between Cubans and Haitians.

[16] The background material for this section is drawn from Zolberg, Suhrke, and Aguayo (1989), pp. 204–224.

[17] Schoultz (1992), p. 160.

[18] Schoultz (1992), p. 178.

4

Relationships Between U.S. Foreign Policies and U.S. Immigration Policies

SERGIO DÍAZ-BRIQUETS

I mmigration policies and foreign policies interact in complex and often unpredictable ways. There is growing appreciation that framers of immigration policies cannot always anticipate the effects of these policies, let alone their unintended and long-term consequences, and that foreign policies can serve as effective tools for the attainment of certain immigration policy objectives, such as reducing unauthorized immigration. More often than not, the nexus between the two sets of policies is ambiguous, and, rather than assessing direct cause and effect relationships, we must focus on the indirect and/or unintended immigration consequences of foreign policies, be they political or economic.

SERGIO DÍAZ-BRIQUETS is with Casals and Associates, a Washington based consulting firm. He was research director of the Congressional Commission for the Study of International Migration and Cooperative Economic Development, and earlier held appointments with the International Development Research Centre (IDRC), Population Reference Bureau, and Duquesne University. Díaz-Briquets is the author or editor of several books, including a series on development and international migration, and has published articles on Cuba and other topics.

In their *formal, explicit* formulation, U.S. immigration policies (other than refugee policies) since the 1960s have been largely driven by domestic agendas. Foreign policy concerns have been rarely taken into account, and when they have, only tangentially. This does not mean that the formulation of U.S. immigration policies has occurred in a foreign policy vacuum. The international environment has provided a backdrop—often of only rhetorical significance—to buttress or undermine the immigration (and foreign) policy options favored by different domestic economic and ethnic pressure groups. The immigration policy decision-making process is further complicated by the leadership role both houses of Congress have assumed regarding immigration initiatives, and by the fact that jurisdiction over immigration matters rests with the Judiciary Committees rather than with the Foreign Affairs Committees. Congressional intent on immigration is often at odds with foreign affairs priorities of the executive branch. Not surprisingly, the end result of this policy-making tug-of-war has been unpredictable. Policies working at cross-purposes with each other have been just as likely as consistent and mutually reinforcing policies.

Almost without exception, the relationship between foreign policies and immigration policies is mediated by the operation of several prominent mechanisms of U.S. immigration law (e.g., family reunification and skill based immigration preferences) and how they are applied. The functioning of these immigration mechanisms is conditioned to an inordinate degree by social networks, or the interpersonal relationships arising from kinship, friendship, and/or a common national origin, arguably the most potent and fundamental determinant of migratory flows.

This inattention to the linkages between foreign policies and immigration policies discussed above has not always been part of the policy formulation process. During the late 1940s and throughout the 1950s, an important element of the immigration policy debate was how immigration policies could be used to advance, or at least not to hamper, foreign policy objectives. That today's policy debate includes references to free trade as a deterrent to undocumented immigration, or that the political and immigration consequences of the economic embargoes of Cuba and Haiti are discussed in the same breath, is a testimony to the current foreign policy relevance of international migration.

Immigration Legislation since the Second World War

The two major immigration acts approved by Congress in 1952 and 1965 were responsive to some degree to the prevailing international political context and, therefore, partly responded to the foreign policy concerns of the day. In contrast, the 1986 and 1990 immigration acts were largely formulated on the basis of domestic considerations, even though the 1986 act had some potentially major international ramifications. The review that follows of these four major immigration acts and other immigration related legislative initiatives highlights those features of the law that in one way or another can be directly or indirectly linked with foreign policy issues.

Immigration and Nationality Act of 1952

The Immigration and Nationality Act of 1952 recodified and revised the immigration and nationality acts of 1917 and 1924. The Immigration Act of 1917 addressed qualitative grounds for exclusion, whereas the Immigration Act of 1924 introduced numerical immigration limitations through the national origins quota system. The 1952 act also codified those provisions of the Internal Security Act of 1950 barring the admission of Communists into the United States. The 1950 act managed, in effect, to begin reorienting immigration restrictions away from race and culture toward ideology.

Mostly regarded as a restrictionist law, the 1952 act was ambivalent about the foreign policy concerns facing the United States during the early days of the cold war. It reflected, on the one hand, a deep fear of the Communist threat. Its advocates regarded the act's restrictionist features as a powerful barrier against Communist infiltration. The country was at war in Korea, and there was concern about the Soviet design for global domination, made even more urgent by the 1949 Communist takeover of mainland China. The 1952 act was as much a response to these fears as were Senator

McCarthy's infamous congressional witch hunts.

The 1952 act made some concessions to the markedly different post–Second World War international environment, with regard in particular to race and cultural considerations. In recognition of the changed international environment, and bowing to growing domestic pressures, the 1952 act did away with racial (and sexual) bars to immigration and naturalization. While liberalizing the admission of immigrants from the Asia-Pacific triangle (in effect, most Asian countries) who until then had been essentially barred from settling in the United States, the 1952 act retained numerical restrictions to severely limit Asian immigration. Further, the 1952 act maintained earlier policies of placing no numerical restrictions on immigration from Western Hemisphere countries. This decision was justified on the basis of geographical proximity and the desire to maintain friendly relations with these countries. For other countries, national annual immigration quotas were set according to a modified version of the national origin quota system in effect since the Immigration Act of 1924. It consisted of one-sixth of 1 percent "of the number of inhabitants in the continental United States in 1920 whose ancestry or national origin" could be attributed to that area. For natives of Asia-Pacific triangle countries, the ceiling was 2,000 immigrants a year, although all countries were assigned a minimum immigration quota of 100.

Passage of the 1952 act represented a resounding defeat to those who had hoped—like President Harry S. Truman, whose veto was overridden by Congress—that "the new internationalism following World War II would bring with it the opportunity for formulating a less restrictive immigration policy."[1] Opponents of the act noted that the racial basis of the 1924 act was "false and unworthy" and contrary to the post–Second World War spirit. The United States was facing the Communist threat in alliance with the same Southern European countries whose immigrants the national origin quota system was intended to minimize. The national origin quota system also discriminated against those would-be immigrants seeking to escape the iron curtain that had descended around Eastern Europe.

Another noteworthy feature of the 1952 Immigration Act was the introduction of a four-point category system for choosing prospective immigrants (immediate relatives of U.S. citizens were exempt and could enter the country independent of the categories or country limits). Under this system, 50 percent of each national quota (first preference) was to be reserved for aliens with "high education or exceptional abilities and their immediate relatives." The introduction of immigrant occupational preferences (in the United States and other developed countries) may have contributed to what later became known as the "brain drain." Some observers feel that skilled emigration had major adverse consequences for the development of many migrant-sending countries, and thus is implicated indirectly in the large-scale international movement of people the world is witnessing today. Thirty percent of the remaining visas were assigned to parents of U.S. citizens (second preference), 20 percent to spouses and children of permanent resident aliens (third preference), and 25 percent of visas unused by the first three preferences to brothers, sisters, and children of U.S. citizens.

Yet another notable feature of the 1952 act was the introduction of the labor certification notion in U.S. immigration. This concept was devised to protect U.S. workers from the adverse effects of non-family based immigration if the secretary of labor determined that there were a sufficient number of equally qualified domestic workers, or if the employment of such alien workers could have a negative effect on the wages and working conditions of persons similarly employed. In due course, the labor certification process would come to occupy an important place in U.S. immigration, especially in terms of whether or not the labor certification requirement hindered the country's ability to remain internationally competitive.

Legislative and Executive Developments between 1952 and 1965

As he vetoed the Immigration and Nationality Act of 1952, President Truman asked Congress to create a bipartisan national commission to "examine the basic assumptions of our immigration policy, the quota system and all that goes with it, the effect of our present immigration and nationality laws, their administration, and the ways in which they can be brought into line with our national ideals and our foreign policy." When Congress did not respond favorably to his request, President Truman issued an executive order to establish the President's Commission on Immigration and Naturalization. The commission's report, *Whom We Shall Welcome*, submitted in January 1953, vigorously objected to the principles underlying the Immigration Act of 1952 and recommended fundamental changes in U.S. immigration law.

Among the commission's principal findings were that the country's immigration laws were based on distrust toward all aliens; discriminated on the basis of national origin, race, creed, and color; and were oblivious to U.S. foreign policy interests. It recommended that the annual immigration ceiling be raised to 251,162 immigrants from the 154,657 authorized by the 1952 act. The report was especially harsh about the impact of the legislation on foreign policy, indicating that it "frustrated and handicapped the aims and programs of American foreign policy," by failing to address the rivalry of the cold war and the refugee crisis inherited from the Second World War.

The years intervening between the Immigration and Naturalization Commission's report and the Immigration Act of 1965 saw several legislative and executive initiatives that eroded the foundations of some of the 1952 act's basic principles. These legislative initiatives were approved in part to tighten or remove some of the statutory limitations conditioning the admission of landed immigrants (aliens admitted for lawful permanent residency). Other legislative initiatives were associated with the lingering refugee situation, or arose in response to new refugee crises caused by the tense international political situation of the early days of the cold war. Among the most important early legislative actions of this period was the Refugee Relief Act of 1953, amended in 1954, which granted entry to Eastern and Southern European refugees, as well as to limited numbers from China and Arab countries. The latter constituted a major departure from the national origin restrictionist principles underlying the 1952 Immigration and Nationality Act and earlier legislation. Other important pieces of legislation during this period were the Refugee-Escapee Act of 1957 and the Fair Share Law of 1960.

On the heels of the 1956 Hungarian revolution, several executive actions were taken to allow thousands of Hungarians to enter the United States outside of the existing quota system under the parole authority granted to the attorney general by the Immigration and Nationality Act of 1952 to temporarily admit aliens in response to foreign crises. In later years, the parole authority was to be invoked several more times, in particular after 1960 to accommodate the entry of Cuban nationals fleeing Castro's revolution.

In retrospect, one of the most consequential pieces of legislation of this period was the 1951 Bracero Program to regulate the flow of legal and temporary Mexican workers. The intent of this legislation was to extend a "temporary" foreign labor program initiated to deal with worker shortages during the Second World War by admitting Caribbean and Mexican workers for temporary work. The 1951 measure was approved in response to the domestic worker shortage produced by the Korean War, and negotiated with Mexico to placate that country's concern about the treatment of its nationals in the United States. Public Law 78 was anomalous in one important respect: it ran counter to the then-current restrictionist immigration legislation by granting Mexican workers almost unlimited access to the U.S. labor market. At first this Bracero Program was associated with foreign policy considerations, but it was later extended five times (up to 1964), propelled solely by the dependency of farm interests on foreign agricultural labor. Regarded as a temporary labor program, and no longer of national security significance, the long-term immigration consequences of the Bracero Program would not be understood until much later.

Immigration and Nationality Act, Amendments of 1965

In response to evolving attitudes toward race and national origins—and domestic and international political currents—the 1965 act rejected the national origin quota system that had guided U.S. immigration policy since the 1920s, and embraced an immigration selection system based on family reunification and needed skills.

Passage of the bill was ensured by a large Democratic congressional majority and widespread popular support for the legislative agenda inherited by the Johnson administration from President Kennedy, a strong immigration reform advocate. This same legislative agenda was responsible for the major civil rights legislation of the mid-1960s. Also contributing to the act's passage were the fact that the immigration quotas for most Northern and Western European countries remained unfulfilled, and the gradual erosion of the national quota system by legislative and executive actions during the 1950s and early 1960s.

Western Hemisphere immigration for the first time (effective in 1968) was subjected to a ceiling (120,000 annually), partly out of concern that rising population growth rates and emigration pressures in Latin America would lead to a major immigration surge from this region. The imposition of a Western Hemisphere ceiling had been opposed by the Johnson administration fearing that relations with these countries could become entangled, given the potentially annoying nature of the ceiling. No per-country numerical immigration restriction was imposed on Western Hemisphere countries, although the law was amended in 1976 and the same per-country limit extended to the Americas.

The most far-reaching, but unintended, consequence of the 1965 Immigration Act was a major increase in Asian immigration, as restrictions based on race and national origins were abolished. Although the purpose of this measure was to increase Southern and Eastern European immigration, the large-scale immigration flow that had been anticipated from these regions did not ensue, as it did from Asia. The annual ceiling for Eastern Hemisphere (the whole world, except for the Americas) immigration was set at 170,-000, with a 20,000 per-country limit. The rising trend of Asian immigration coincided with a surge in Western Hemisphere immigration, despite the introduction of the new regional ceiling. The current dominance of Asians in the U.S. immigrant stream can be traced back to the legislative changes introduced in 1965.

Another important feature of the 1965 Immigration Act was its departure from the use of occupational characteristics and toward the use of family ties as the principal criterion for selecting immigrants. Some observers have suggested that an underlying reason for reemphasizing family reunification was to preserve the country's ethnic composition while doing away with the discriminatory nature of national origin quotas. The assumption was that the only foreigners likely to immigrate were those with relatives already here. Senator Robert Kennedy even predicted that with the new regulations there would not be a surge of Asian immigration!

Under the preference system, the 1965 act assigned only 20 percent of visas to occupational categories, as opposed to the 50 percent allotted by the 1952 act. One-tenth of all visas were reserved for members of the professions and scientists under the third preference, while the sixth preference assigned the remaining 10 percent to skilled and unskilled workers with occupations in short supply in the U.S. labor market. Seventy-six percent of the visas were allocated to close relatives of U.S. citizens and permanent residents as follows: first preference (20 percent for unmarried adult children of U.S. citizens); second preference (20 percent to spouses and unmarried children of permanent resident aliens); fourth preference (10 percent to married children of U.S. citizens); and fifth preference (24 percent to brothers and sisters of U.S. citizens). The remaining visas, 6 percent, were allocated to refugees under the seventh preference. Immediate relatives of U.S. citizens were not restricted and entered the country exempt from the immigration ceiling.

Major revisions to the labor certification system were part of the 1965 act. The issuance of labor certifications became mandatory for all non-family based admissions since the new law required the exclusion of aliens, unless the secretary of labor certified that no adverse labor market consequences would follow from the admission of occupational preference immigrants.

The 1965 act also included provisions for the temporary entry of agricultural labor (H-2 visas). This temporary labor visa, mostly used in later years by seasonal workers from the English-speaking Caribbean, has its antecedents in the labor programs instituted by the United States during the Second World War.

Legislative and Executive Developments between 1965 and 1986

Legislative initiatives approved by Congress during this period were largely driven by the major refugee flows that arose in the aftermath of the war in Vietnam, and in response to the domestic and international debate regarding the definition of what constitutes a refugee. The focus of the debate was the proper role of ideological versus humanitarian criteria in the selection of refugees. This debate culminated in the Refugee Act of 1980. However, during this period, several important amendments were made to the Immigration Act of 1965. These included legislation to adjust the status of Cuban refugees (in 1966); applying a modified preference system and extending the same country limit to Western Hemisphere nations (in 1976) that had applied to immigrants from Eastern Hemisphere countries since 1965; and introducing a global immigration ceiling (in 1978). The immigration of immediate relatives of U.S. citizens continued to be unrestricted and not governed by the national country limit or the global ceiling.

Immigration Reform and Control Act (IRCA) of 1986

This legislation, under consideration for more than fifteen years, followed a series of compromises among a variety of domestic interest groups. IRCA's primary concern was illegal immigration, in particular the growing presence of undocumented aliens in the country, and closing the illegal immigration back door. IRCA's main components were the legalization of undocumented immigrants, including some temporary agricultural workers; the enforcement of employer sanctions and companion antidiscrimination provisions; and improved border controls. The logic of the legislation was that by acting in concert, these three components would cope effectively with the undocumented migration problem.

Since most illegal immigrants came from Western Hemisphere countries, and most of all from Mexico, it was anticipated that

Mexico would suffer the brunt of IRCA's provisions. To address this concern, during the debates leading to IRCA's passage, some members of Congress proposed to increase Mexico's (and Canada's) legal immigration quotas to ease the shock of a new immigration regime in which undocumented entries from Mexico would be curtailed. Despite IRCA's projected adverse impact on Mexico, and several entreaties made by the United States to begin a dialogue with Mexico about immigration matters, the Mexican government refused to hold discussions with Washington.

The Mexican refusal was justified on several grounds. Immigration, Mexico claimed, is the sole prerogative of host states, and thus Mexico should not intervene in U.S. internal affairs. But there were also other unstated reasons why Mexico turned down the U.S. offer to negotiate. First of all, Mexico did not want to be drawn into the bilateral control of undocumented migration. Second, given the past history of U.S. interventions in Mexico, Mexicans are extremely sensitive about safeguarding national sovereignty, and were concerned that the United States would use the immigration issue as a bargaining chip to negotiate other bilateral issues. Mexico also recognized that the immigration status quo was the best it could hope for. Finally, the Mexican government was of the opinion that its input into the pending legislation would be minimal, since domestic interests ultimately carry the day on immigration matters. Even though Mexico refused to address the undocumented migration issue in a bilateral forum, in response to domestic pressures and in partial recognition of the legislation's foreign policy impact, Congress mandated the creation of a bipartisan Commission for the Study of International Migration and Cooperative Economic Development. The commission's task was to:

in consultation with the governments of Mexico and other sending countries in the Western Hemisphere . . . examine the conditions in Mexico and other such sending countries which contribute unauthorized migration to the United States and [explore] mutually beneficial, reciprocal trade and investment programs to alleviate such conditions.

The commission, after extensive consultations with Mexican government officials, including Presidents Miguel de la Madrid Hurtado and Carlos Salinas de Gortari, officials from Caribbean Basin countries, and a collaborative research effort involving investigators from the United States and the migrant-sending countries, recommended a set of policy measures to accelerate economic growth in migrant-sending countries and to reduce emigration pressures. One of these recommendations was that the United States enter into a free trade agreement with Mexico.

IRCA's main accomplishment was the legalization of close to 3 million undocumented aliens. Far less was gained regarding employer sanctions, and even less concerning the legislation's intent to improve border controls. Illegal immigration did not cease, with the number of undocumented immigrants apprehended in the 1990s approaching the number of the early 1980s, just before IRCA's approval. Among IRCA's major predictable but unintended consequences were the strengthening of migratory networks via the legalization process (and the family reunification provisions), and the likely modification of long-established Mexican immigration patterns, as formerly undocumented and temporary Mexican immigration may have become authorized and permanent.

Immigration Act of 1990

After dealing with undocumented immigration in 1986, Congress addressed legal immigration with the Immigration Act of 1990. A major revision of the Immigration and Nationality Act, the 1990 act increased the number of annual admissions to 675,000 under a flexible cap (beginning in Fiscal Year 1995), following a temporary period (FY 1992-94) in which the annual immigrant ceiling was fixed at 714,000. This figure does not include immigrants not subject to numerical limitations, namely, immediate relatives of U.S. citizens, returning permanent residents who had resided abroad for longer than one year, and persons reclaiming U.S. citizenship. For the first time ever, the ceiling sets the annual number of immigrants that may be admitted by subtracting from it the number of immediate relatives entering the United States the previous fiscal year. Previously, immediate relatives of U.S. citizens had been excluded from the numerical limits. However, the cap is "pierceable" and may be increased since the number of family sponsored immigrants may not drop below a 226,000 visa floor. Whereas the increase in the admissions ceiling responded to pent-up demand for immigrant visas, the legislation made an attempt to accommodate restrictionist sentiments by the introduction of the immigration ceiling.

An important development associated with the Immigration Act of 1990 was the reformulation of the preference system by dividing it into family based and independent immigration. Family based immigration was set at 226,000 visas annually, and distributed in four preferences, as follows: 10 percent to unmarried adult children of U.S. citizens (first preference); 50 percent to spouses and unmarried children of permanent resident aliens (second preference); 10 percent to married children of U.S. citizens (third preference); and 30 percent to brothers and sisters of adult U.S. citizens (fourth preference). The new category of independent immigration was allotted 180,000 visas (plus any unused visas under the family based preferences) and divided into various employment based categories (priority workers, professionals with advanced degrees, non-advanced degree professionals and skilled and unskilled workers, special immigrants, and investors) and "diversity" immigrants to allow immigration from underrepresented countries. After Fiscal Year 1995, the diversity immigration category is to be increased by 15,000 visas annually. By increasing the number of employment based visas, it was assumed that U.S. international economic competitiveness would be enhanced by attracting highly skilled immigrants.

Also addressed by the act were a number of immigration matters needing resolution, some of which had a foreign policy dimension. The 1990 act granted undocumented Salvadorans temporary protected status (TPS) and work authorization for a limited period of time. Fears about the economic consequences of forcibly repatriating the immigrants to a country at war—aside from human rights concerns—were determining factors in granting TPS to the Salvadorans. The 1990 act also gave the attorney general authority to extend TPS to citizens of countries facing natural or human-made crises, and included provisions to regularize the status of relatives of undocumented migrants legalized under IRCA. It revised as well the previously ideologically-driven provisions for exclusion and deportation in effect since 1952, when Congress approved the Immigration and Nationality Act.

The Relationship between U.S. Foreign Policies and U.S. Immigration Trends and Policies

These relationships cannot be broken down into neatly separable categories, but can be roughly organized according to the *direction* of the effect and the *intent* of the policies. Direction, although not always apparent, refers to a policy's potential capacity to initiate or intensify a migratory flow, or to curtail or slow it down. Some policies are specifically designed to arrest migratory flows, whereas others unwittingly may promote these same flows. The more readily apparent distinction regarding intent is between the *intended* and *unintended* consequences that arise from the implementation of policy. When relevant, policies can be further subdivided according to their *implicit* or *explicit* policy objectives. Here I discuss five major relationships: 1) foreign economic policies as complements to immigration policies; 2) foreign policies as complements to immigration policies; 3) unintended immigration consequences of domestic and foreign economic policies; 4) unintended immigration consequences of foreign political involvements; and 5) foreign policies and the relationship between nonpermanent and permanent immigration.

Foreign Economic Policies as Complements to Immigration Policies

Trade, investment, and foreign assistance policies are among the foreign policy tools that can most effectively be used to promote desirable political, economic, and social outcomes, including the reduction of undocumented migration pressures. As a rule, these foreign economic policies are more likely to be applied in neighboring countries producing unauthorized immigrants than in more distant countries, from which unauthorized immigration is presumably easier to control. The ultimate intent of trade, investment, and foreign assistance policies is, of course, to improve economic conditions in migrant-sending countries, and thus to gradually reduce the motivation to emigrate. These policies are predicated on the argued migration-reducing impacts of increased job creation and improving living standards.

The Relationship between Economic Development and Migration. If the intention of trade, investment, and foreign assistance policies is to reduce emigration pressures in sending countries, they must confront the dilemma that over the short term, these policies are likely to have a perverse effect. While economic development may manage to reduce emigration pressures over time, early on it is likely to increase the motivation to emigrate. Major transformations in a country's productive structures usually accompany accelerated economic growth. Rural to urban labor shifts and productivity increases are part and parcel of the development process. Labor displaced from low productivity, rural occupations joins urban labor markets already saturated by rapid demographic growth. In countries with a tradition of emigration, many of the workers competing for urban jobs may seek to go to other countries. As development proceeds, the pool of potential migrants also expands: city residents are usually better informed about conditions elsewhere, and also have access to higher incomes with which to cover transportation expenses.

In the 1980s and 1990s increases in aid, investment, and foreign assistance were generally conditioned on the beneficiary country's implementation of economic restructuring policies to reduce the interventionist role of the state and grant market forces a more prominent place. While ultimately beneficial, in the short term these structural adjustment policies have an adverse impact on employment and living standards. As state owned enterprises are privatized, government bureaucracies trimmed, and formerly protected national markets exposed to competitive international pressures, redundant workers are released, thus aggravating emigration pressures.

Over time, as suggested by the historical experiences of some European and Asian countries, demographic pressures abate, labor conditions improve, and wages and living standards begin to rise. Facing gradually improving economic prospects at home, workers are no longer compelled to emigrate. Many of these countries (e.g., Spain, Italy, Japan, Malaysia) now attract immigrants from other nations.

The Border Industrialization Program. Since the mid-1960s the United States has used trade, investment, and foreign assistance policies as either primary or incidental mechanisms to reduce emigration pressures from neighboring countries. The first such instance was in conjunction with the Border Industrialization Program begun by Mexico after the Bracero Program was unilaterally terminated by the United States in 1964, to provide alternative employment to the many return migrants Mexico was expecting (as well as for those who otherwise would be emigrating).

While not begun as a result of a U.S. policy initiative, the Border Industrialization Program rested on the trade preferences granted by the United States to Mexico and other developing countries. The program's success was contingent on the locational advantages of the border area, the ready availability of a supply of low-wage Mexican workers, and a tariff regime—the Generalized System of Preferences (GSP)—that allowed U.S. firms to ship American-made components to Mexico for further processing, and, once processed, to bring them back while paying duty only on the foreign value-added. Foreign investors, mostly from the United States, took advantage of the trade preferences and the border location, with the pace of foreign investment quickening considerably during the 1980s.

By 1990 there were about 2,000 *maquiladoras* (as the border assembly plants are known) employing close to half a million workers. There has been considerable debate, however, as to whether or not the Border Industrialization Program met its objective of offering alternative employment opportunities to surplus Mexican workers. Critics of the program argue that in one important respect the *maquiladoras* had an effect opposite to that intended. Most *maquiladora* workers are women (although the male share has been increasing), whereas most Mexican seasonal migrants are men. Thus it would appear that the goal of creating employment opportunities for returning migrants or would-be emigrants may not have been met. These critics also point out that the prosperous border towns attract migrants from the Mexican interior, who may travel from there to the United States in search of work. Empirical investigations found ambiguous evidence as to the latter assumption.

The Caribbean Basin Initiative. The Caribbean Basin Economic Recovery Act (CBERA), better known as the Caribbean Basin Initiative (CBI), was launched by the Reagan administration in 1983 and extended in 1990. Designed primarily to promote political stability and economic prosperity in Caribbean and Central American countries during the turbulent 1980s, the CBI was advanced also with claims that it would contribute to controlling emigration. The key element of the CBI was the unilateral granting by the United States of nonreciprocal, duty-free treatment to Caribbean Basin exports. Its potential effectiveness was diluted, however, when such duty-free treatment was not extended to certain goods that could be competitively produced in the region, such as textile and leather products. The CBI was further crippled by the absence of an incentive package to attract foreign investments to the region. The government of Puerto Rico attempted to fill this investment vacuum, and protect its own tax exemption privileges, by securing congressional authorization to invest in CBI countries part of the tax-sheltered funds generated by U.S. corporations operating in the island under Section 936 of the U.S. Internal Revenue Code, but with only limited success.

Even under the best of circumstances, the employment generation potential of the CBI, despite its promise, is limited. The CBI's export-led development strategy cannot by itself cope with the serious regional unemployment problem. Complementary strategies must include sustained efforts to give more dynamism to domestic markets and reactivating the agricultural sector.

The North American Free Trade Agreement. More recently, the U.S. Congress and the Canadian and Mexican legislatures ratified the North American Free Trade Agreement (NAFTA). Although NAFTA was not primarily intended to reduce Mexican emigration, its supporters frequently noted that one of the agreement's benefits would be to diminish undocumented Mexican immigration. As foreign investment increased in Mexico and exports expanded, they argued, the attractiveness of the emigration option would decline. Emigration pressures should mount over the short term, however, as the trade liberalization measures of NAFTA negatively affect several Mexican economy sectors that, prior to the agreement, enjoyed considerable protection against foreign competition. Special concern has been voiced about the economic survival prospects of several hundred thousand small bean and maize farmers engaged in rain-fed agriculture because of their inability to compete against more efficient American and Canadian producers. Many of these farmers, as well as displaced landless agricultural workers, will migrate to cities, be absorbed by U.S. oriented export agriculture (e.g., winter vegetables), or emigrate. The expectation is that in due course, and as economic prospects improve in Mexico, fewer and fewer of these workers would have to emigrate. There are concerns that NAFTA's trade preferences may damage the CBI countries' economies. Responding to these concerns, the Clinton administration has proposed that trade parity be extended to the CBI countries.

Foreign Assistance. Foreign assistance is the third foreign economic policy mechanism that can be used in conjunction with trade and investment policies to achieve immigration-reducing objectives. Foreign assistance has one advantage over trade and investment policies: it can be designed by governments to target migration concerns directly. In contrast, trade and investment policies can only do so indirectly since they respond primarily to market signals in the pursuit of private interests. An overall current scarcity of financial resources, however, hampers the effectiveness of foreign aid as a U.S. immigration policy instrument.

Foreign assistance may influence migration flows and trends in a multitude of ways. Because of the complexity of the relationship, it has been suggested that foreign assistance programs must be sensitive to their migratory consequences, just as development programs must be cognizant of their environmental consequences. Some analysts have argued, for example, that by emphasizing export oriented strategies in countries like Haiti, U.S. foreign assistance policies have aggravated rather than ameliorated emigration pressures. Such policies are seen as exacerbating poverty levels by reinforcing existing patterns of social and economic inequality, while at the same time leading to the neglect of the domestic economy, agriculture in particular. These critics argue that for foreign assistance to effectively deter emigration, it should be channeled directly to the poor, be planned and administered by the beneficiaries themselves, and satisfy the population's consumption needs, rather than those of foreign markets. A balanced approach to development is the one most likely to succeed.

But even if we were to assume that a shift in development strategies could reduce emigration pressures, a massive amount of foreign assistance would be needed to attain this goal. It has been estimated, for example, that the now peaceful Central American countries would require approximately $2 billion dollars in aid annually for several decades to create the number of jobs necessary to make a substantial difference on emigration pressures. This level of assistance would exceed annual U.S. aid provided to this region during the 1980s, when, because of the cold war, economic assistance levels reached unprecedented figures.

Further, even if resources were available, foreign aid provided with the intention (among others) of reducing emigration pressures would have to be carefully directed in support of emigration-reducing objectives (e.g., structural reform, regional and small business development) for it to be effective. Just as important, considerable levels of assistance would have to be offered to Central America for an extended period of time, even if at first emigration propensities were to increase rather than decline.

Foreign Policies as Complements to Immigration Policies

In recent years, the United States has directly engaged in or supported the efforts of other countries to curtail illegal immigration flows from neighboring countries. The most controversial and best known—discussed elsewhere in this volume—is the U.S. Coast Guard interdiction of would-be Haitian emigrants begun by the Reagan administration and maintained by its successors. This policy, while formalized through a bilateral accord, was imposed on Haiti by a Washington concerned about the continued arrival of undocumented Haitian immigrants.

In 1994 the U.S. government, in a major policy reversal,

removed the welcoming mantle that had been extended to Cuban emigrants for more than three decades and began to interdict Cuban rafters attempting to reach South Florida by sea when the Cuban government started to encourage their departure. In a telling statement, President Clinton referred to the rafters as "illegal immigrants," rather than as "refugees," the term used by successive U.S. administrations since President Eisenhower.

The United States has also provided financial support to Mexico for a land interdiction program along the Mexico-Guatemala border to prevent Central Americans from using Mexico as a land bridge to enter the United States illegally. The genesis of this program lies in repeated U.S. requests to Mexico for better enforcement of border controls along its southern frontier. The interdiction program began as closer economic relations were being forged between the two countries, culminating in 1993 with the signing of the North American Free Trade Agreement. Another reason explaining improved border enforcement was Mexico's own concern about the growing domestic presence of undocumented Central American immigrants.

Unintended Immigration Consequences of Domestic and Foreign Economic Policies

Domestic economic policies with international ramifications and international economic policies are implicated, if only indirectly, with the rate at which migratory streams may flow by either increasing or decreasing emigration pressures. The migratory consequences of these policies are hardly ever evaluated by the policy maker, and, until recently, were seen as not even remotely connected with migratory streams.

Domestic Price Support Programs. Trade measures used to limit access to the U.S. market for commodities and manufactured goods produced in migrant-sending countries encourage emigration by adversely affecting the economy of these countries. Two examples are the nontariff barriers that have been used to prevent the growth of winter vegetables exports from Mexico and other Caribbean countries to protect Florida producers, and the barriers, referred to earlier, to apparel and other manufactured goods imports included in the legislation authorizing the Caribbean Basin Initiative.

The more notorious and best-known example is the sugar price support program, approved by Congress in 1981, designed to protect a small but influential group of U.S. sugar producers. The price support program maintains domestic sugar prices artificially high by limiting foreign imports through a quota system, thus allowing high-cost domestic producers to survive and prosper economically. Higher domestic prices, and the increased preference of U.S. consumers for sugar substitutes, have drastically reduced the demand for imported sugar. Further, as sugar demand has declined in the domestic market, so have international prices due to a surplus of sugar in the global marketplace.

Major losers from this policy were the Caribbean producers that traditionally held an important share of the U.S. sugar market. The policy has had particularly dire consequences for the Dominican Republic, one of the main suppliers of legal and undocumented migrants to the United States. The Dominican Republic lost three-quarters of its sugar export quota in less than a decade. Ironically, as the adverse effects of this policy were being felt, the United States initiated several economic assistance programs to arrest economic decline and partly to ameliorate emigration pressures from this and other Central American and Caribbean sugar-producing countries. Also hard hit were several English-speaking Caribbean countries that supplied labor for the harvesting of Florida sugar cane under the H-2 seasonal labor program of the Immigration Act of 1965. Between 1982 and 1988 the domestic price support program led to the loss of approximately 400,000 jobs and hundreds of millions of dollars in export revenues in the Caribbean Basin, a region already ravaged by severe unemployment pressures, while U.S. consumers were forced to subsidize domestic producers to the tune of $3 billion annually.

Domestic Economic Policies with Adverse Foreign Economic Impacts. Domestic economic policies that adversely affect the economies of migrant-sending countries can also accelerate emigration by increasing the cost of borrowing in international capital markets and by aggravating their foreign debt burden. Extensive U.S. borrowing in international capital markets and deficit financing during the 1980s increased domestic and international interest rates, and thus harmed the economies of migrant-sending countries. U.S. efforts to address the Latin American debt crisis through the Baker and Brady plans during the late 1980s and the 1990s, however, were major influences in the region's eventual economic recovery.

Foreign Economic/National Security Policies: Immigration Impacts. Foreign economic policies dictated by national security considerations often have an indirect immigration impact. It is not difficult to conclude, for instance, that the economic embargoes imposed by the United States on Cuba and Haiti, two neighboring countries with histories of extensive U.S.-bound migration, can only make more acute existing emigration pressures. In other instances, the relationships are not so readily apparent.

The Philippines offers another perspective on how national security, foreign economic policies, and immigration are related. Much of Filipino immigration is mediated, of course, by its historical colonial relationship with the United States. Early Filipino immigration followed from the economic dependency of the Philippines on the United States, the free entry accorded Filipinos as colonial natives, the business linkages between the mainland and the islands, and labor recruitment at the turn of the century (mostly for work in the Hawaiian sugar cane fields). Other important explanatory variables are the social linkages arising from the U.S. presence there, including interethnic marriages and the recruitment of Filipinos into the U.S. armed forces. But Gus Ranis argues that the perpetuation of the migratory flow, both legal and undocumented, can be attributed in part to direct and indirect large-scale U.S. economic assistance policies that have permitted successive Filipino governments to postpone needed economic reforms. These U.S. policies were largely dictated by national security, specifically, the large military bases maintained by the United States in the Philippines, and the leverage that Manila had over Washington regarding the continued use of these facilities. Had U.S. economic assistance been smaller and needed Philippine economic reforms been implemented, economic conditions would have improved markedly enough to reduce emigration pressures. As Ranis notes:

Unlike the east Asian countries in the 1960s, and unlike some of the south-east Asian countries more recently, the Philippines has so far refused fundamentally to restructure its economy towards mobilizing its rural sector in a balanced growth context, and towards the full exploitation of its potential for labor-intensive industrial exports. The system's ability to continue on this inefficient path for several decades has been based in part on the financing made possible by the country's diversified natural resource export base, and in part by the willingness of foreigners, in particular the commercial banks in the 1970s, and official donors throughout, to continue to support it.[2]

Unintended Immigration Consequences of Foreign Political Involvements

Foreign policy ventures often have unintended immigration consequences, in part because foreign policy makers have generally been oblivious to the immigration consequences of overseas interventions. Among the more notorious are the refugee flows associated with U.S. political and military interventions abroad (discussed elsewhere in this volume), such as the war in Vietnam (1960s and 1970s) and the conflicts in Central America (1980s and 1990s).

Less evident are the immigration flows that follow from U.S. political and economic interventions abroad. Many observers have suggested that migratory flows can be perpetuated and intensified by foreign policy actions that disrupt the normal course of socioeconomic development in countries that currently supply migrants to the United States. It has been alleged, for example, that the Central American military conflicts of the 1980s and the ensuing U.S.-bound migratory flows would not have occurred had the United States not repeatedly intervened (e.g., Guatemala and Nicaragua) and/or supported repressive regimes (e.g., El Salvador, Guatemala, Nicaragua) in the region to block socioeconomic reforms. By helping to perpetuate highly inequitable social systems and politically repressive regimes, the reasoning goes, U.S. foreign policy made revolutions in these countries inevitable. Some have used comparable arguments to explain the tortuous Cuban-American political and immigration histories.

Caution must be used, however, when invoking this argument to explain the onset or intensification of migratory flows. In other cases, it has been alleged that it was United States *failure* to intervene that resulted in emigration. In 1994, for example, a good many members of Congress were suggesting that the only way to stop Haitian emigration was through a U.S. invasion, followed by a multiyear U.S. or international occupation to stabilize the country and help restructure its political and economic institutions.

Foreign Policies and Administrative de Facto Immigration Policy Making. Foreign policy interacts with immigration policy in still another way. Under certain circumstances, the rigor with which immigration regulations are administered abroad has been found to produce long-term immigration consequences. In particular, issuance of temporary or permanent immigration visas as a means to cope with perceived short-term foreign policy threats has been related in more than one instance to the onset of large-scale immigration flows. Behind the liberal application of immigration regulations is the assumption that the emigration safety valve can be used to prop up unstable friendly regimes by siphoning away their political opposition or by invigorating their economies (through the receipt of foreign labor remittances). What is at first a modest emigration flow soon becomes the ethnic anchor around which a sizable immigrant community develops through the family reunification provisions of U.S. immigration law.

It has been alleged, for example, that in the mid-1960s, emigration from the Dominican Republic was facilitated by the application of more liberal immigration administrative procedures to help stabilize the country and prevent it from embracing a radical revolutionary path similar to that of neighboring Cuba. A similar claim has been made regarding Haitian emigration to the United States during the early 1960s. Fearing another Cuban-style revolution, the United States condoned the brutal repressive practices of the Francois Duvalier regime, and helped relieve some of the political pressure by allowing many of his opponents to come to the United States with nonpermanent visas and remain here illegally. Some analysts have suggested that Central American immigration during the 1980s was facilitated, likewise, by the liberal dispensation of nonimmigrant visas by U.S. consular officials, although this view has been questioned by other researchers who have examined the immigration consequences of U.S. foreign policies in the region. The more obvious instance of the use of immigration as a foreign policy complement is Cuba since the Castro revolution. The admission of Cuban refugees to the United States served the symbolic purpose of showing the world that the Cuban people rejected Socialist rule, and thus helped legitimize U.S. policy toward the island. Several instruments were used to facilitate the entry of Cuban nationals, ranging from the liberal granting of immigrant and nonimmigrant visas in Havana (until 1961, when diplomatic relations between the two countries were severed), to the approval of a bilateral migration agreement in 1965 and the passage of the still current (but diluted by President Clinton through an executive action in 1994) Cuban Adjustment of Status Act of 1966. To this day, the issue of Cuban immigration continues to be at the center of U.S.–Cuban relations.

In other instances, explicit and implicit immigration policies have been used to help stabilize a friendly government or prevent a crisis from erupting in a neighboring country. An example of the first policy was the decision by the Bush and Clinton administrations to "temporarily" allow undocumented Salvadoran migrants to remain in the United States by having the attorney general repeatedly grant the Salvadorans "temporary protected status," as authorized by the Immigration Act of 1990. Although the statute authorizes the granting of temporary protected status to nationals of countries "subject to armed conflicts or natural disasters," its intent has been stretched to give a postwar El Salvador breathing room by postponing—temporarily, but most likely permanently—the repatriation of tens of thousands of emigrants.

A number of observers have suggested that in the case of Mexico, the ineffective domestic enforcement of immigration law has at times been used as an implicit foreign policy instrument. When undocumented immigration from Mexico increased during the economic crisis of the 1980s, it is alleged that the U.S. government chose to relax the enforcement of immigration laws to prevent the crisis from worsening. By allowing emigration to relieve domestic pressures, the argument goes, Mexico was able to preserve its stability. This view is controversial, of course, and disputed by other observers who attribute the lack of enforcement simply to a dearth of human and financial resources and to the unwillingness of the American public to pay the political and civil rights price entailed by rigid enforcement.

Foreign Policies and the Relationship between Nonpermanent and Permanent Legal Immigration

Permanent immigration policies (e.g., the visa preference system, the worldwide immigration cap, or country ceilings for permanent immigrants) generally, but not always, have predictable outcomes. Whereas the purpose of the preference system is to regulate the type and number of permanent immigrants admitted in any given year (except for the numerically exempt immediate relatives of U.S. citizens), nonpermanent immigration visas are issued to serve other domestic and international purposes. However, as has become apparent in the United States and elsewhere, permanent settlement is a corollary of nonpermanent immigration. Nonpermanent immigration flows, furthermore, are often triggered by the pursuit of foreign policy objectives.

Temporary Skilled Immigration. Some major permanent immigration flows are traceable to how temporary immigration regulations were used to admit nationals from countries where the United States has had important foreign policy stakes (aside from refugees and temporary unskilled labor programs). Nonimmigrant visas are not allocated randomly. Their country-specific demand (and issuance) is determined by a complex set of determinants, the most important (aside from geographical proximity) being the nature and intensity of the bilateral relationship. Not surprisingly, the closer the relationship, the higher the demand for U.S. nonimmigrant visas. Economic and trade ties between Japan and the United States, for example, give rise to a considerable volume of business travel, and also to foreign study, cultural and scientific exchanges, and tourism. Since Japanese visitors enjoy high living standards at home, few remain here. Nationals of many other countries, however, use nonpermanent visas to circumvent the legal permanent immigration system. Not surprisingly, some of the more numerous hyphenated American ethnic communities originate in countries that were U.S. allies in one or another foreign policy venture.

The traffic of visitors to and from the United States from these countries (e.g., Korea, Taiwan) has been substantial. This international movement of people results in part from the binational official and private economic linkages arising from the assistance provided by the United States for national security reasons. These visitors come to acquire specialized skills, or in connection with the foreign operation of official development assistance projects or private sector business ventures. After graduating from a college or university, for example, a student may adjust his or her status to that of nonimmigrant worker (e.g., H-1b visas), and ultimately, through his or her labor market contacts, manage to be sponsored as a permanent immigrant by a U.S. employer willing to request labor certification for an employment based immigration category. Once a U.S. foothold is established, family based immigration preferences take over and immigration flows acquire a durable character.

Several examples can be used to illustrate this process. The flow of South Asian immigrants, particularly from India and Pakistan, started in earnest soon after the United States, for national security as well as for humanitarian reasons, began extensive economic assistance programs in these countries in the 1950s (and with the passage of the 1965 Immigration Act eliminating earlier bars to Asian immigration). Students and other nonpermanent immigrants from these countries arrived in the United States shortly thereafter. Communist China is a more recent case. Thousands of Chinese students came during the 1980s following the political and economic rapprochement between Washington and Beijing. As a result of the Tiananmen Square events and President Bush's executive order of April 1990, tens of thousands of Chinese students were granted the right to adjust to permanent residence status. While extreme, this episode exemplifies how the issuance of nonpermanent visas for foreign policy reasons can lead to permanent immigration.

In some instances, this status adjustment process appears to even have been institutionalized, regardless of how it began. It has been suggested that in countries such as India, students choose to attend certain universities to increase their chances of being admitted to graduate study in the United States and in other developed countries. Admission to a U.S. graduate technical program is seen as a ticket to permanent admission. In other countries that have pursued active policies to promote emigration, such as the Philippines and Korea, potential migrants, including students, are provided with specialized training and other assistance.

Temporary Unskilled Immigration. Temporary unskilled labor programs often have effects similar to those associated with the issuance of nonpermanent visas to skilled workers and students. The large-scale influx of legal and undocumented Mexican immigrants since the 1960s can be traced to the "temporary" importation by the U.S. government of unskilled Mexican workers during the Second World War to address domestic labor shortages. In this instance, the short-term immigration policy goal of coping with an acute shortage of agricultural workers coincided with the foreign policy goal of defeating the Axis. Given the priority assigned to the national war effort, the long-term immigration consequences of the Bracero Program were ignored, not recognized, or assumed to be unimportant. IRCA's enactment in 1986 was a belated recognition of the long-term immigration consequences of importing Mexican temporary agricultural workers.

Policy Implications

A crucial policy recommendation can be drawn from the preceding review: policy makers should always be aware that foreign policies and immigration policies and trends coexist in a state of dynamic tension. More often than not, one triggers a response on the other. The problem is anticipating whether there will be a response, and if so, the form the response will take, whether immediate or in the long term. These are difficult goals to accomplish, given the complex constellation of political, economic, and social factors determining migratory flows. Among the toughest policy decisions will be those made knowing full well about the trade-offs between foreign policies and immigration policies, and recognizing that these trade-offs often involve unintended, but predictable and inevitable, immigration responses.

For the foreseeable future, the foreign policy and immigration policy communities are likely to remain focused on two significant and seemingly intractable issues: refugee movements (discussed elsewhere in this volume) and undocumented migration. Concern with undocumented migration most likely will translate into three types of policy responses. The first one, tightening immigration and border controls, while most appealing to policy makers, is not likely to work unless vigorously enforced. Vigorous enforcement of immigration laws, however, will be adamantly resisted by pressure groups that fear its domestic ramifications for a kaleidoscope of political, social, and ethnic reasons.

The second policy option is for the United States to embark on a cooperative long-term regional economic development strategy based on trade, investment, and foreign assistance to gradually reduce emigration pressures from Mexico and countries in the Caribbean Basin. A third policy option—and the one most likely to be implemented—brings together elements of the first two. The North American Free Trade Agreement, a revitalized Caribbean Basin Initiative, and future hemispheric-wide trade accords are building blocks leading in a logical progression toward the full implementation of this policy option, as are encoded passports and visas, and the ongoing debate regarding the feasibility of a reliable national identification system and other enforcement mechanisms.

For the regional emigration-reducing development strategy to succeed, it must be developed in concert with the governments of migrant-sending countries, be coordinated with other bilateral and multilateral donors, stay the course even when facing short-term perverse results, focus on employment and income generation, and target assistance programs to areas with well-demarcated emigration pressure-reduction objectives. The strategy must be devised with a clear understanding of the country-specific advantages and disadvantages that trade, investment, and foreign assistance policies offer for the attainment of its goals, and with commitments from migrant-sending countries to do everything in their power to get their political and economic houses in order.

A comparable development strategy option for countries beyond the Western Hemisphere, or even beyond the vicinity of Mexico and the Caribbean Basin, is not as pressing or may not even be feasible. Improved enforcement measures may be perfectly capable of handling undocumented migration flows arriving from more distant shores.

Notes

[1] This chapter draws heavily on "U.S. Immigration Law and Policy," a 1988 report prepared by Joyce Vialet for the Subcommittee on Immigration and Refugee Affairs, Committee on the Judiciary, U.S. Senate.

[2] Ranis (1994), pp. 180–181.

5

The Impact of U.S. Refugee
Policies on U.S. Foreign Policy:
A Case of the Tail
Wagging the Dog?

KATHLEEN NEWLAND

Throughout the period of the cold war, U.S. refugee policy was consciously and, until the passage of the 1980 Refugee Act, explicitly a handmaiden of foreign policy. It was meant to contribute to the overarching objective of damaging and ultimately defeating Communist countries, particularly the Soviet Union. (Refugees from Communist China were never accorded the blanket welcome given to Soviet and East European refugees.)

The political impact of U.S. cold war refugee policy on its intended targets is far from clear. Although it was unequivocally

---

KATHLEEN NEWLAND is senior associate, Immigration Policy Program, Carnegie Endowment for International Peace, in Washington, D.C. Newland was senior researcher at Worldwatch Institute from 1974–82. She spent five years at the United Nations University in Tokyo, and served as lecturer in international relations at the London School of Economics. In 1989 she cofounded (with Lord David Owen) and directed Humanitas, a nonprofit educational trust in the United Kingdom devoted to promotion of debate on international humanitarian issues. The author would like to thank Kate Nahapetian for valuable assistance in the research and writing of this chapter.

aimed at destabilizing "enemy" regimes, its results were often mixed. A National Security Council memorandum of 1953 characterized the Refugee Relief Act of 1953 as a means to encourage defection and thereby inflict psychological and economic damage on the Soviet bloc.[1] It is, however, difficult to point to real damage done to the Soviet economy or political system because of U.S. refugee policy, apart from the loss of prestige caused by high-profile defections.

In some cases, generous U.S. reception policies allowed unfriendly regimes to rid themselves of their most acutely discontented citizens and those most politically active in opposition. There were also economic benefits to be gained from mass departures. Short-term benefits included the collection (or, sometimes, extortion) of "exit fees" (applied to Soviet Jews and ethnic Chinese from Vietnam, for example) and the ability to seize the assets and redistribute the housing of those who left. Long-term benefits came in the form of remittances that refugees, once established, sent back to their families remaining in the home country. Such flows have been major sources of foreign exchange for Cuba and Vietnam, among others.

As a political safety valve and economic crutch, the U.S. cold war policy of encouraging refugee flows from "enemy" states may have done more to stabilize than to destabilize unfriendly regimes. This argument was used, implicitly, to justify a turnaround in policy toward Cuban refugees in 1994. The withdrawal of open admissions, in response to the 1994 upsurge in Cuban outflows, generated relatively little opposition from Cuban-American activists and their political allies. They accepted—and sometimes made—the argument that Castro should not be allowed to release the discontented. The implication was that the would-be migrants should work to change the system in Cuba rather than escape from it.

In the past, such policies of discouraging refugee flows often served merely to abandon dissidents to their fate. The United States was reluctant to admit as refugees the Greeks fleeing from the Colonels' coup in 1967, Chileans escaping from Pinochet's Chile after 1973, and Salvadorans, Guatemalans, and Haitians seeking asylum from right-wing dictatorships. In some cases, however, American reluctance to admit refugees was coupled with other policies that actively encouraged political change. Examples include support for the Solidarity movement in Poland (1981), tightening of the economic embargo and other measures against the Cuban government (1994), and humanitarian support for civilian populations in Bosnia (1992). In such cases, the policy of discouraging refugee flows can be seen as part of a strategy of opposition to the government in power rather than a sign of support for it.

With the passage of the 1980 Refugee Act, the legal basis of refugee admissions to the United States changed from political realism to humanitarian principle. The act eliminated the geographical (Europe and the Middle East) and ideological (anti-Communist) grounds for granting refugee status. Actual practice, however, changed very little. In 1993 the overwhelming majority of U.S. resettlement places for refugees from abroad still went to people from the former Soviet bloc and Indochina, relatively few of whom would meet the international standard for a claim on international protection.

This picture of stasis is somewhat misleading, however, for U.S. policy on refugee issues is changing in fundamental ways. Even some of the advocates for the ex-Soviet and Indochinese entrants acknowledge that the programs that gave these groups special treatment as refugees are winding down, and that the current pipelines will be allowed gradually to empty. Refugee allocations are becoming more and more difficult to justify in the light of changing conditions in the countries of origin of these two groups; however, historical obligations, family ties, and powerful domestic advocates may ensure that the refugee programs are replaced by special immigration programs.

As the cold war era receded through the mid-1990s, the outlines of a post–cold war refugee policy were slow to emerge with any clarity. However, a pattern of U.S. response to the refugee crises of the 1990s suggested that it was becoming more common for foreign policy to be designed to achieve certain objectives in refugee policy, rather than exclusively the other way around. Even in cases where refugee flows were not a lead factor shaping policy, the implications for refugee flows of certain foreign policy decisions

were much more likely to be high on the policy agenda. An examination of a number of refugee crises and responses in the 1990s
shows that preventing, responding to, controlling, or ending refugee outflows is an increasingly important objective of U.S. foreign
policy in a number of settings. This chapter will examine some of
those situations, the refugee constituency pressures that influence
them, and the policy responses to them.

Refugee Policy in the Driver's Seat?

There are relatively few instances even now in which refugee
policy can be said to drive U.S. foreign policy, but these few are
important. Supplementing them are an increasing number of
situations in which an actual or threatened flow of refugees is in
the forefront of the policy environment. Both categories include,
but are not limited to, situations in which the United States is the
direct recipient of refugee flows as a country of first asylum. The
new prominence of refugee issues is apparent in a string of foreign
policy crises descending in a line from the war in Iraq in 1990/91
and the subsequent Kurdish uprising to the confrontations with
Haiti and Cuba in 1994.

Northern Iraq

In northern Iraq, in the aftermath of a failed uprising following
the war to reverse the annexation of Kuwait, some 400,000 Kurds
fled to the Turkish border during a three-week period in April
1991. It was one of the largest and certainly the most rapid refugee
exoduses the world had seen up to that point. U.S. policy, despite
the war with Iraq over the annexation of Kuwait, had not included
any challenge to Iraqi sovereignty in Iraq; indeed, this was part of
the reason the United States did not support more actively the
Kurdish uprising. U.S. policy makers were unwilling, however, to
see their Turkish allies destabilized by a large-scale influx of Kurds
from Iraq at a time when Turkey was (as it still is) engaged in
armed confrontation with its own Kurdish minority. They were
determined, therefore, not to put pressure on Turkey to open its
border to the refugees.

As the Kurds began to suffer and die on the desolate hillsides opposite the border, pressure from congressional advocates, media exposure of the plight of the refugees, and, finally, public opinion drove the Bush administration to action. It instigated a military operation first to bring humanitarian relief to the Kurds, and eventually to secure a safe haven for them in northern Iraq. The refugee crisis, in this instance, overturned the position that Iraqi sovereignty should be respected even in defeat, as well as the strongly held view that U.S. troops should leave the theater of war as quickly as possible. In fact, at this writing, U.S. troops are still there, protecting the Kurds who would otherwise become refugees and taking casualties in the process. Operation Provide Comfort and its aftermath rewrote the rules for humanitarian intervention; the reverberations of that aspect of U.S. policy are still being felt.

Rwanda

The 1994 refugee crisis in Rwanda pulled the United States into a form and degree of foreign involvement that it did not seek or desire—and, indeed, went some way to avoid. Lacking historical ties, cultural affinity, strategic interests, or geopolitical concerns, U.S. policy makers were extremely reluctant to be drawn into active involvement in Rwanda—even indirectly through support for a UN peacekeeping mission involving no U.S. troops. When the crisis broke in April 1994, a UN force of 2,500 troops was present. It was drawn down to less than 500 by early May, as the main troop contributors (Belgium and France) withdrew their forces and the Security Council decided that the remaining force was too small to carry out its mandate.

As the UN secretary-general called for intervention to stop the massacres in April and May (massacres that continued well into July), the Clinton administration made Rwanda the first test case for its new, restrictive policy on UN peacekeeping. Announced in May as Presidential Decision Directive 25, the new policy redefined UN peace operations as "a tool to provide finite windows of opportunity to allow combatants to resolve their differences and failed societies to begin to reconstitute themselves." It declared that the United States would base its support for them on consider-

ations of whether the mission supported U.S. national interests and enjoyed domestic support. Neither could be said of Rwanda.
U.S. insistence on a painstaking review of the proposal for a newly mandated UN peacekeeping force delayed deployment in a period when an estimated 10,000 people a day were being killed, not in combat but in a carefully planned campaign of genocide.[2] The Security Council, with the United States in a leading role, repeatedly deflected calls from Secretary-General Boutros-Ghali to increase the UN presence in Rwanda in order to shield civilians from the ongoing massacres.

The U.S. policy response to the crisis in Rwanda was one of determined disengagement, and it remained so throughout the period of the civil war. Apart from subduing action in the United Nations, U.S. officials in April and May confined themselves to deploring and condemning the unfolding horrors, and offering some humanitarian aid to refugees. Despite calls for a more robust response from congressional leaders in mid-June, and a report from the UN Human Rights Commission in late June characterizing the massacres in Rwanda as genocidal, the administration refused to invoke the 1948 Convention on Genocide. Indeed, officials were cautioned to avoid use of the word, fearing that it would force them into action.

The policy of noninvolvement changed only in response to the refugee crisis that developed in July 1994. In the week of July 13–19 alone, some 1.2 million people flooded across the Zairean border, most of them in the vicinity of the town of Goma. With as many as 3,000 people an hour reported to be crossing the border into this particularly desolate region, President Clinton assigned the administrator of the Agency for International Development, Brian Atwood, to visit the burgeoning refugee camps in Zaire to assess the humanitarian needs there. By that time, a cholera epidemic was beginning to sweep the camps, and relief supplies and systems were completely overwhelmed.

Upon his return to Washington, Atwood's meeting with the president was delayed, and the suppressed fury of refugee advocates erupted. With the complexities of intervention in the midst of a civil war no longer an obstacle, the delay in responding to the refugee crisis was denounced in strong terms, the message amplified by the press and in congressional hearings.

Stung by the accusations that U.S. indifference was allowing the tragedy of Rwanda to be compounded, the president met with Atwood ahead of schedule, and announced a stepped-up program of financial and logistical support for the refugee relief effort. The program escalated throughout the following week, until by July 29 nearly half a billion dollars of aid had been committed, along with tons of equipment and 2,000 U.S. soldiers to deliver and distribute it. The president, vice president, chairman of the Joint Chiefs of Staff, national security adviser, and deputy secretary of defense, among others, made the announcements. There was no doubt that the United States was, by August 1994, firmly and concretely engaged in Rwanda.

Cuba

U.S. refugee policy toward Cuba was, until August 1994, an outpost of cold war policy in a post–cold war world. Virtually all Cubans who fled the island were admitted to political asylum in the United States and allowed to proceed quickly to permanent residency. As the United States moved to more restrictive asylum policies generally, demanding high standards of proof of persecution from most asylum seekers, Cubans were still admitted even if their admitted motivation was the pursuit of a better life in economic terms rather than the "well-founded fear of being persecuted" that defines a refugee under international and U.S. law. One of the rafters who arrived in Florida in August 1994 told the *New York Times* that "she just wanted something different for herself and her family. 'I was born in 1960. I was born with Fidel, and I want to have what I've never had before', she said. 'We never celebrated Christmas in Cuba.' "

The change in U.S. policy toward Cuban refugees was set in train in July 1994 after an attempted hijacking of a Cuban ferry boat was thwarted by the Cuban authorities, with heavy loss of life among those who were hoping to use the boat to reach the United States. The incident set off anti-Castro riots in Havana. In response, Cuban President Fidel Castro let it be known that Cuban authorities would not stop people from leaving on their own small craft. During the summer months, more than 35,000 "rafters" were picked up by the U.S. Coast Guard as they headed for Florida; an unknown number perished in the attempt.

The exodus raised fears in the United States of another Mariel boatlift, which in 1980 had brought 125,000 Cubans and much political turmoil to the United States. Administration officials were keenly aware of the electoral disadvantages of presiding over a refugee influx seen to be out of control. (Mariel related events were implicated in the defeats of both President Jimmy Carter and then–Arkansas Governor Bill Clinton in 1980.) Similar disadvantages were perceived in conceding any bargaining advantage to Castro. The double policy imperative in approaching the crisis became a) control the outflow from Cuba, b) in a way that could not be perceived as a political victory for the Cuban president.

The first part of this imperative required opening negotiations with the Cuban government. The second severely limited their scope. Only action by the Cuban authorities could bring order to the departures in the short run. But a lasting solution to the outflow of Cuban migrants would require not only political liberalization but also an improvement in economic conditions in Cuba, where a failed command economy staggered under the impact of continuing mismanagement, the loss of Soviet subsidies, and the effects of a comprehensive U.S. economic embargo. Any negotiations to trade off the lifting of political repression and the regulation of migration for the lifting of the economic sanctions were anathema to the conservative Cuban-American forces most vocal on this subject. They continue to see the economic misery in Cuba as the most potent threat to Castro's continuation in power.

On August 18, 1994, President Clinton announced that thenceforth Cubans rescued at sea would not be allowed to enter the United States but would be offered safe haven at the U.S. naval base in Guantanamo, which was already in use as a safe haven for some 15,000 Haitian refugees. With that, he ended the twenty-eight-year-old policy of automatic political asylum for Cubans and with it the implication that all Cubans are subject to persecution. At the end of August, the administration entered negotiations with Cuban officials, in effect conceding the point that the United States could and would deal with Cuba as a partner on matters of practical concern (as it had done repeatedly in the aftermath of the 1980 Mariel boatlift). The talks concluded successfully on September 9 with Cuban agreement to discourage boat departures and U.S. agreement to increase sharply (to a minimum of 20,000 per year) the number of visas for Cubans wishing to emigrate legally to the United States. With the agreement, the United States committed itself to extend extraordinary immigration privileges to Cubans, even those without U.S. relatives, special skills, or claims to refugee status. The U.S. negotiators refused to discuss a loosening of the embargo as the Cuban government had insisted; indeed, a tightening of the economic embargo was announced to placate domestic critics.

To some administration officials, the tightening of the embargo was an "own goal" against the long-term policy of relieving emigration pressures in Cuba through political and economic liberalization. In their view, as reported in the *New York Times* on September 11, 1994, "The best way to promote a peaceful transition to democracy in Cuba is to increase, not decrease, the flow of Western ideas to Cuba, and that means increasing travel, telecommunications and student exchanges," among other things. Nonetheless, some saw the refugee negotiations as establishing a basis of communications that could lead to wider ranging discussions in the future. It may be too early to conclude that the need to bring an end to the refugee influx from Cuba brought about a fundamental change in the U.S. foreign policy stance toward Cuba. It did open practical negotiations on the immigration front. More importantly, it elevated the issue of Cuban-American relations on the foreign policy agenda, opening the prospect of an eventual resolution of the cold war in the Caribbean.

Haiti

For most of the cold war period, Haiti was a backwater of U.S. foreign policy. Its dictators were minor but useful anti-Communist allies in the Caribbean, whose larcenous habits and appalling human rights abuses were largely overlooked as a result. They also cooperated with the U.S. government in its efforts to control the

flow of Haitian refugees and would-be migrants into the United
States. In 1981 an agreement was concluded between the two
countries that allowed the U.S. Coast Guard to intercept Haitian
vessels bound for the United States and return to Haiti those who
were determined, on the basis of the most cursory inspection, to
have no basis for an asylum claim. Between 1981 and 1991 some
24,600 Haitians were intercepted by the Coast Guard. Only
twenty-eight were permitted to enter the United States to apply for
asylum; the rest were returned to Haiti.

This pattern persisted until 1991, when Haiti's first democratically elected president, Jean-Bertrand Aristide, took office. During
his tenure, the U.S. Coast Guard found few Haitians at sea to
intercept. After a military coup deposed Aristide on September 30,
1991, however, the departures soared. In the nine months following the coup, more Haitians were apprehended at sea than in the
previous decade.

With operations aboard the Coast Guard cutters overwhelmed,
President Bush opened a processing center for the Haitians at the
U.S. naval base at Guantanamo Bay. Nearly a third of those
screened were found to have a credible fear of persecution and
were allowed to proceed to the United States. In May 1992, with
the numbers of Haitians in Guantanamo mounting steadily and
the screening procedures under court challenge, President Bush
issued an executive order to halt the screening and summarily
repatriate all the Haitian boat people intercepted at sea. To soften
the blow, the administration pledged to monitor the conditions of
returnees, and opened processing centers in Haiti where people
could apply for refugee status. Though the order was challenged as
a violation of U.S. and international refugee law, the Supreme
Court ultimately allowed it to stand.

President Clinton came to office in the midst of the controversy
over Haitian refugees, having severely criticized the Bush policy of
forcible return. From the beginning of the new administration,
U.S. policy toward Haiti was driven by the refugee issue. Fearing
an overwhelming influx of Haitian boat people to the United
States early in his presidency, President Clinton announced that
he would temporarily retain the policy of interdiction and sum-

mary return. But he pledged a serious and concerted political effort to pressure the military junta to step down and permit the return of the elected president.

The pressures on the new administration were both internal and external. Clinton came to office with a stronger human rights orientation and constituency than his predecessor. Many of those he brought into office were uncomfortable with the policy of interdiction and return. Moreover, among the strongest advocates for Haitian refugees were the members of the Congressional Black Caucus, natural allies of the president whose support would be crucial to the success of his legislative program. Along with many others, the members of the Black Caucus objected strongly to the differential treatment given to Cuban and Haitian asylum seekers. The former were routinely paroled into the United States and given asylum, while the latter were turned away without so much as a hearing and returned to a country in which political murder was an everyday occurrence. It was particularly painful to this president to be accused of having a racist refugee policy.

Weighed against the concerns of two of its core constituencies, the Democratic administration was keenly aware of popular aversion to an uncontrolled influx of Haitian refugees, particularly in the electorally important state of Florida. Furthermore, key decision makers were convinced that a more generous asylum policy would act as a magnet, drawing to the United States not only the politically persecuted, but many economically motivated migrants as well.

The need to halt the flow of refugees drew the administration into a more activist foreign policy toward Haiti, aimed at securing a return of legitimate government. To this end, limited sanctions were sought and imposed on Haiti through the United Nations in June 1993. A protracted negotiating process culminated in the Governors Island Agreement, signed in July 1993, under which the military would relinquish power and Aristide would return. The agreement was, however, abrogated by the Haitian military when the time came for them to relinquish power.

The demise of the Governors Island Agreement unleashed a heightened sense of frustration among refugee advocates in the

United States. With hopes of a negotiated solution dashed, political violence in Haiti escalating, and the policy of interdiction still in place, pressure to change the refugee policy increased.

In March 1994 the Black Caucus introduced a bill in the House of Representatives to tighten the economic embargo against Haiti, cut commercial flights to and from the United States, block Haitian financial assets held in the United States, and stop the summary return of Haitian asylum seekers interdicted at sea. Over the next several months, all of these steps became administration policy, although the bill was never brought to a vote. It became increasingly clear that, for the refugee flow, the only cure was prevention, and the only acceptable form of prevention was the restoration of elected government in Haiti. This became the focus of U.S. policy.

Perhaps the most significant of the many turning points in the development of the U.S. stance came as a direct result of pressure on the refugee issue. The African-American activist Randall Robinson embarked on a hunger strike in April 1994 to protest the policy of interdiction and summary return. On May 8 the administration announced that Haitian refugees picked up at sea would have their claims to refugee status adjudicated at sites in the region. The president also announced that he would consider using U.S. military force to eject the ruling junta and restore the elected president, if all other methods of persuasion failed. In describing the U.S. interests that would justify such a move, he cited on May 19 Haiti's proximity to the United States and the likelihood of a continuous "massive outflow" of refugees to U.S. shores.

This theme was repeated by administration officials throughout the summer. For example, in a June 8 State Department briefing Deputy Secretary of State Strobe Talbott said:

But the two principal ways in which the Haitian crisis . . . impinges on the vital interests of the United States are, first, it represents an affront and a potential reversal to the trend of democratization in this hemisphere. . . . And second, of course, because that catastrophe is so severe, one of its results is an outpouring of refugees, many of whom of course do want to come to the United States. And if all of them came . . . that would put a considerable burden on the United States.

In July the policy of screening Haitian boat people gave way to a policy of offering temporary safe haven to all who expressed a fear of returning to Haiti. The U.S. base at Guantanamo again became host to thousands of people awaiting a change of regime in Haiti that would make it safe for them to return home. U.S. policy makers made it clear that such a change must take place in the near future, and obtained a UN resolution authorizing the use of "all necessary means" to restore democracy to Haiti.

President Clinton addressed the nation on September 15, 1994, to explain the reasons for the impending U.S. intervention, which began four days later. He dwelt on the impact of the refugee exodus from Haiti at some length:

Thousands of Haitians have already fled toward the United States, risking their lives to escape the reign of terror. As long as Cedras rules, Haitians will continue to seek sanctuary in our nation. This year, in less than two months, more than 21,000 Haitians were rescued at sea by our Coast Guard and Navy. Today, more than 14,000 refugees are living at our naval base in Guantanamo. The American people have already expended almost $200 million to support them, to maintain the economic embargo, and the prospect of millions and millions more being spent every month for an indefinite period of time looms ahead unless we act. Three hundred thousand more Haitians, 5 percent of their entire population, are in hiding in their own country. If we don't act, they could be the next wave of refugees at our door. We will continue to face the threat of a mass exodus of refugees and its constant threat to stability in our region, and control of our borders.

The most extreme act of foreign policy, the use of armed force, was thus explicitly justified as an outgrowth of a refugee crisis.

Refugee Constituencies
and U.S. Foreign Policy

The impact of refugee policy on broader U.S. foreign policy objectives is often magnified—and in some cases virtually created—by concerted political action on the part of refugee communities resident in the United States. A number of diaspora groups have developed sophisticated political lobbyists, with strong influence on politics and policies in the countries where they or their forebears found refuge.

The word "refugee" invokes visions of despair, displacement, and powerlessness. The political vitality of refugee communities is often overlooked, and their political activism discounted, because of this passive image—and because new refugees lack the power to vote. But many refugees have acquired that status precisely because of their political activity, and are likely to continue their political activism in exile. Among them, foreign policy has a high priority, since it has defined their current exile and is likely to be shaping the lives of family and friends left behind in the home country.

Many refugee groups focus their political energies on developments in their country of origin or within the expatriate community. They may support parties, candidates, or clandestine organizations at home. Some devote themselves to preparing for return, or to establishing support for political movements in exile—the Ayatollah Khomeini in Paris and Benito Aquino in Boston being two prominent examples. Refugees often have a strong impact on political events in their home countries, whether through direct action or through "political remittances"—the transmission of values, experiences with democratic institutions, habits of loyal opposition, and appreciation of a free press.[3]

In many cases, the factionalism of home country politics dogs refugee politics and robs it of efficacy. Cambodian refugees—split among Khmer Rouge, Royalist, Republican, and Phnom Penh factions—have had little impact on the policy debate in the United States. The Oromo and Amhara may pursue their mutual grievances with each other in exile without generating larger awareness or support for Ethiopian issues in the U.S. polity at large.

As refugee communities put down roots in the United States, however, some groups succeed in grasping the levers of the domestic political systems as other immigrant groups have before them. Their influence gains momentum as adjustment and naturalization proceed. Over time, for some groups, political activity ceases to be confined to inward-looking exile circles and is projected into the national foreign policy debate. Refugee communities—including the native-born descendants of refugees—who combine political skill, focus, and financial commitment have come to exert considerable influence on particular aspects of U.S. foreign policy. The Cuban, Jewish, and Armenian communities are well-established political forces, and Vietnamese-Americans are beginning to exercise their collective political muscle.

Cuban-Americans

One of the most impressive examples of refugee influence in foreign policy can be found among Cuban-Americans. Cuban-Americans were a relatively small population in the United States until refugees began pouring into the United States after Fidel Castro took power in 1959. Between 1960 and 1970 more than 400,000 Cubans came to the United States, settling in particular around Miami, Florida. Today Cuban-Americans number over 1 million. Such a large constituency concentrated in one city has a strong political punch in the state and the country. As Robert Bach notes, "No other immigrant group to the U.S. . . . has been able to use as effectively its opposition to the new government to influence US foreign policy."[4]

Several factors account for the Cuban-American community's strength. To begin with, the exile population is, in general, educated, skilled, and prosperous. In addition, the large Cuban-American community served and continues to serve as a social and economic safety net. Adjustment to the United States is made much easier through an established and generous Cuban-American community.

The early refugees were politically active in Cuba and had many contacts in Washington. Political activity continues at a high rate among Cuban-Americans. They register and vote at levels much higher than the average U.S. population. Also, the Cuban-American constituency offers a largely cohesive and united voice against the Castro government, which is relayed to Washington almost exclusively by one powerful lobby, the Cuban-American National Foundation (CANF). Lastly, the U.S. government is keenly interested in Cuba. During the cold war, Cuba, as the Soviet satellite nearest the United States, was an especially sore spot on the U.S. foreign policy agenda. As a cold war maneuver to show the superiority of American capitalism over Cuban communism, U.S. policy encouraged Cuban refugees to come into the country and offered them generous assistance. Even though the East-West conflict is over, Cuba remains an unresolved nemesis, and the Cuban-American lobby uses this irritation to its advantage.

The CANF is the most influential Cuban-American lobby by far, described by some as "a millionaires' club of right-wing exiles with a hefty campaign war chest."[5] The foundation has over 50,000 members and sixty-five directors who contribute $10,000 each to the organization, in addition to pledging $10,000 more to political campaigns.

One of the first major successes of the CANF was the establishment of Radio Marti in 1983, a Voice of America broadcast program to Cuba. The bill that founded Radio Marti with $10 million was strongly supported by Florida's congressional delegation, spurred by large Cuban-American constituencies. However, Radio Marti has received strong criticism from less hard-line observers for serving as a CANF mouthpiece at a cost of $15 million a year in public funds.

A large constituency and budget spell political power and access. The continued isolation of Cuba, even after there is no longer a Soviet threat, can be attributed to Cuban-American pressure, especially from the foundation. As one Bush administration official said, "The foundation has had a chilling effect on the debate. Anytime anyone starts to think creatively about Cuba we're told: What do you want to do, lose South Florida for us?"[6]

The conservative exile groups were able to overcome objections from both the Bush administration and U.S. allies in order to pass the Cuba Democracy Act of 1992, which forbids foreign subsidiaries operating in the United States to trade with Cuba. Representative Robert Torricelli (D-NJ), the sponsor of the act, was likely motivated by the 85,000 Cuban-Americans of his state who could provide crucial support for his future election prospects.

President Bush opposed the act until presidential candidate Clinton was winning more Cuban-American votes with his endorsement. Clinton merely stated, "I like it [Cuban Democracy

Act]," and managed to raise $125,000 for his campaign from the Cuban-American community.[7] As president, Clinton continued his predecessors' policy of isolating Cuba. The conservative Cuban-American constituency continues to dominate the U.S.–Cuba policy debate, even though the cold war is over and a liberal administration is in office.

Jewish-Americans

An even stronger show of political power on the part of a former refugee population can be seen among American Jews. Most American Jews or their forebears came to the United States to escape religious persecution, many in the aftermath of the Holocaust. Today American Jews number 8.1 million, and the United States continues to admit Soviet Jews through refugee programs at the rate of 35,000–50,000 per year.

The American Israel Public Affairs Committee (AIPAC), the Jewish-American community's most powerful voice, is often used as an example to emulate among other ethnic lobbies in the United States. With an annual budget of about $15 million and a membership of 50,000, AIPAC is well equipped to press its agenda forward. For AIPAC, as for numerous other politically active Jewish organizations, foreign policy is high on that agenda. For this among other reasons, Israel is the single largest recipient of U.S. aid, with a total of $3 billion a year. Monetary assistance to Israel does not stop there, however. In 1992, $10 billion in loan guarantees were granted to Israel in order to resettle hundreds of thousands of Soviet Jews. Members of Congress received 50,000 telephone calls in support of the appropriation, and according to one estimate, 1,200 Jewish-American activists worked to secure its passage.[8] However, the loan guarantees experienced considerable opposition from President Bush, who was concerned about the effect of further Jewish settlement in the West Bank and Gaza on the Middle East peace process. The lobbying efforts were only one factor that influenced the final outcome; more importantly, a new Israeli government under Yitzhak Rabin promised to curb Jewish settlement in the occupied territories.

Most of the Soviet Jews who are not resettled in Israel settle in the United States. In 1988 there was considerable controversy over the almost unquestioned admission of Soviet refugees, in some cases without even a claim of actual persecution. Soon after, refugee processing in Moscow was more strictly administered, though not without substantial protests from the Jewish-American community. Leaders from the community met with Attorney-General Dick Thornburgh and Immigration and Naturalization Service (INS) Commissioner Alan Nelson. In addition, the Hebrew Immigrant Aid Society (HIAS) had a fifty-two-page legal memorandum prepared by the Fried, Frank, Harris, Shriver & Jacobson law firm. Finally, Jewish-American constituent pressures triggered the Morrison-Lautenberg Amendment. Representative Bruce Morrison (D-CT) and Senator Frank Lautenberg (D-NJ) initiated an amendment that lowered the persecution threshold for refugee status for certain groups, including Soviet Jews. In the Senate, the Lautenberg Amendment received a 97-to-0 vote (not one senator spoke against the legislation), and the House voted 358-to-44 to pass the Morrison Amendment.

The natural result has been a high acceptance rate of Soviet Jews for resettlement in the United States. More than 133,000 Soviet Jews (about 30 percent of all refugee arrivals in the United States) have resettled in the United States since Fiscal Year 1990. In addition, Soviet Jews account for about 80 percent of refugee admissions to the United States from the former Soviet Union—a result of effective lobbying by the Jewish-American community.

The recent Jewish refugee arrivals from the former Soviet Union are becoming yet another political force within the Jewish-American population. The Soviet Jews have chosen to develop their own political and social identity and are reliving the stages of political development that their sponsors experienced; they are now beginning to organize. The Soviet Jewish community does not yet have the political clout, but the seed, the desire to influence policy, has already been sown. One Soviet Jewish activist commented, "We have thousands of experienced people. The goal is to continue to make a unit of our community to involve more and more people . . . and in the tradition to be a Jew. To help our friends, our relatives in Israel, to help our friends and relatives in Russia. . . ."[9]

Today's generous response to the Soviet Jewish refugees sparks a stark contrast to a half-century ago when a boat load of Jews fleeing the Holocaust was turned away. The Jewish-American voice was barely audible then. Today the numbers and the political and economic abilities of the Jewish-American population make it impossible to ignore their concerns.

Armenian-Americans

Like the Jews, Armenians have fled from religious and ethnic persecution. The majority of Armenians came to the United States after fleeing genocide in Ottoman Turkey. The first wave came in the mid-1890s. The first of the mid-1890s massacres began in 1894 and resulted in the arrival of 50,000 Armenians in the United States that year. By 1899, 70,000 Armenians had fled to the United States. Today their descendants number about 1 million. The heaviest concentrations of Armenians are in Southern California, Massachusetts, and Michigan.

Several organizations represent the Armenian-American community's political concerns: the Armenian Assembly, the Armenian National Committee of America (ANCA), and the Armenian American Action Committee. Their political clout can be seen in very large aid packages for Armenia. Armenia is the smallest republic of the former Soviet Union; yet in 1993 this small nation received the second highest amount of U.S. aid to former Soviet republics ($335 million)—second only to Russia. Also, Armenia had the highest per capita aid at $98 per person; Russia received only $14 per capita.

Armenian-American political pressure can also be seen in the 1992 Freedom Support Act, which extended aid to all former Soviet republics except Azerbaijan, the republic that has since 1988 been at war with Armenia over the enclave of Nagorno-Karabakh. The Armenian-American lobby successfully pushed for a provision of the act (Section 907) that denies Azerbaijan U.S. government aid (excepting only humanitarian assistance) until the country ceases its blockade on Armenia and Nagorno-Karabakh. Despite recent efforts at repeal, this provision still stands.

Perhaps the most emotional and controversial issue for Armenian-Americans is the recognition of the Armenian genocide, which Turkey continues to deny. Every year the Armenian community mobilizes to honor the victims and lobby their congressional representatives to do the same—a gesture extremely unpopular with a strategic NATO ally. Nevertheless, the lobbying efforts and voting power of the Armenian-American population have proved to be powerful pressures. In April 1994 more than 100 senators and representatives spoke in Congress to commemorate the Armenian genocide.

Lastly, the Armenian-American lobby also influenced the previously mentioned Morrison-Lautenberg Amendment. Unlike the Jewish-American community, the Armenian-American population was unclear on its position toward Armenian refugees from the Soviet Union. Many political activists from the community did not want Soviet Armenians to be considered as one of the persecuted categories. Armenians in America felt that a massive exodus from the homeland would drain the already weak country. Lori Titizian, the western regional director of the Armenian National Committee, stated, "As a policy we do not like to see Armenians leave the Soviet Union. We do not consider them political refugees."[10] In addition, Levon Marashlian, an Armenian historian, has said, "They [Armenians] are not really victims of persecution in Soviet Armenia. Virtually all Armenians organizations are against this emigration."[11] As a result, Soviet Armenians, who are Christians, were excluded from the Morrison-Lautenberg Amendment, even though the amendment included Evangelical Christians as a persecuted category.

Vietnamese-Americans

There are many other refugee voices in the United States. For instance, the Vietnamese community may not be as politically potent as the aforementioned lobbies, yet it does have an impact. The community is fairly new, beginning serious growth only in 1975, but it has already increased to over 1 million, 300,000 of whom are U.S. citizens. A recent *Los Angeles Times* poll reported nearly 60 percent of Vietnamese-American citizens in Southern California are registered to vote, and 79 percent believed it was important to participate in American politics. Their political activity is likely to gain momentum as more and more Vietnamese naturalize. Over 80 percent of the noncitizens within the Southern Californian community expect to naturalize in the next few years.[12] The Vietnamese-American community is working to empower these new voters. Several leaders have been promoting an aggressive voter registration drive.

Vietnamese-Americans have shown impressive organizational and political skills, having survived, integrated, and organized politically within twenty years. There are a number of organizations working to influence U.S. foreign policy: the National Congress of Vietnamese Americans (NCVA); National Association for Education and Advancement for Cambodian, Laotian and Vietnamese Americans (NAFEA); Boat People SOS; Families of Vietnamese Political Prisoners Association; and the Vietnamese-American Political Action Committee, among others. The Vietnamese-American lobby has scored at least four foreign policy successes in recent years. They include the enactment of Radio Free Asia, a lawsuit victory against the State Department, the freeing of Vietnamese political prisoners, and the "Vietnamese Human Rights Day" Bill.

Vietnamese-American activists have been pushing for Radio Free Asia for over a decade, through letter campaigns and meetings with members of Congress. Unlike a divided Chinese-American community, the Vietnamese offered a united voice in support of the radio that helped pass the bill in April 1994.

The Vietnamese-American community has also influenced U.S. policy toward Vietnamese refugees. In March 1994, 250 Vietnamese-Americans sued the State Department to force it to review the U.S. immigration applications of Vietnamese boat people held in Hong Kong, rather than repatriating them and forcing them to reapply for immigration to the United States from Vietnam.

The involvement of Vietnamese-Americans has also been instrumental in releasing thousands of political prisoners in Vietnam. Vietnamese-Americans were members of the first delegation to speak with Vietnamese government officials about releasing political prisoners. The April 1989 meetings were the first in which the Vietnamese government had agreed to meet with expatriates from the United States. These talks helped lead the way to an agreement between the United States and Vietnam to resettle Vietnamese political prisoners in the United States. In the agreement's first five years, 100,000 Vietnamese have resettled in the United States under its terms. Seventy thousand more Vietnamese are expected to be released within the remaining three years of the agreement.

Another political success was the designation of May 11, 1994, as "Vietnam Human Rights Day." The bill, introduced by Representative Leslie Byrne of Virginia, urges the Vietnamese government to protect human rights and hold free elections—two foreign policy priorities among the Vietnamese-American community.

Conclusion

The refugee debate in America is often focused on the costs of resettlement and the goods and services that refugees receive. Such discussions paint a distorted picture of a rather passive group that waits to be acted upon. However, the above illustrations show several vibrant communities that are keen to utilize their political powers to help themselves and the homeland they—or their parents or grandparents—fled.

The political activism of Cuban-, Jewish-, and Armenian-Americans is seen as a model by other refugee communities such as the Vietnamese and Haitians. If new refugee groups come to be as successful in presenting a unified front and in mobilizing financial resources to press their agenda, it is likely that today's refugee admissions will influence tomorrow's foreign policy.

Broader Implications for Foreign Policy

The influence of refugee crises and constituency groups can be seen in certain specific areas of foreign policy, some of which have been discussed above. However, the effects on foreign policy of U.S. refugee policies as conducted in the 1990s reach well beyond the particular issues to which they are designed to respond. The broader implications of refugee policy include the disposition of funds for foreign policy implementation, the freedom of action of

212

KATHLEEN NEWLAND

major powers, and the future of multilateralism. These wider implications add up to a strong case for earlier, preventive action when refugee crises threaten to develop.

The disposition to respond to humanitarian needs only after a mass displacement has reached the crisis phase raises the costs of intervention.

When the Rwandan crisis broke, the UN Security Council voted to reduce the UN peacekeeping mission (UNAMIR) to less than a quarter of its existing size, against the advice of the secretary-general. The remaining UNAMIR troops lacked the logistical capacity to rescue Tutsi refugees who had gathered at sites in Kigali and the surrounding area. Those left behind were easy prey for murderous militias; the small and ill-equipped UN force could do little but bear witness to the horrors unfolding around it. With hindsight, many in the relief community argue that an early investment of perhaps $10 million in preventive protection could have saved thousands of lives and millions of dollars that must now be devoted to relief and reconstruction. As a Western diplomat based at the United Nations told the *New York Times* on July 23, 1994, "There is no question that we are going to have to spend 10 times as much money and 10 times as much effort to deal with refugees in Rwanda than we would have if we had had the political will to go in and quell the fighting." With the price tag for the international relief operation for Rwanda now approaching $1 billion, that assessment now looks like an underestimate.

The funds for massive refugee relief operations like that in and around Rwanda, or military operations to intercept, shelter, or return refugees compete with other budgetary items. The U.S. contribution to Rwandan refugee relief is nearly $500 million. Seeking a supplemental appropriation to cover some $270 million of that, Secretary of Defense Perry warned in August that the diversion of Pentagon funds to emergency relief could threaten U.S. military preparedness. In September the Defense Department estimated that an invasion of Haiti would cost a minimum of $427 million, on top of the $200 million already spent on interdicting and sheltering Haitian refugees.

Ultimately, it is feared that such crisis response and emergency relief operations will divert funds from longer-term development efforts—precisely the kinds of investments that may blunt some of the pressures that give rise to refugee-generating conflicts in the first place. In 1994 the budget of the office of the UN High Commissioner for Refugees (UNHCR) exceeded that of the UN Development Program for the first time. At $1.4 billion, the UNHCR budget is twice what it was in 1989. A refugee policy that responds to emergencies only at the eleventh hour is an expensive policy.

The United States is not alone in its reluctance to get involved in refugee crises that are physically remote and involve no direct threat to national security. As a matter of policy, however, the widespread adoption of this stance risks a return to great power spheres of influence in the Third World. Faced with an array of refugee-generating conflicts, the United Nations Security Council has approved U.S. intervention in Haiti, French intervention in Rwanda, and Russian intervention in Georgia. The pattern makes the veneer of multilateralism look increasingly thin, and is likely to erode global support for such actions in the future.

A more positive result of the aversion to direct involvement in refugee crises remote from the national interest is the increasing tendency to look to multilateral institutions, often working with private sector organizations, to cope with mass displacements. The capacities of organizations like UNHCR and the International Organization for Migration (IOM) have been augmented. Handing over responsibility for refugees to the UN agencies, the Red Cross movement, and international private relief agencies has to some extent pushed the U.S. government toward the "assertive multilateralism" foreseen in the 1992 presidential campaign, from which in other areas it has pulled back. On the other hand, handing over tasks without handing over the resources to fulfill them can only be seen as an evasion of responsibility.

If a reactive, short-term refugee policy holds dangers for broader U.S. foreign policy objectives, a more considered refugee policy focused on early preventive action holds promise. Prevention worthy of the name addresses the causes of refugee flows—rather than simply bottling them up—and dovetails with broader objectives such as observance of international human rights standards, mediation of ethnic conflicts, the rule of law, and representative government. A foreign policy that is consistent and rigorous in the pursuit of these objectives is effective refugee policy as well. Over the long term, it is likely to reduce the high cost in blood, treasure, and political credibility of late responses to full-blown emergencies.

Notes

[1] National Security Council, "Psychological Value of Escapees from the Soviet Orbit," Security Memorandum, March 26, 1953, cited in Zolberg (1990).

[2] See, for example, the testimony of Jeff Drumtra (Africa policy analyst, U.S. Committee for Refugees) on "U.S. Response to the Crisis in Rwanda/Central Africa" before the Senate Foreign Relations Committee, Subcommittee on African Affairs, July 26, 1994.

[3] Rick Swartz, "Immigration and Refugees: Issues, Politics & Democratic Pluralism," unpublished paper, March 1985.

[4] Bach (1985), p. 91.

[5] Robbins (1992), p. 163.

[6] Robbins (1992), p. 163.

[7] Robbins (1992), p. 167.

[8] Winston Pickett, "The Day Bush Shocked the Jewish Lobby," *Ethnic News-Watch*, September 25, 1992.

[9] Singer (1992).

[10] Chorabjian (1982), p. 71.

[11] Chorabjian (1982), quoted from the *New York Times*, July 9, 1988.

[12] Doreen Caravajal, "Southland Vietnamese Support Renewed Ties," *Los Angeles Times*, June 13, 1994.

6

The Effects of
International Migration
on U.S. Foreign Policy

CHARLES B. KEELY

C ommon sense dictates that international migration must affect U.S. foreign policy. International migration anywhere
on the globe may affect vital U.S. interests. Recall the potential for
unrest that displaced persons in Western Europe represented after
World War II both for economic growth and a return to political
stability without Communist influence.

Beginning with the Mariel boatlift from Cuba to the United
States in 1980, the potential for unexpected mass migrations to the

---

CHARLES B. KEELY is the Donald G. Herzberg Professor of International Migration and professor of demography at Georgetown University. He has written or edited six books and over fifty articles on U.S.
immigration policy, global temporary labor migration, and international
refugee policy and programs, and he has just completed a study of the
operation of the Office of the U.S. Coordinator of Refugee Affairs since
its inception in 1978. He is currently working on a study of the use of
nonimmigrant temporary visas and corporate personnel strategy as well
as a theoretical book on the nation, the state, and international migration.
Before joining the faculty at Georgetown in 1987, he was senior associate
at the Population Council in New York for ten years.

216   CHARLES B. KEELY

United States affected hemispheric policy. Domestic political issues were also pulled into the vortex of mass asylum, including regionalism (the impact on Florida), ethnic politics (Cubans specifically and Latinos generally), and racial politics (policy on Haitian asylum seekers).

Finally, as Oliver Wendell Holmes noted in 1893 in *The Poet at the Breakfast Table*, "We are all tattooed in our cradles with the beliefs of our tribe; the record may seem superficial, but it is indelible." Immigrants and their descendants (ethnics) can influence domestic and foreign policy through lobbying groups or other organized attempts to shape decisions of the United States.

While they do not exhaust the connections between international migration and U.S. foreign policy, international migrations affecting stability elsewhere in the world, the threat of mass migrations to the United States, and ethnic lobbies have the greatest salience.

International Migration around the Globe and U.S. Foreign Policy

Past Examples

Population redistribution after the 1948 Indian partition, Palestinian refugee camps, ethnic slaughter during the Idi Amin regime in Uganda, Pol Pot's demented vision of a Socialist country in Cambodia, civil wars in Africa, Kurdish rebels in Turkey and Iraq, and ethnic cleansing in former Yugoslavia are examples over the last five decades of migrations in other countries that affected U.S. foreign policy. New movements and possible requirements for preventing them, as in the former Soviet Union, engage policy makers. Prior reviews about international migration elsewhere and its influence on U.S. foreign policy were made in the context of the cold war by Michael S. Teitelbaum, Gilbert Loescher and Laila Monahan, Leon Gordenker, and Peter H. Koehn, among others.[1] These analyses now need updating in view of the recent tidal changes in geopolitics.

A New International Order

An exploration of conditions affecting international migrations and their character must attend to five developments: the reemergence of self-determination; the reawakened force of nationalism; the disappearance of state mechanisms; the articulation of a "right to stay" for refugees; and the effects of economic globalization and regional integration on the free movement of people, goods, and capital.

Reemergence of Self-Determination. Self-determination by nationality groups, which was the normative model for restructuring states after the First World War, hardly led to homogeneous nation-states as implied by the concept. The redrawn European map had to be supplemented by minorities' treaties to deal with the loose ends of what was an impossible task, given overlapping claims to the same territory.

Self-determination was not given the same prominence by the Allies after the Second World War. Forced repatriations were the order of the day in Europe until 1946, implying almost the opposite of self-determination. People belonged to their state of citizenship, and were to go there regardless of their support for the government. Subsequently, self-determination was hardly operative except for decolonization. Aside from colonial independence, Bangladesh is the only case of secession until the events of 1989.

The eclipse of self-determination took place because of an inherent paradox in the process. A state is not a state until other states recognize it as such; for weak states, external support is mandatory. Except in the case of decolonization, UN resolutions ruled out self-determination that involved secession. The multiplication of states, as measured by United Nations membership, underplayed the fact that self-determination was practically a dead letter in other contexts.

The reemergence of the normative power of self-determination was signaled by the separatist demands of Eritreans. The secession of a breakaway state on the African continent was particularly disturbing, given the Organization of African Unity (OAU) charter provision recognizing inherited colonial boundaries. Yet the same justification of decolonization was presented in the Eritrean case, based on the history of Ethiopia as an empire and the forced incorporation of Eritrea in the 1930s.

While Ethiopia/Eritrea may have been allowed to pass as an example of colonialism, reference to empire raises the issue of distinguishing between illegitimate incorporation versus nation building. What criteria distinguish among Eritria, Brittany, Northern Ireland, and the Baltic states? The longstanding policy of nonrecognition of the Baltic republics' incorporation into the Soviet Union meant that secession was a distinct possibility. The fall of the Soviet Union in 1991, the reunification of Germany, the velvet divorce of the Czech and Slovak republics, and the dissolution and bloody aftermath of Yugoslavia revived self-determination as a normative principle. The proliferation of states can introduce unpredictability and instability into international relations. If the new international order means anything, it must include a return to territorial stability as the norm for the international community.

Nationalism Newly Rampant. As erudite an observer as Eric Hobsbawm, in a series of lectures delivered in 1985, predicted the coming end of nationalism.[2] Hobsbawm ended his book with a "singular conceit" by noting that nationalism's becoming a legitimate field of study was evidence of its coming demise. Moynihan summarized Hobsbawm's book and its thesis curtly, but accurately, as "a work of great learning, it is equally a work of vast delusion."[3]

The reemergence of nationalism is related to the new-found force of self-determination beyond former colonial boundaries. For almost five decades, the Soviet hegemony in Eastern Europe and northern Asia froze nationalist expression as a political force. In the thaw following the cold war, nationalism spread its tendrils.

The former Soviet Union is not alone in hosting revived nationalism. In the European Union, nationalism arises in many guises, from the plebiscites on the Maastricht Treaty, to monetary policy, to asylum policy. The Uruguay Round of the General Agreement on Tariffs and Trade (GATT) was held up over the unsolved issue of U.S. television programing's access to European airwaves.

While events since 1989 make it difficult to delude oneself about the staying power of nationalism, its full impact on international migration is difficult to assess. Many factors will influence events, including the tolerance of the world community and regional powers for secession, forced migration, and civil unrest. That nationalism can lead to violence and forced migration is a matter of historical record. What is not clear are the limits of tolerance by states individually and collectively.

Decline and Fall of the State. When Catherine the Great, Empress of All the Russias, made stately progressions through her realm, her favorite and minister, Count Gregory Potemkin, would precede her. The count assured an impression of prosperity for the empress by having elaborate building facades constructed, with nothing behind them. Thus the phrase "Potemkin villages."

In the decolonization era after World War II, many new states appeared. France and the United Kingdom kept close ties to former colonies. Their involvement provided political and economic support needed by the new states. Other colonial powers, like Italy, Belgium, and Portugal, did not involve themselves after departure to nearly the extent of the larger colonial powers.

In addition to support from former colonial rulers, the great power rivalry of the United States and the Soviet Union assisted successor states. Competition for spheres of influence and ideological supporters sometimes slipped into military support in armed conflicts. Proxy wars permitted the leading powers of East and West to test one another. Vietnam, Cambodia, Afghanistan, the Horn of Africa, Angola, Nicaragua, and El Salvador are among the conflicts.

With the end of the cold war, the republics of the former Soviet Union lack the capacity to engage in such foreign adventures, even were they to have the desire to do so. The economic problems of other European countries in the 1980s and the demands of integration have resulted in their pulling back from support of former colonies.

One result of this withdrawal of external supports may be termed "state implosion." The characteristics include no sitting government in control and no operative justice system. Infrastructure crumbles without the resources or organization to maintain it. Schooling, organized medical care, and other basic social services are unavailable. Internal markets are primitive and virtually no export market exists. Banking and monetary systems become more worthless, sometimes by the hour. There is an increasing litany of countries that have names on a map but no functional state: Afghanistan, Somalia, Angola, Liberia, Rwanda. Others, like Zaire, are waiting in the wings. The system of states, to an appreciable extent, is becoming a Potemkin village.

The new international order must include rebuilding state capacity to participate in the global economic and political systems. The task is complicated when one or more rival "governments" resist, claiming violation of sovereignty, regardless of the lack of state capacity. Perhaps a new international trusteeship system will have to be developed. How the political will and the resources will be found and whether the United Nations can be the agency for organizing this system is unclear. The lack of clear techniques and models for building capacity adds to the gravity of the challenge.

Forced international migration has been integral both to the proxy wars of the cold war and to the collapse of states. Proxy wars dragged on because international sponsors were unwilling to allow their proteges to be defeated. Yet sponsors would not arm either side to the point of permitting a clear victory for fear that regional wars would escalate into East-West confrontations. Military stalemates meant that few refugees were repatriated while conflicts dragged on. Refugee counts have grown since the 1970s with each new civil war.

The demise of states, like proxy wars, can also produce large numbers of refugees. While an emergency response can be mounted to deal with refugees, peacemaking and development are hollow words when, at best, a country lacks a coherent government and is run instead by rival feudal barons. Dwindling state capacity is not viable long term. Unless the collapse of states is addressed, refugee movements from the same country will be recurring events.

The Right to Stay and the Right to Leave. In the mercantilist era, the sovereign right to control movement of people over borders focused on the right to prohibit emigration. Rulers sought to prohibit the loss of skilled people and recruits for armies. To rule was to populate. The United States fought the War of 1812 with Great

Britain partly over the right of British subjects to expatriate themselves.

Circumstances change. The Universal Declaration of Human Rights of 1948 declares a person's right to leave his or her own country and to return thereto, but the declaration enunciated no right to enter another country. Sovereignty had been transformed to embody the right of a government to control who enters and with what restrictions.

The UN High Commissioner for Refugees, Sadako Ogata, proposed to make repatriation a high priority of her time in office. She also espoused the right of people not to be forced to move. While such an idea seems self-evident, assuming the most modest notion of human rights, it is a double-edged sword. It may encourage development of the idea of humanitarian intervention, with its many dangers for independence. The right to stay can be perverted into justification for limiting the right to seek asylum—a right to stay can become a duty to stay. Concepts like safe countries and safe zones and efforts to contain emigration potential in violent situations seem to limit the right of exit. The American request to Cuba in 1994 to control illegal exit verges on requesting violation of the right of exit.

In developed countries, the number and nature of asylum applications have led to efforts to reform asylum systems. In developing countries, the flow of refugees from ethnic strife and the breakdown of states continue. It is not at all clear that the post–cold war refugee flows will be of shorter duration than the refugee flows from the proxy wars of the 1970s and 1980s. The flows have been acute, as in Somalia, Liberia, and Rwanda, but the collapse of states may mean they will result in long-stayer refugee situations. Mozambique is the best-case scenario to date in restoring a semblance of order that allows for large-scale return after state collapse. The killing and bloodshed were so great that people simply tired of it and reconciliation took place.

International Migration and the New International Order. International migration will be a defining characteristic of the new international order, for three reasons. First, the world is full of multinational countries with potential for the violence that produces refugees. Second, as long as self-determination has force, the potential for secession and irredentism remains. Third, economic unions, which usually include a goal of free migration among contracting states, are in the ascendancy.

The future shape of the emerging international structure and rules of state behavior is unclear. To what extent freer movement within economic unions or forced migration due to political development will take place is unknown. New ingredients are redefining geopolitics: the reemergence of the normative power of self-determination; resurgent nationalism; the withering of state apparatuses; and the redefinition of the international community's responsibility toward victims of war, disaster, and bad government. While recent history can provide counsel, the end of the bipolar struggle that colored virtually every facet of international relations for the last half century means that it does not furnish blueprints.

The New Meaning of Security

A new notion of security is emerging in the cold war's aftermath. In Europe, discussion of asylum policy includes the threat to internal stability posed by migration. The concern is not just that migrants bring different ways, or that extreme rightists commit violent acts. Ordinary citizens are unwilling to abandon their belief in "the nation" for a pluralistic society that means the abolition of a culture and way of life. The question is seriously entertained whether liberal democracies, rooted in an ethnically based nation-state, are still acceptable and viable. When migration leads to questioning the current constitution and viability of liberal democratic states in Europe, it is a security issue.

In a February 1993 article in *Atlantic*, Robert Kaplan saw impending anarchy in the combined threats of environmental degradation, poverty, crime, corruption, migration, and disease spreading across the world. Such a chaos thesis proposes environmentally-driven anarchy, including uncontrolled migration, as the national security issue of the next century.

Samuel P. Huntington, in a provocative and widely read article in *Foreign Affairs*, proposed that a "clash of civilizations" is likely to dominate geopolitics in the coming years.[4] Culture, rather than competing political ideologies rooted in Western philosophy and economic theory, will be the new battleground. Unlike Kaplan, Huntington acknowledges that "nation states will remain the most powerful actors in world affairs" but posits clashes between civilizations as the principal conflicts to come.

Myron Weiner[5] raised, in a rather less sweeping and normative way than Kaplan or Huntington, the change in the meaning of security away from an exclusively military definition to a broader concept that includes culture, social stability, environmental degradation, population growth, migration, and other soft security issues.[6]

Recent U.S. government reorganization in the State and Defense Departments and the Central Intelligence Agency reflects implicitly a new definition of security. Similarly, private think tanks are turning their attention to issues ignored as unimportant when they were otherwise engaged with the correlation of forces, MIRVs, and throw weights.

Policy influentials, both within and outside government, are in the initial stages of adopting a broadened view of security. While it is premature to form firm conclusions about U.S. foreign policy and international migration, some initial judgments can be offered.

Conclusions about Contemporary International Migration

How U.S. foreign policy relates to contemporary and future international migration depends on how the United States and other states respond to the factors encouraging and inhibiting forced and voluntary international migration, and on how states redefine security. Certain foreign policy objectives in this domain are clear, even if the means to achieve them are not.

Self-determination should be allowed to change borders in rare cases. The pendulum must swing back to allow self-determination to proceed as one principle of state formation, yet be balanced by general stability of states needed for international relations to take place. A corollary is that, in most cases, nationalist aspirations must be channeled in directions other than civil wars undertaken with the hope of independence or reunion with a purported homeland. If territorial change is denied as an option, the temptation to take up arms will lessen among nationalists.

To meet these objectives requires a willingness by and capacity of the international community to undertake "humanitarian intervention" to stop persecution, genocide, forced removals, and other actions that foster international migration. Requiring respect for human rights as a *sine qua non* of state behavior appears to be more of a realist than an idealist position than heretofore, because human rights violations are palpable threats to stability. International rules of state behavior must be enforced; international recognition of a government and of its sovereignty must be conditional on adherence to minimal rules of behavior. These ideas are fraught with problems, not least that "humanitarian intervention" proposals are suspect because they usually emerge from the capitals of big power states, rather than from medium and small countries. Consequently, arrangements for mounting humanitarian interventions are suspect as based on a double standard. A Haiti or even an Iraq has felt the weight of internationally organized intervention for human rights violations, but a China will not.

The Potemkin village trait of the international system of states must be addressed. The difficulty of finding the political determination to impose such mechanisms and the states willing to undertake the role of guarantor of order and trainer of a generation to assume governance are not easy. It should not be presumed that only European or North American states be candidates for trusteeships.[7] Nor do we know how to train a generation to assume leadership of its own country. The difficulties suggest that delay in addressing the issue will be the short-term preference of the international state system.

It would be unfortunate if the United States should adopt the chaos thesis as proposed by Kaplan. Among its faults is the mistake of assigning states in general or nation-states in particular to the dustbin of history. "Nation states, with their armies, governments, laws and legitimacy . . . are—and will remain—the dominant force in world affairs."[8] It is this conclusion that underlies the proposal to redevelop a trusteeship system.

That self-determination may need to be reined in does not deny its integral role as an expression of nationhood, which remains the fundamental ideological legitimation for the state. The main justification for a claim to territory and the right to self-governance remains a community, a nation, which, like a species, is its own irreducible justification for the right to exist. There is tension between self-determination as the expression of the right of a people to continue through time, on the one hand, and the need of states for stability on the other. Because states remain the basic building blocks of the international system, there is an immense need to attend to faltering states. Neither world government nor the vision of the peaceable kingdom is in the immediate future.

If states remain at the core of security interests, then the chaos thesis should not be adopted as security doctrine. Chaos theory is not the functional equivalent of George Kennan's containment strategy to guide us in contending with the apocalyptic horsemen of disease, drugs, environmental degradation, and population dynamics out of all control.

Mass Migration to the United States

Asylum

Throughout the 1980s, asylum applications soared in the industrial countries. Applications in Europe, North America, and Australia rose from 90,000 in 1983 to about 825,000 in 1992. In the United States, applications rose from 20,000 in 1983 to 150,000 in 1993.

The drafters of the 1980 Refugee Act took up the topic of asylum as an afterthought. The focus of the bill was to regularize refugee resettlement in the United States from overseas camps. The instigating issue was the Indochinese refugees admitted through a controversial use of "parole," an immigration law provision intended for emergency temporary admissions, but frequently used since the Hungarian rebellion in 1956 to admit refugees. Hundreds of thousands of Indochinese had been admitted/paroled in 1975 and 1976, and Vice President Walter Mondale, as head of the U.S. delegation to a Geneva refugee conference in 1979, promised that the United States would admit up to 144,000 a year outside of congressional authorization to help respond to the Vietnamese boat people issue.

The new legislation specified that each year, up to 5,000 persons who were granted asylum would be permitted to adjust to immigrant status. The ink from President Carter's signature in March 1980 was hardly dry when the Mariel boatlift began in April. Eventually about 125,000 Cubans and an additional 65,000 Haitians were admitted outside the refugee provisions of the 1980 Refugee Act.

Mariel took the U.S. government by surprise. Concerned over the failed mission to rescue the hostages in Iran some three weeks earlier, the Carter administration was unclear about how to respond. Castro seemed to control American policy. Military solutions were dangerous and entailed opening two possible fronts. To impound boats and arrest Americans for rescuing family was a politically tenuous proposition. Yet thousands were coming to South Florida, with huge impacts on the capacity of federal, state, and local governments, as well as nongovernmental organizations, to cope. In addition, it became evident very early in the episode that Castro was forcing boat captains to transport convicts and mentally ill people.

The new provisions of the 1980 Refugee Act required federal reimbursement of state and local governments for costs related to Mariel entrants if the president declared them refugees. To avoid this, he admitted them using the same controversial parole provision previously used for refugee admissions. Under the 1980 act, the president could no longer legally parole refugees. But by paroling them and calling them something other than refugees, he could allow them to stay while avoiding the need for federal reimbursement to Florida and other jurisdictions. The paroled Marielitos and Haitians were dubbed "Cuban and Haitian Entrants, Status Pending." The Florida congressional delegation soon remedied the reimbursement situation by forcing special federal legislation covering the Mariel entrants.

Mariel took place in an election year, and President Carter lost Florida. President Clinton, in whose state of Arkansas some riots took place among Marielitos in detention centers, also lost his 1980 bid for reelection as governor. The lesson was simple, and Mariel was translated into an unarticulated policy that the United States was not to become the Thailand of the Western Hemisphere. Subsequent action toward Haitians through the 1980s, Central American asylum seekers, and Cubans in the summer of 1994 supports the assertion of such an unarticulated policy.

Deflection of Haitians began with the policy of interdiction at sea enunciated by President Reagan in 1981. The Kenebunkport Declaration by President Bush in 1991 changed the policy to return interdicted boats without hearing of passengers' asylum claims. President Clinton continued the Kenebunkport policy, despite his strong denunciation of it as a candidate, until late spring of 1994, when he returned to the Reagan policy of interdiction and provision of safe haven outside the United States, primarily at the U.S. naval base at Guantanamo.

The Central America issue differed from the asylum challenge from the Caribbean countries. Central Americans joined a well-worn overland path of illegal entry from Mexico. The major method to discourage Central American asylum applications was to deny petitions; the approval rates were generally below 5 percent for Guatemalans and Salvadorans. Even in the case of Nicaragua during the period of the Sandinista government, the asylum approval rate, although higher than for other Central American countries (as high as 30 percent in some years), was lower than the overall average. The coordinator for refugee affairs in the Reagan administration, Eugene Douglas, reported that the Nicaraguan policy was partially dictated by a desire to discourage exit and to keep in place a moderate opposition to replace the Sandinistas.[9] Such a policy—to keep a moderate opposition in place in a country with a Communist government—represented a clear departure from policy since World War II.

In Central America, the change of government in Nicaragua and the peace negotiations and agreement in El Salvador have reduced (but not eliminated) the justifications and the incidence for asylum claims. Attention to human rights in Guatemala is also seen as reducing the legitimacy of widespread claims of persecution justifying refugee status and asylum under U.S. law. U.S. politics about Central American asylum during the Reagan and

Bush presidencies was largely a function of disagreements about Central America policy. While not totally eliminated, the scope and intensity of disagreement in the Clinton presidency are reduced.

One aftermath of Mariel was the reported *démarche* to Premier Castro by President Bush during the 1992 presidential election, warning that dire consequences would result should another mass boatlift develop. The Clinton administration responded to the increased flow of rafters permitted by Castro in the summer of 1994 by ending the special treatment of Cubans. In a holdover from the cold war, past Cuban escapees had been treated more generously than the law required. The change in geopolitics and Cuba's relative isolation, its deteriorating economy, and the lesser reliance of a Democrat administration on the Cuban ethnic vote contributed to the new Cuban policy. The politics of the Florida gubernatorial election provided leverage to the Cuban lobby in forcing a policy of pressuring Castro rather than engaging in dialogue and constructive engagement of the two societies. The mailed fist was put on to assuage the Cuban lobby, rather than a velvet glove, along the lines of Germany's *Oestpolitik*.

While migration is integral to U.S. policy toward Cuba or Haiti, it is not the only factor. The strategic value of either country for U.S. national interests is a theme that weaves through policy discussion and analysis in and outside of government. Yet without the asylum flows, U.S. engagement with either country would probably be much less. A strong requirement that any policy must honor is not to allow, much less encourage, uncontrolled mass movement to the United States.

Shifts in asylum policy also applied to petitioners from other parts of the world. After the changes of governments in Eastern Europe, the word went out quickly that asylum would generally be denied to petitioners from former Warsaw Pact countries. Liberal democratic countries with a policy of free markets, almost by definition, did not produce refugees.

Nevertheless, asylum applicants, particularly from Third World countries, continued to come. Once in the United States and having applied for asylum, the length of the procedure and the general policy of granting work authorization was an open invitation to abuse. In addition, applicants rely on the lack of detention facilities at major airports to facilitate early release. Like other industrial countries, the United States instituted procedures to discourage fraudulent applications, such as withholding work authorization for 180 days.

It has proved to be an endless cat-and-mouse game. Each innovation to "beat the system" is countered, and an ever more clever evasion then appears. A major victim is the politically important mechanism of asylum. The possibility of persecution within the state system requires agreement about standards and responsibilities of states to innocent victims. Otherwise, any barbarity must be tolerated in order not to infringe on sovereignty. The capacity to conduct international relations and economic interactions would eventually break down. Asylum is not only humanitarian; it is also provided for reasons of state.

In sum, the United States has three types of mass asylum problems: by sea, primarily from the Caribbean; overland, mainly from Central America; and by air from various, mostly Third World, countries. The policy of avoiding becoming a mass first asylum country affects options in all cases.[10]

Harmonizing Migration Policies

An important issue for the European Community (EC) has been the harmonization of policies on migration needed for a single Europe with free movement of goods, capital, and people. More difficult has been the coordination of policies on asylum, not only by the twelve but also by European countries generally. The break-up of the Soviet Union has not made it any easier to coordinate European policy on asylum, much less about overall migration.

In North America, the North American Free Trade Agreement (NAFTA) contained migration provisions that covered only a small number of commercial travelers. But NAFTA could have major migration consequences. The stimulation of the Mexican economy, some of it in anticipation of NAFTA, already has led to migration over Mexico's southern border. In the short run, NAFTA might stimulate migration to the United States. If economic growth continues, Mexico might become the Italy of North America. Just as Italian migration to EC partners in the 1950s and 1960s diminished to a trickle, in ten to fifteen years Mexico may become a net immigration country. The southern border of North America would functionally become not the Rio Grande, but the Mexican-Guatemalan border.

The NAFTA partners already share interests about migration into their region in the form of would-be refugees and economic migrants from Central America, and the use of Mexico by international smuggling rings. The three states already meet in bilateral and trilateral groups on migration issues, but outside the formal NAFTA framework.

In both the North American context and as a partner (as is Canada) with European industrial countries, the United States is addressing a shared challenge that requires cooperation with other countries to deal with smuggling rings, multiple applications to many countries by asylum seekers, and sequential applications by asylum seekers after being denied in one country.

Ethnic Lobbies

The most direct and controversial relationship between international migration and foreign policy is the putative influence of ethnic lobbies.

Why Are Ethnic Lobbies Suspect?

Rooted in the Magna Carta, the right of petition was asserted in the resolutions of the Stamp Act Congress of 1765, the Declaration of Independence, and the First Amendment to the Constitution. James Madison gave his imprimatur when he wrote in the *Federalist Papers* (No. 10) about the favorable outcomes of pursuit of private interests in a democracy. Why is something so basic to traditional usage a problem? Three reasons are notable: foreign policy in a democracy; single-issue interest groups; and nativism in American life.

Democracy and Foreign Policy. Alexis de Tocqueville wrote that "although democratic liberties applied to the internal affairs of a nation as diverse as the United States bring 'blessings greater than ills,' this was assuredly not the case in the conduct of foreign relations." De Tocqueville noted that, from Rome through the Great Britain of his day, an aristocracy conceived and carried out the grand designs that embodied their influence.

The suspicion of foreign policy as an elite affair is reflected in the accusation that an "eastern establishment" with connections to old money, Ivy League schools, and white, Anglo-Saxon, Protestant pedigrees is synonymous with the "foreign policy establishment." Despite increased access by Americans of various ethnic backgrounds, the accusation of dominance (with judicious cooption of talented outsiders) remains.

Diplomats and policy makers often decry the lack of a constituency for foreign policy, underscoring their perception of the difficulty in obtaining attention and resources for vital American interests. Yet foreign policy is surrounded with an air of the esoteric, requiring long experience, linguistic skills, and special knowledge of arcane subjects from nuclear strategy to international monetary policy. That foreign policy is no place for amateurs seems to be the real position, and ethnic lobbying groups only get in the way.

Single-Issue Lobbies. Woodrow Wilson expressed the view that single-issue groups are a special threat based on experience of ethnic lobbies and neutrality, as well as his attempts to remake the map of Europe at war's end. President Jimmy Carter made a high art of castigating single-issue groups. Not only presidents deplore the single-issue lobby. That an influential lobby can apply a litmus test to candidates for election, whether about gun control, abortion, or policy toward Israel, has come in for wide criticism.

Ethnic lobbies have multiple objectives in principle. Nevertheless, because the issues are focused on a specific country, the presumption is that they are single-issue groups.

Nativism. In his classic book on American nativism and immigration, John Higham defined nativism as an "intense opposition to an internal minority on the ground of its foreign (i.e., 'unAmerican') connections."[11] Almost by definition, Americans organized to champion the interests of another country or to use the power of the United States to dislodge a government represent "some influence originating abroad [that has] threatened the very life of the nation from within."

In sum, ethnic lobbies stir up deep animosities. Influentials who deal with foreign policy issues see them as a bother. Politicians group them with single-issue gadflies who see the world with blinders. Worst of all, ethnic lobbies have an aroma of being un-American, if not anti-American. They may imperil the country from within because their attachment to another country could undermine the national interest.

The National Interest

What exactly the national interest is, or how anyone can know it unambiguously, is often cloudy. Agreement about the national interest emerges concretely from the political process.

How Can the National Interest Be Determined? The Assembly of Captive European Nations was founded in 1954 with the avowed objective of freedom for Eastern Europe. In the 1960s it helped delay most-favored-nation status for Yugoslavia, organized boycotts of Polish hams, and helped cancel a large contract involving the Firestone Rubber Company and Rumania. These actions impeded President Johnson's policy to build bridges to Eastern Europe.[12] Who was right, the assembly or the president?

With the break-up of the Soviet Union in 1991, there was an embarrassing question asked of the Sovietologists and the intelligence community: how did they miss the coming end of the cold war and the demise of the Soviet Empire? Daniel Patrick Moynihan, the senior senator from New York, recounts in his book, *Pandaemonium,* more than a decade of warning signals from demographic data, health statistics, and nationality tensions in the republics and in the Soviet military itself that were overlooked or ignored in the continuous overestimation of the Soviet Union's vitality. Consensus intelligence estimates pegged Soviet gross national product at 62 percent of the U.S. level in the mid-1970s and estimated per capita income of East Germany as *higher* than that of West Germany as recently as 1985 (East Germany at $10,440 and West Germany at $10,220).

Given that the scholars whom Moynihan cites were correct and the intelligence community and experts who ran foreign policy were wrong, were the Reagan policies of military build-up and simultaneous tax decreases, with their attendant deficit increases, in the national interest? Was the downfall of the Soviet Union inevitable, if, in fact, it was already well underway by 1980? Was Moynihan correct when he wrote: "Surely, the cold war might have come to an end on its own without the U.S. having become a debtor state in the process." While Moynihan's book will not be the last word, it questions the confidence to be placed in an assertion that a policy like Reagan's military build-up is in the national interest. Sovietologists' myopia concerning the USSR's vitality illustrates that entrenched interests are not peculiar to ethnic lobbies. "We had got into the routine of counting missiles . . . ," Moynihan quotes a senior U.S. intelligence officer. As the Librarian of Congress and distinguished Russian historian James Billington said:

The greatest investment any nation ever made in international study . . . failed . . . utterly to help America predict—or even allow for the possibility of—any of the great overseas crises this nation has faced in the last quarter century: Vietnam, Iran, Iraq and now Yugoslavia. . . . We failed equally to anticipate or even allow for the possibility of the great positive breakthroughs in Poland and Russia. . . .[13]

Sources of Ethnic Lobbies' Power

If ethnic lobbies are so suspect, whence comes their power? Ethnic lobbies' strength is based on their organization, the imperatives of the electoral system, and the merits of their cases.

Politically Organized Groups. Ethnic lobbies have power because a committed constituency is organized, contributes resources, and demonstrates that officials will pay a political price if their demands are not heard and addressed. Simply put, the fundamental power of ethnic lobbies comes from old-fashioned political muscle, based on organization.

To assume that every ethnic group can affect foreign policy in some rough correlation to its size or growth is mistaken. A fashionable assertion that recent Mexican immigration to the United States bodes ill, because another ethnic foreign policy lobby is in the offing, is not self-evident. Large numbers do not insure unanimity or a committed faction to support a lobby. It is not clear that Mexican-Americans would be for or against the current government and dominant political party in Mexico.

The civil rights voting legislation produced a "politics of numbers" in which an ethnic or racial group's size allows claims on domestic resources that previously could not be pressed without political organization.[14] But the ability of ethnic group leaders to impact foreign policy on the basis of the size of their groups is not credible.

Political influence based on organization is also unlike a foreign government's paying for professional representation in Washington. Paid lobbyists have influence based on access of their principals or useful advice about ways to sway opinion and ultimately to impact decision makers.

The Election Imperative. Organization as the source of ethnic lobbies' power rests on the periodic elections for Congress and the presidency. The ability to deliver votes, as well as money and other campaign resources, provides access to office holders and office seekers. Elections and the congressional committee structure are tailor-made for influencing the American political system.

The Merits of the Case. Finally, lest complete cynicism take over, a lobby may have a case that merits support. While the merits of a case are not the only issues to be considered and are not necessarily determinative, a good case, well presented, makes a lobby's job easier. The Greek lobby had merit on its side when it protested the Turkish invasion of Cyprus. Invasion of a sovereign country is difficult to justify.

Ethnic Lobbies in American History

Ethnic lobbying is not new to American politics. The earliest examples of important pressure applied by organized, ethnically based interest groups attempted to preserve American neutrality preceding World War I.

Neutrality and World War I. Isolationism has deep ideological roots in the United States. Early colonial settlers often came to the New World to escape the evils of Europe. George Washington warned against entanglements in Europe's disputes. This ideological legacy, along with transportation technology, weak central government, and the Civil War, sufficed to confine attention to domestic issues during the republic's first century.

Industrialization and urbanization in the last quarter of the nineteenth century changed the capacity and interests underlying a more activist U.S. foreign policy. From about 1890 to 1912, the country emerged as a world power, albeit still untried, as progressivism, with its mixture of idealism and moralism, gripped the American imagination.[15] Coincidentally, mass migration reemerged at that time, now from nontraditional sources of Southern and Eastern Europe.

As the Great War developed in Europe, Irish- and German-Americans sought to have Wilson maintain his neutrality policy. Other ethnic groups supported abandonment of neutrality, as well as additional policy objectives; groups like Zionists, Slovaks, and Czechs (Bohemians) sought independent homelands.

Preventing U.S. entry into the war was the central objective. The American public broadly shared Wilson's isolationism. Ethnic groups supporting neutrality were not trying to change policy but to preserve a policy with deep American roots.

Isolationism as the norm survived World War I. Ethnics weighed in on the League of Nations, and their view prevailed over the president's. Overall, there is no consensus on the relative importance of general isolationist sentiment versus ethnic power in the decision to stay out of the League.

Delayed Entry into World War II. During the interwar period, Irish- and German-American predilections for isolationism continued. There also was a resurgence of isolationism in the 1930s among the general population. According to Manfred Jonas, " 'Ninety-nine Americans out of a hundred,' the *Christian Century* estimated in 1935—probably correctly, 'would today regard as an imbecile anyone [who suggested] that, in the event of another European war, the United States should again participate in it.' "[16] Jonas concludes that ethnic support for isolationism, which mirrored general opinion, had marginal policy influence. Isolationism predated

Irish, German, and, certainly, Italian mass migration. Further, the isolationism of such influentials as Herbert Hoover, Hiram Johnson, and Hamilton Fish did not depend on a personal ethnic background or an ethnic constituency. The leading isolationist publications of the 1930s included *The New Republic, The Nation,* and *The Saturday Evening Post.*

The propositions that Irish, German, or Italian ethnics were the mainstays of American isolationism and delayed American entry into World War II are hard to support. Conversely, the evidence that Jewish or Polish ethnics pushed the United States into the war is extremely thin. As Jonas states it, the evidence of a relationship between immigration and foreign policy, through the vehicle of ethnic groups, "has been greatly exaggerated."[17] While not all agree with the conclusion,[18] the general consensus is that ethnic interests for and against American entrance into World War II on the Allied side were far from determinative.

Post–World War II. Ethnic lobbies blossomed in the postwar period. The general thrust of lobbies also changed from isolationist to interventionist. In this, ethnic lobbies continued to be in the mainstream, which now flowed in a different direction.

Perhaps most discussed, because presumed to be the most effective, is the Israeli lobby. Jewish participation in foreign policy was muted before World War II. The access of Jews to President Franklin Roosevelt increased active attempts to mold policy, but they were of a quiet and behind-the-scenes character for fear of arousing anti-Semitism. The Holocaust and the new Jewish state of Israel spurred American Jewish activism.

Instances of policy differences between the United States and Israel are many. Generally, however, the United States government has been extraordinarily supportive of Israeli governments' policies. The American Israel Public Affairs Committee (AIPAC) is credited (or blamed) for the record of U.S. support of Israel.

The Israeli lobby's record raises the issue of national interest. Most analysts support the position that in the main, U.S. support for Israel has been and continues to be in the American interest. But on specific issues, that is not clear. Was the sale of the F-15s to Saudi Arabia, debated in 1978 and approved by Congress over the objections of AIPAC, blackmail to keep oil flowing? Or did Israeli and Saudi interests coincide regarding Soviet influence in the region, a concern they shared with the United States. Further, no matter how important or special a U.S.–Israel relation, it is not exclusive.

The impact of the 1974 Jackson-Vanik amendment, a success for the Jewish lobby, in achieving its goal of opening Jewish emigration from the Soviet Union is controversial. It strained overall U.S.–Soviet relations. Whether in retrospect that was good or bad is debatable. But an impression was left that a gamble was taken for the sake of human rights and emigration goals without proper regard for other, and some would say the larger, issues of geopolitical stability.

The Jewish lobby's role is procedurally important because of its successful tactic of focusing on Congress. The increasingly activist role of Congress in foreign policy in the postwar period can be traced partially to lobbies' emboldening, and thereby empowering, Congress to set increasingly specific terms and limits on foreign policy.

The Greek lobby also affected important East-West policies. A major concern of the Greek-Americans' lobbying has been Turkey. Because both Greece and Turkey are members of the North Atlantic Treaty Organization (NATO), the issues often touched on policy toward the Soviet Union. The temporary withdrawal of Greece from NATO, the invasion of Cyprus and subsequent arms embargo on Turkey, and its closing of U.S. bases and listening posts set up a dangerous situation on Europe's southern flank. The Greek lobby's effort to maintain the embargo delayed its removal and, at least debatably, threatened NATO and, thereby, the United States, Greece, and Turkey's collective interests.

The third major ethnic lobby with notable success in influencing U.S. foreign policy is the Cuban lobby. The Cuban lobby has primarily focused on toppling Castro and reversing the revolution. It is a conservative group, supportive of the Republican party, and vocal in its anticommunism. As homegrown as any ethnic lobby, it retains an air of an exile group.

The increase in Cuban "rafters" in the summer of 1994 led to a change in U.S. policy toward would-be refugees from Cuba. The exceptionalism toward Cubans seeking asylum, particularly in contrast to practice toward Haitians and Central Americans, has been glaring. Governor Lawton Chiles's reelection campaign led to the Clinton administration's reversal of policy of special treatment for escapees from Communist Cuba. This supported the governor and was possible for a Democratic administration that lacked great political support from the Cuban-American community of Miami.

The Cuban-American lobby could not be completely ignored. It pushed the administration to continue its hard line toward Cuba, keeping the embargo and limiting travel and remittances from the United States. The lobby's argument was that the parallelism with Haiti should extend not only to the treatment of asylum seekers, but also to the efforts to dislodge a nondemocratic dictatorship. While the Cuban-American lobby lost out on continued special treatment of Cuban asylum seekers, it won continued support for its goal of toppling Castro through economic sanctions.

Beyond the Israeli, Greek, and Cuban lobbies, other groups have had less sustained success in being a force in U.S. foreign policy. That does not mean that there have been no successes, as the discussion of the Assembly of Captive European Nations indicated. The role of African-Americans in foreign policy, including South African and Haitian policies, deserves note.

Given the influence of ethnic lobbies, the issue arises whether recent immigration, especially from Latin America and Asia, signals the emergence of additional ethnic lobbies. The primary group of interest is Mexican-Americans. While the size of the group could probably support an organized ethnic lobby, as previously suggested, the interest and the consensus are not evident at this point. The specter of a Mexican-American lobby is just that, a worry that has not yet materialized.

On the contrary, Asian-American groups, which have grown as a result of the ending of the national origin quota system in 1965, have had some notable successes. Philippine-Americans reportedly influenced Senator Richard Lugar who, in turn, influenced President Reagan in support of replacing Ferdinand Marcos with Corazón Aquino in a relatively bloodless coup. However, the 1995 U.S. budget dropped the prior, special foreign assistance program to support Philippine stabilization. Korean-Americans have supported the two Kims, and Indian lobbying regarding Pakistan, notably in relation to nuclear policy, has also taken place. While none of these efforts has had the scope and persistence of more established lobbies, they are notable and could have deeper and more abiding impact.

What Difference Do Ethnic Lobbies Make?

This analysis presents ethnic lobbies historically as an ordinary part of American political life, hardly subversive of the political system and generally espousing mainstream positions about "national interests." What difference, then, do ethnic lobbies make? Four consequences, as discussed by Lawrence H. Fuchs, are striking: the impact on Anglo-American friendship; mitigation of class conflicts; weakening political party discipline; and bolstering the congressional assertion of a foreign policy role.[19]

Anglo-American Friendship. In addition to the controversy prior to both world wars about America's entrance, there were other incidents in the nineteenth and early twentieth centuries (e.g., treaty compromises concerning Canadian fisheries, difficulties over a Venezuelan boundary dispute, and Chinese policy) that involved areas of the world that many saw as requiring coordinated Anglo-American relationships. Even after World War II, the policy of Dean Acheson for a close Anglo-American alliance came in for heavy criticism, especially with the charge of twenty years of treason emerging from Republican Senator Joseph McCarthy. Opposition to British policy in Northern Ireland by segments of the Irish-American group put strain on the Anglo-American relationship. That tie continues to be a pillar of the NATO alliance, still a bulwark of U.S. interests.

Class Tensions. The importance for ethnics of U.S. policy affecting other countries mitigates potential class tensions in two ways. First, the ethnics identify with their peers and thereby submerge differences based on other cleavages of interests. Second, whether successful or not, ethnics may feel the anger of other Americans because of the actions of their "homeland." The effect of World War I on the role of German language and culture in the United States was extremely large.

Ethnic affiliation does not singly determine the fate of all members. Ethnicity can submerge other dividing lines that mark boundaries of shared interests. This insight underlies classic analyses of ethnicity in American life from Will Herzberg's 1955 *Protestant, Catholic, Jew: America's Triple Melting Pot* to Nathan Glazer and Daniel Patrick Moynihan's 1963 *Beyond the Melting Pot.*

Weaken Political Party Discipline. Ethnic constituencies do not always follow party lines. Election goals of an incumbent may lead to breaking with party leadership. The size of the Congress allows for many pressure points, and electoral goals, as pointed out, make Congress amenable to pressure.

Bipartisanship, so often extolled in foreign affairs, is not always compatible with party discipline, and it can even lose elections. An extreme example of bipartisanship was the restraint of the 1948 Republican presidential campaign. In the name of bipartisan foreign policy, the agreements of Teheran, Cairo, and Yalta were not attacked. It may have cost Governor Dewey the election.

Congressional Role in Foreign Affairs. The more recent pattern of ethnic lobbies targeting Congress has been noted. Congress is vulnerable to even small groups, if they are highly organized and effective in delivering election needs. Congress has increased its involvement in foreign affairs by means of the purse and oversight. While the president has the major constitutional role in foreign affairs, and until the end of World War II had very wide latitude, exclusive responsibility of the president now is challenged in word and in deed. The attention that lobbies give Congress contributes to its activism in foreign affairs, which, in turn, provides an entry wedge for lobbies.

Summary

Ethnic lobbies historically have been a force in American political life and an element in foreign policy. They espouse views that are ordinarily in the mainstream and hardly seem antithetical to U.S. interests at the time. Many of their causes and objectives are widely supported, but their views are not always determinative. To the contrary, Americans organized as ethnic lobbies, like other constituencies, represent a wide range of sophistication and have their shares of victories and defeats.

Ethnic lobbies are part of contemporary American politics and unlikely to fade in the foreseeable future. Despite being criticized, they are not indisputably a detriment to or subversive of the national interests. They are not all-powerful or a force out of control. They can be an effective check, and provide viewpoints that may be otherwise overlooked.

Conclusions

International migration is on the upswing around the world primarily because traditional alignments, rules of behavior, and economic structures are changing. Until these become clearer, firm commitments to new foreign policy strategies are premature. Nevertheless, to abandon traditional attention to states and their interests is a mistake. The new challenges requiring interstate cooperation, whether on environment, control of migration, or economic integration, do not spell the end of the state system or of the nation-state as an ideological model, for the foreseeable future. To elevate civilizations, economic forces, or the chaos of pollution, disease, crime, and corruption that know no borders to a level that transcends the ambitions of states and their leaders badly misleads. When the causes of disorder are being addressed, as they must be, the agency of human beings (leaders) and social structures (states and international regimes) must be kept firmly in sight.

Mass asylum flows, coming unbidden and uncontrolled, require change in the asylum system in the United States and in industrial countries in general. Those who unreflectively criticize attempts of industrial countries to curb abuses of asylum systems may be more guilty of destroying asylum than the governments that they accuse of abandoning the practice.

The tactics of forced repatriation of those found ineligible for asylum, interdiction on the high seas, requiring transportation carriers to insure proper documentation for passengers, use of safe zones and safe countries for containing mass flows, agreements on which state should have responsibility for reviewing asylum claims and prohibiting multiple or serial applications, and sharing information among states on asylum applicants have all been discussed and implemented at least on an experimental basis. The consequences are not entirely clear, nor is the debate finished about the acceptability of these practices. To decry any change and to deny that the asylum system is under pressure almost excludes one from being considered a serious policy discussant. The abuse of asylum is eroding support for asylum policies and practices among electorates. Unless confidence is restored in a system that is intended to protect true victims of political persecution, asylum will wither.

On a more positive note, cooperation or harmonization of asylum and migration policies is a concomitant of the growing interrelatedness characteristic of the global economy in the post–cold war world. Thus the United States needs to continue discussions to clarify common aims and routes of cooperation with North American partners in NAFTA and with European industrial countries.

Finally, ethnic lobbies are part of the American political scene, unlikely to go away and, historically, quite mainline in their objectives. Ethnic lobbies serve as a useful voice and can even be a corrective to conventional wisdom. They certainly can claim as much right to present views about the national interest as any Americans.

International migration and foreign policy will continue to have important and, arguably, even greater relevance to one another in the twenty-first century. While important, migration will rarely rise to the level of a first-order issue. It will be one of many issues, often interrelated in complicated ways, that form the substance of ongoing interaction with allies, neutral states, and enemies. The United States will benefit from closer attention to international migration, as it will to such topics as the environment and drugs. But the focus should be squarely on states and their interests, even as closer attention is paid to those interests as affected by migration, pollution, crime, and other soft security issues. As the definition of security is expanded to include international migration, the framework of the state system should not be abandoned.

Notes

[1] Teitelbaum (1984), Loescher and Monahan (1989), Gordenker (1987), and Koehn (1991).

[2] Hobsbawm (1990).

[3] Moynihan (1993), p. 28.

[4] Huntington (1993).

[5] Weiner (1992/93) and (1993).

[6] I thank Astri Surhke for suggesting the phrase "soft security issues" to describe the expanded areas of concern among international relations analysts who specialize in strategic studies.

[7] Paul Johnson, "Colonialism's Back—And Not a Moment Too Soon," *New York Times Magazine*, April 18, 1993, pp. 22–24.

[8] Jeremy D. Rosner, "Is Chaos America's Real Enemy?" *Washington Post*, August 14, 1994, p. C1.

[9] Keely and Barrett (1992).

[10] Mitchell (1992b), Dominguez (1990) and (1992), Bach (1990), and Stepick (1992).

[11] Higham (1963), p. 4.

[12] Mathias (1981), p. 986.

[13] James H. Billington, "Commencement Address," Georgetown University School of Foreign Service, Washington, D.C., May 30, 1993.

[14] Skerry (1993).

[15] O'Grady (1967), pp. 2–3.

[16] Jonas (1990), p. 63.

[17] Jonas (1990), p. 67.

[18] See, for example, Tucker (1990).

[19] Fuchs (1968).

7

Refugees: Concepts, Norms, Realities, and What the United States Can and Should Do

CARL KAYSEN

I n our world of sovereign states, a refugee is defined in international law as a person who:

CARL KAYSEN is the David W. Skinner Professor of Political Economy, Emeritus, in the School of Humanities and Social Science at the Massachusetts Institute of Technology. He is now a senior lecturer at MIT. From 1981 to 1987 Dr. Kaysen served as director of the Program in Science, Technology, and Society; he remains a member of the program, and of the Program on Defense and Arms Control Studies. Before coming to MIT, Dr. Kaysen was director of the Institute for Advanced Study at Princeton, and prior to that, a member of the Economics Department of Harvard University, where he was Lucius N. Littauer Professor of Political Economy and associate dean of the Graduate School of Public Administration (now the Kennedy School of Government). Dr. Kaysen's scholarly work has ranged widely in the areas where economics, sociology, politics, and law overlap. His most recent work has focused on arms control and international politics. In addition to his academic work, Dr. Kayson served as deputy special assistant for national security affairs under President Kennedy, and has been chair of or served on many public and private commissions concerned with a wide variety of public policy issues.

owing to well-founded fear of being persecuted for reasons of race, religion, nationality, membership of particular social group(s) or political opinion is outside the country of his nationality and is unable to or owing to such fear is unwilling to avail himself of the protection of that country; or who, not having a nationality and being outside the country of his former habitual residence . . . is unable or unwilling to return to it.

The treaties embodying this definition establish the basic right of refugees not to be forcibly returned.[1]

These concepts and the legal norms embodying them were essentially the legacy of the Second World War, which displaced an estimated 30 million people in Europe and left 11 million outside their own countries and in need of assistance at its end. They also reflect the experience of the First World War, when the total displaced reached a peak of 9.5 million in 1926.[2] In both situations, international organizations urged and helped states to provide some combination of temporary asylum, resettlement, and repatriation to deal with what were seen as transient problems.

When the United Nations High Commissioner for Refugees (UNHCR) was established in 1951 to succeed the International Refugee Office of the immediate postwar years, the problems were still thought to be temporary. In fact, they persisted and changed their character. Rather than being transient phenomena attendant on interstate war in Europe and diminishing after its end, refugee flows have become the continuing by-product of what appears to be endemic intrastate violence in many parts of the Third World.

The single most important fact about the world's refugee problem and the problems of the refugees today is that they are chiefly a problem of the poor people and countries of the Third World. Of the grand total of nearly 20 million refugees reported at the end of 1992, 70 percent were in Africa, Asia, and Latin America. Of the 23 percent (4.4 million) in Europe, nearly half were in the former Yugoslav republics, displaced by the ongoing civil wars. Most of the refugees were in countries near their original homes; about 2.6 million had been given asylum in the rich countries of Western Europe, North America, and Oceania.[3]

The second most important fact is that the problem is increasing. Civil war, repression of and official and unofficial violence against minorities of all sorts, state breakdown, and the consequent disappearance of elementary law and order and personal security are on the increase in much of the world, and the number of refugees these conflicts create grows accordingly. Further, there are even more "internal" refugees, persons displaced for the same reasons and typically even more in need of help and protection, remaining within the borders of their own countries than international refugees—25 million in 1993—again mostly in the poor countries of the Third World.[4]

While the status of refugees and their right not to be forcibly returned are established in international law, no corresponding right of asylum is. The grant to refugees of asylum, in the sense of the right of permanent residence and the right to work and otherwise integrate themselves into the host society, is at the discretion of the receiving state.

State sovereignty in respect to admitting non-nationals remains absolute, both in legal theory and in practice. Although the various human rights declarations and conventions urge states to grant asylum on humanitarian grounds, all recognize the absolute discretion of states in doing or not doing so.[5]

The final conflicting element in the set of norms governing the treatment of refugees is the command embodied in human rights declarations and conventions that everyone should be free to leave any country, specifically including his or her own.[6] This norm does generally guide the conduct of democratic governments; it is flouted by most dictatorial and authoritarian governments.

In crude summary, the international law of refugees says "let those people go"; "don't send them back where they came from"; but it does *not* say "take those people in."

The capacity of states to control their borders and, to the extent that they can, their policies in respect to how they exercise that control are much more important than the international norms in governing the fate of refugees. So are the opportunities for movement available to those who would become refugees. In practice, it is the joint operation of these two sets of factors that determines the fate of those suffering the violence, oppressions, and deprivations that make refugees.

The rich nations of Western Europe, North America, the

Pacific Rim, and Oceania (the "North") all have, in greater or lesser degree, the capacity to control their borders, and all have a strong desire to do so. Most of the poorer nations of Africa, Asia, and Latin America have little capacity for effective border control; many have weak governments that could not set policy even if they had the capacity to execute it.

The question of the willingness of the nations of the North to offer long-term asylum and resettlement to refugees must be seen in the context of their attitudes toward immigration in general. As the economic pressures for immigration created by the widening (absolute) economic gap between North and South increase and the costs of movement decrease, almost all the nations of the North have become more restrictive in their immigration policies. The relatively high levels of unemployment of the last decade in Western Europe and North America have further reinforced these attitudes. So has the substantial flow of illegal immigrants, in the many cases where less than perfect border control and the contiguity and easy access of large numbers of relatively poor people make tight restriction impossible—the United States in respect to its southern border, France and Italy in respect to North Africa, Germany in relation to Eastern Europe. The consequence is a decrease in the willingness of the rich countries to grant asylum to refugees as such, and an increase in the rigor with which the separation of "true" political refugees from economic refugees from poverty is made by their bureaucracies.

Finally, and importantly, the element of cultural and ethnic difference also enters the equation. In the period immediately following the Second World War—when, as we observed above, the conceptualization of the refugee problem embodied in the legal norms and international institutions now in place was crystallized—the refugees were Europeans, and the countries of potential asylum were European or their overseas daughters. Further, these countries had been participants—in different ways, to be sure—in the wartime events that resulted in the refugee streams, and so felt some degree of moral involvement and even responsibility for the problem. Thus an appeal for the need for asylum and resettlement could and did meet a sympathetic reception.

Today the overwhelming majority of refugees are truly alien to the people of the countries most able to offer long-term asylum and opportunities for resettlement: different in race, religion, and culture. Nor do the peoples of these countries or, for the most part, their political elites feel either involvement in or responsibility for the events that have occasioned the refugee stream. To say this is not to deny the strong humanitarian response that many people in the North have made and are making to the terrible experiences of the refugees through a variety of channels: churches, voluntary associations, nongovernmental organizations focusing on refugee problems. But for most countries, the attitudes and sentiments underlying the exclusionary response have far more political weight and longevity than those of humanitarian sympathy.[7]

The characteristic response of the rich countries has been to fund assistance for refugees, and in particular to support the work of the UNHCR. The High Commissioner's programs in 1992 expended more than $1 billion in assistance to refugees. The United States, the European Community, and its member states provided nearly 80 percent of these funds through government contributions on a voluntary basis, i.e., outside of their regular and special UN assessments.[8] For 1992 this amounted to $50 per refugee per year, not a very high level of support. To be sure, private contributions through voluntary organizations increase this total, but it is not known by how much.

This response is clearly inadequate, and the gap between needs and available resources grows. Further, the basic fact is that most refugees go to neighboring countries, especially in Africa and Asia, usually countries as poor as the ones from which the refugees come and unable to provide either the organizational or the economic resources required, or, in some cases—as for the Rwandan refugees in Zaire—even basic security. Thus the costs fall chiefly on those least able to bear them, next to the refugees themselves, and these are the costs of what is, for the most part, palliation; in no way do they support fundamental solutions.

Fundamental solutions to the refugee problem require either permanent resettlement or repatriation. At a deeper level, they depend on prevention: the avoidance of the kind of violent civil conflict and government repression and persecution of its citizens that generate the refugee flow. As we have seen above, the opportunities for permanent resettlement are severely limited, and more likely to shrink than to grow. This is clearly true of the countries of the North as places of permanent resettlement, and it is not much better elsewhere. In 1991 and 1992 the UNHCR sought to resettle somewhat over 125,000 refugees and found places for only 54,000, truly a drop in the bucket.[9]

Repatriation and prevention require similar and similarly difficult conditions: for the first, the creation of civil peace and the end of repression and persecution by governments of some or all their citizens; for the second, the maintenance of those conditions: civil peace and reasonably liberal governments respectful of the human rights of all their citizens. This is a tall order. A tall order, but not impossible.

The recent history of Central America gives us a success story, one that, even if not total and complete, is enough of a success story to provide an example of possibility and hope.[10]

From the beginning of the 1980s Central America was ablaze with violence. In Nicaragua a left-wing authoritarian regime that followed the collapse of the conservative dictatorship was attacked by right-wing guerrillas financed and armed by the United States. Conservative military governments in El Salvador and Guatemala fought peasant revolts led by left-wing parties who had some degree of Cuban and Nicaraguan support. As many as 2 million people were displaced from these countries over the decade 1980–89. More than a million refugees were scattered throughout the nearby countries, from Costa Rica to Mexico, only 150,000 of whom were documented as recognized refugees, benefiting from UNHCR protection and assistance. Many of the rest had fled to the United States, mostly as illegal immigrants.

Beginning with the efforts of the Contadora Group—Colombia, Mexico, Panama, and Venezuela—in 1983, Latin American governments tried to mediate the struggles in Central America and substitute political discussion for warfare. Their early efforts failed, primarily because of the vigorous opposition of the United States during the Reagan administration, which saw the Central American struggles in ideological terms, as a battle in which the right side had to prevail. With the succession of George Bush to the U.S. presidency in 1989, the end of the cold war, and then the collapse of the Soviet Union, the situation changed radically. The circle of mediating countries widened, the UN Security Council was brought into the situation, and the United States ceased to press its ideological crusade. By the end of 1992, an elected civilian government had replaced a repressive military one in Nicaragua; the newly elected government of El Salvador had negotiated with the rebel leaders for an end to the civil war and the disarmament of the guerrillas, and the reincorporation into the society of the rebel leaders; Guatemala had an elected civilian government. Many of the officially recognized refugees had been repatriated, and more repatriations were in prospect.

What made all this possible was the active role of the international community, led by the neighbors of the countries torn by violence, but involving a widening circle of others and finally the UN Security Council, in substituting political discussion and negotiation for violent conflict, and seeking to ensure the maintenance of governments that respected the rights of all their citizens.

In this story, the role of the United States was crucial, if in a rather perverse way. For most of the decade, the insistence of the United States on victory for the side it was supporting in the several civil wars and its continued endorsement of repressive conservative governments frustrated the efforts of the neighboring countries to promote peaceful settlements. When the United States withdrew its intervention and even supported Security Council involvement in the conflict in El Salvador, these efforts came to fruition.

Cambodia provides another example of at least partially successful international intervention to end internal conflict and allow the repatriation of refugees. Again, as a consequence of the end of the cold war, the chief outside powers supporting the opposing sides in the Cambodian civil war—Vietnam, helping the government they had installed after invading Cambodia at the end of 1978 and expelling the Khmer Rouge government, which, in turn, conducted a guerrilla war against the new regime; and China, which supported the Khmer Rouge insurgency—changed their positions. After much exploratory discussion involving these principal actors, the Cambodian factions, which had grown to four; the neighboring states of Southeast Asia, France, and Australia;

and the permanent members of the Security Council agreed on a peace plan for Cambodia in August 1990, which was formally endorsed by the Council in Resolution 668 the following month. A formal peace agreement was signed in Paris in October 1991 by the four contending factions in Cambodia, the five permanent members of the Security Council, and twelve other states from the region. This was followed by the creation of the United Nations Transitional Authority in Cambodia (UNTAC), the largest and most complex operation the UN has ever undertaken. Though faced with obstruction by the Vietnamese-installed government, continuing cease-fire violations, and harassment by the Khmer Rouge, UNTAC succeeded in carrying out a remarkably fair and peaceful election in most difficult circumstances in May of 1993: almost 90 percent of the eligible voters participated. The Khmer Rouge, which did not participate, was isolated, and the remaining factions formed an uneasy coalition government.[11] As of September 1994 the coalition was functioning, and although some guerrilla warfare still continued, there was a certain degree of peace and order in much of the country. Whether it will last is hard to predict. Nonetheless, in the year following the Paris Peace Accord, more than 365,000 refugees returned to Cambodia from refugee camps in Thailand, where most of them had been for more than a decade.[12]

Recent events in Mozambique offer another partial success story, also incomplete, and even more fragile than that of Cambodia. Here again, the end of the cold war allowed a successful negotiation between the left-wing Mozambican government and the rebellious RENAMO, which had been supported by South Africa and, to some extent, the United States. The resulting agreement, signed in Rome in October 1992, permitted the deployment of a UN peacekeeping party in June 1993, and enabled the UNHCR to begin an organized program of repatriation for the 1.4 to 1.7 million Mozambican refugees scattered through the neighboring countries.[13]

However, the successes are still few, and the failures many. In Africa, the brief U.S. intervention in Somalia failed to resolve the continuing conflict or restore internal order, and the residual UN force seems powerless. The civil war in Angola continues; so does the repression of non-Muslims in the southern Sudan. In the summer of 1994, the horrors of Rwanda created more than a million new refugees. The ethnic war in Bosnia is in its third year at this writing; so is the inability or unwillingness of the United States, the European Community, and the Russians to do anything effective to end it.

The successes and failures both underline the central proposition of this chapter: the major effort of the international community in responding to the growing refugee problem must be directed at settling conflicts, and not be limited to the efforts of the UNHCR at protection and help for refugees, necessary and admirable as these are.

The "international community" is, of course, a heterogeneous mix of actors of all sorts: all the 178 member nations that constitute the UN, the five permanent members of the Security Council, the UN bureaucracy starting with the secretary-general, the hundreds of nongovernmental organizations that lobby both the UN and governments, as well as the publics to whom governments respond, the press, both print and electronic, and, at its base, so to speak, the politically attentive publics all over the world. In the complex interactions among all these that shape outcomes, the actions of the U.S. government play a particularly significant part. Indeed, it is hardly an exaggeration to say that U.S. action is a necessary condition—if not always a sufficient one—for international action, and that U.S. leadership is frequently needed to make something happen. For all its economic difficulties and political weaknesses, the United States remains the leader of the international community in three very important ways. It is overwhelmingly the most powerful country in military terms; it is the richest country; and, for all its shortcomings, it embodies as well as any nation the political ideals that are proclaimed in the corpus of United Nations declarations and conventions on human rights, political, economic, and social, and is widely seen as doing so.

Recent U.S. actions on refugees show both the possibilities for leadership and the lack of any long-run policy. After nearly three years of inconsistent and contradictory pronouncements and actions in violation of international law and at least the spirit of our own domestic law, the United States, at the end of September

1994, finally took decisive action to end the repressive rule of the ruthless military dictatorship in Haiti and restore to power its democratically elected refugee president. Absent the U.S. decision, the murderous repression in Haiti would have continued as it had done for the previous three years, as would the stream of refugees it had generated. Tens of thousands of Haitians fled by sea on everything from small boats to rafts. By the beginning of 1993 more than 40,000 had been intercepted at sea by the U.S. Coast Guard and either returned to Haiti in violation of the principle of non-refoulement, embodied in the 1951 Convention on the Status of Refugees and the 1967 protocol, or taken to camps at the U.S. military base in Guantanamo.[14]

It is clear that the strong desire to halt the flow of refugees played a large part in the administration's decision finally to use the threat of imminent force, and, indeed, to begin the first phase of an invasion of Haiti in order to force the military junta to resign. This, in turn, was heavily influenced by two factors in domestic politics. One was the strong negative response in Florida to an increasing flow of poor black refugees. At the same time, the general level of liberal outrage at the repression in Haiti continued, and the Congressional Black Caucus transmitted that outrage and its own resentment of what it rightly saw as a racist policy, in contrast to our treatment of Cuban refugees.

Some of the same political forces led the United States to its other strong action on refugees at nearly the same time. The outburst of boat people from Cuba in the late summer and early fall of 1994, triggered by Castro's decision to allow people to leave, received a decidedly mixed reception. The anti-Castro Cubans in Florida, led by the Cuban-American National Foundation, gave them the traditional welcome for refugees from Cuban communism. But many Floridians and the state's political leadership saw them as a further unwelcome economic burden on an already burdened community. Both in and beyond Florida, there was a resentment against what was seen as Castro's deliberate direction of dissident and disgruntled Cubans to the United States. The result was a negotiation between the United States and Cuba, in which the United States agreed to set the quota for Cuban immigrants at 20,000 per year, and Cuba agreed to shut off the flow of

undocumented emigrants. This was not only a complete reversal
of more than thirty years of the U.S. policy of encouraging refugees from Communist countries, particularly Cuba, and making
special provisions for them both by legislation and executive action, but also an agreement in direct contravention of the Declaration of Human Rights and the Final Act of Helsinki, which define
the right to leave a country as a basic human right.[15] But here
again, domestic politics made foreign policy, not unusually, but in
this case, a policy in contradiction to the principles we profess and
urge on others.

How can the United States go beyond the ad hoc responses to
particular spikes in the flow of refugees that hit the then-current
administration in a politically sensitive nerve? Is there some feasible policy path, pursued consistently and persistently, that can
address the underlying problem of refugees (and persons displaced
within their own countries by the same forces as well), instead of
merely trying to help a small fraction of the tens of millions affected?

I believe that there is. It is to give worldwide promotion of civic
peace and democratic order by international action a central role
in our security policy. With the end of the cold war, the threats to
our security arising from a powerful and formidably armed hostile
coalition have disappeared. The proliferation of weapons of mass
destruction has risen in salience as a threat. But an even greater
threat is the spread through the Third World of a mixture of
anarchy and repressive anti-Western governments. The best
counter is to build the institutions of the international community
that can mediate internal conflict, try to transform it into political
competition, and to make plain in every way that lawless governments that repress their own populations are not acceptable in a
wider world. This requires the use of the whole range of policy
instruments, from quiet diplomatic discussion and economic incentives through public condemnation and isolation, economic
sanctions, and even the use of military force.[16] Such a program can
be carried out effectively only if done internationally; any one
country or small group of countries cannot be seen as imposing its
will on the rest of the world.

The Clinton administration has on occasion embraced, at least in words, major elements of such a policy. But it has not yet given it the salience it deserves, or shown the commitment to assuming international leadership in advocating it and devoting the effort and resources to building the institutions that would make it possible. Such an effort needs at least the commitment and persistence we devoted to the cold war, and deserves no less.

Is such a policy politically feasible, domestically and internationally? It is the task of U.S. political leadership to show that it can be made so.

Notes

[1] Quoted from the 1951 convention as amended by the 1967 protocol on the Status of Refugees in United Nations High Commissioner for Refugees (1993), Annex II.2 p. 163. One hundred twenty states are parties to the convention or the protocol. The list is on p. 167; Article 33 of the convention prohibiting expulsion or return is on p. 163.

[2] See Zolberg, Suhrke, and Aguaya (1989), pp. 18–27. The two figures are given on pp. 21 and 18, respectively.

[3] United Nations High Commissioner for Refugees (1993), Annex 1.1, pp. 149–153.

[4] Deng (1993), p. V.

[5] See Goodwin-Gill (1983), pp. 225–226, and Annexes IV and VII, pp. 247–79 for the texts of the 1952 Convention on Refugees, the 1967 protocol thereto, the U.N. Declaration on Territorial Asylum adopted by the General Assembly in 1967 and the unapproved Draft Convention on Territorial Asylum produced in the UN Conference on Territorial Asylum held in Geneva in January and February of 1977. A few states, notably Austria and the Federal Republic of Germany, give those formally recognized as refugees a legal right to asylum. See Goodwin-Gill (1983), p. 209.

[6] See United Nations High Commissioner for Refugees (1993), pp. 163–165, for the relevant excerpts from the Universal Declaration of Human Rights adopted by the UN General Assembly in 1948; the International Convention on Human Rights, entered into force in 1976; and the American Convention on Human Rights, signed in 1969 at San Jose, Costa Rica.

[7] There are exceptions. Sweden had a refugee population of 324,000 at the end of 1992, one refugee per twenty-seven Swedes. This was more than twice the ratio for Canada, the next most hospitable nation of the North, at one per forty-eight. United Nations High Commissioner for Refugees (1993), Annex 1.2, p. 154. The United States had fewer refugees (473,000) than Canada (538,000), with nearly ten times its population. See Annex 1.1, p. 153.

[8] See United Nations High Commissioner for Refugees (1993), Fig. IIID and IIIE, p. 177. The United States was the largest single contributor, at $241 million. The European Community and its member states contributed more than twice that. If contributions per head of population are taken as a measure of generosity in responding to refugee needs, the four Scandinavian countries lead the list:

Norway, $12; Sweden, $11; Denmark, $8; and Finland, $6. The United Kingdom and Germany gave slightly more than $1 per head; Japan, the United States, and the European Community slightly less; Canada, $1.50.

[9] United Nations High Commissioner for Refugees (1993), p. 174.

[10] The brief account that follows draws on Kaysen, Pastor, and Reed (1994). See especially, Ch. 5, "Collective Mediations in the Caribbean Basin" by Luis G. Solis; Ch. 6, "Regional Initiatives for Peace and Democracy" by Alicia Frohmann; and the "Introduction" by Carl Kaysen and Robert Pastor. See also United Nations High Commissioner for Refugees (1993), pp. 117–124, the section on "Central America at the Crossroads."

[11] See the successive summaries on the Cambodian situation in *SIPRI Yearbooks 1991–94*. Stockholm International Peace Research Institute. For 1991, pp. 363–364; 1992, pp. 439–450; 1993, pp. 107–112; 1994, pp. 66–67. For a somewhat fuller discussion of the negotiations, see *Strategic Survey 1991–92*, International Institute for Security Studies, pp. 142–149. *Strategic Survey 1993–94* has a brief discussion of UNTAC, pp. 176–177.

[12] United Nations High Commissioner for Refugees (1993), p. 104.

[13] United Nations High Commissioner for Refugees (1993), pp. 108–109.

[14] United Nations High Commissioner for Refugees (1993), p. 42–43. As of the end of August 1994, about 14,000 refugees were in Guantanamo in safe haven status; only 523 had been admitted to the United States. In 1982 a federal district court found the return of the refugees in violation of the 1980 Refugee Act, but the Supreme Court overturned the decision by an eight to one vote, showing its usual deference to the executive in foreign policy matters, arguing that refugees intercepted at sea were not entitled to the same protection as those reaching the U.S. borders.

[15] See Loescher and Scanlon (1986). See *New York Times*, September 4, 1994, Section 4 p. 1ff. for a summary of the events.

[16] The role of forcible military intervention in "enforcing peace" raises wide issues well beyond the scope of this chapter. There is an emerging international consensus that forcible intervention is justified in situations not falling within the strict terms of breaches of (international) peace and acts of aggression defined in Chapter VII of the UN Charter. See Reed and Kaysen (1993). For the role of the threat of force in supporting diplomacy and leading to resolution of conflicts without war, see George (1991).

8

How the International System Copes with Involuntary Migration: Norms, Institutions, and State Practice

TOM FARER

The Evolution of a Normative Structure

Roots

Were they but accessible, Philistines and Hebrews of Biblical times could attest that mass migration is nothing new, either as a phenomenon or a problem: sometimes for the migrants, sometimes for the peoples they encounter, sometimes for both.

TOM FARER is professor and director of the Joint-Degree Program in Law and International Relations at The American University in Washington, D.C. He is former president of the Inter-American Commission on Human Rights of the OAS and of the University of New Mexico. Professor Farer has been a senior fellow of the Carnegie Endowment and the Council on Foreign Relations, special assistant to the general counsel of the Department of Defense and to the assistant secretary of state for inter-American affairs, and legal consultant to the director of the UN operation in Somalia. Author and editor of ten books and monographs on international law and international relations, his numerous articles have appeared in such journals as *Foreign Affairs*, *Foreign Policy*, the *New York* and *London Review of Books*, the *Harvard* and *Columbia Law Reviews*, the

Indeed, one could structure an entire history of the human race in terms of the great migrations—of Vandals and Visigoths, Arabs, Mongolians, and Turks, Jews and Huguenots, Spanish and English, Zulus and Dutch, Irish and Italians, Russians and Armenians, impelled at a certain moment (by duress, ambition, dreams) to move from the known place to one that could at best be imagined. Through great migrations we humans have filled the once empty spaces of the earth until now there are none, other than the regions of water and ice.

Some migrants came quietly; some, like the Jews and Huguenots, were welcomed in certain times and places. Many others came with trumpets and pikes, came as conquerors and stayed to rule. Whatever happened when people sought to migrate or resist migration, for millennia it happened without the guidance or restraint of commonly accepted rules and principles. Those who were strong took what they wished; those who were weak accepted what they must.

International legal regulation of anything, much less migration, is a relatively recent development, conventionally dated from the middle of the seventeenth century. The foundation of the system of principles and rules accepted by the leading states, the concept and value that first lent the system coherence, was sovereignty, the sovereignty of princes initially, later the sovereignty of nation-states. The operational essence of the idea of sovereignty was exclusive legal authority within the recognized limits of the sovereign's domain. That authority included discretion to determine who could enter, who could remain, and, although this was rarely an issue, who could leave.

As long as sovereignty was, with trivial exceptions, a property of hereditary rulers, it did not portend much for migration, because a ruler's authority was contingent not on his or her special relation-

Human Rights Quarterly, and the *American Journal of International Law.* He periodically comments on foreign policy for National Public Radio, the Canadian Broadcasting Corporation, the World Service of the BBC, and the Voice of America. Professor Farer serves on the boards of Americas Watch, the International League for Human Rights, and the International Human Rights Law Group.

ship to a determinate people in a determinate place, but on heredity and hence on the fortuities of marriage, death, and descent. That a people should change their sovereign and a sovereign his people was in no way anomalous. In addition, many boundaries were vaguely demarcated and disease could, in the space of a historical moment, strip people from the land. In ages of high infant mortality and brief adult lives, moreover, when perforce most of Europe was thinly populated and skilled artisans, shrewd bankers, and adroit merchants at a premium, rulers would often welcome migrants, for they added to the territory's sparse human capital. The rich and the skilled continue to find a warm welcome in many countries.

The French Revolution marked a great change. It restored to prominence a principle of political organization salient in the Greco-Roman world on whose shattered base modern Europe had been built. It restored the principle of citizenship. A particular people for a particular place. A people with a right to that place and claims to govern it, whether themselves or through proxies. A people made one by history, distinct from other peoples, with mutual obligations by virtue of their shared distinction. A national community. In Prussia and Russia and Austria-Hungary, there were subjects, not citizens. Subjects came and went along with territories won, lost, and exchanged. Most people lived very close to the land. Outside army duty, they might in their whole lives not travel more than a few miles beyond their village. To a peasant, the man wandering over from the next valley was "foreign." One owed him as little as one owed someone who had wandered in from the other side of Europe.

The makers of the Revolution proclaimed an end to all that. Those who accepted the Revolution and happened to live within that agglomeration of territories haphazardly assembled by the generations of monarchs who had called themselves French were "citizens." Others were not. Without the "other," without the "foreigner," there could be no citizen. When all were subjects, no one in theory had rights. If subjects were themselves without rights, the foreigner's lack of them was neither a denial nor a distinction. The declaration of common citizenship was a declaration of shared rights, shared not promiscuously, however, but shared among the people of France. So it was also a declaration of who did not and could not share, if Frenchness were to mean anything, much less be a reason to die. For die was what a vast number of the French did for the next quarter century in the defensive wars that opened the revolutionary era and in the aggressive ones that led by tortuous steps to its close.

The French were Europe's teachers. By assembling at the call of their government and hurling themselves against the professional armies sent by the rest of Europe to restore the old order of things, they demonstrated the power generated when a great mass of people contiguously inhabiting a large territory began to think of themselves (or could be induced to think of themselves) as forming a single community separate from and competitive with communities living on the other side of some notional, adventitious line on maps most of them had never seen.

But while, in transforming the French from subjects of the king to citizens of the nation, the Revolution implied a hierarchy of rights defined by citizenship, like the American Declaration of Independence it so quickly followed, the Revolution insisted that the rights central to a dignified existence were the common property of all people everywhere. The right to enter a country, to remain and enjoy benefits and opportunities coextensive with those of long-settled inhabitants, was not among them. In theory, it still is not today, but theory is palpably eroding under the pressure of hard facts, conflicting interests, and moral uncertainty.

A regime is a mental device invented by some clever academics in part as an aid in explaining why there exists a degree of peaceful stability, even cooperation, among states that cannot be easily accounted for by theories stemming from the hypothesis that every government all of the time exploits power differentials to maximize gains—the hypothesis, in other words, that states are reflexive predators. In lay language, regimes are the rules and principles (and related institutions) states develop to guide and coordinate their activities with respect to the various items on their agendas like trade, narcotics, fishing rights, pollution of the oceans, and many more.

Not all of the clustered rules and principles that form a regime may be regarded as "legal" by the private persons and public officials who pursue their ends within it. What is "law" at any given time is finally a subjective judgment, hence a matter of degree. If most governments think that a particular rule is legally binding, if they are prepared to regard deviation as law breaking and to complain and demand compensation on that ground, and if they correspondingly feel some restraint about deviating themselves, then for the parties concerned, the rule is a "law." A regime will invariably have many such rules; but it may also have some to which most parties are only provisionally committed, informal understandings recognized as such and hence subject to unilateral adjustment.

With respect to certain issues, like who could do what to whom on the high seas, regimes began to take shape centuries ago. In the case of migration, until the twentieth century, nothing like a regime could form because all governments agreed that, absent a specific agreement to the contrary, each of them was at liberty to exclude anyone for any reason. In the nineteenth century, the only generally conceded restraint on a government's discretion that related to migration was the requirement of decent treatment for aliens once they had been allowed to enter. With respect to what we would today call human rights, such as the right to a fair trial, not only could an alien's government demand equal treatment, but his or her treatment also had to satisfy an international minimum standard.

But though the last century had nothing one could reasonably call a migration regime, it was the temporal site of certain practices that in some respects augured the regime that would eventually arise. The principal augury of today's regime was the practice that gradually spread of including in extradition treaties a "political offense" exception. Extradition treaties themselves proliferated because international law was not seen to impose any obligation on states to hand over to other states at their request persons accused or convicted of crimes in the asking state. Moreover, some governments, like that of the United States, were inhibited by their own constitutions from picking up the citizens of another state and turning them over for trial or punishment, in the absence of authorization by the legislature *or* an extradition treaty. The political offense exception made the treaty inapplicable when the crime attributed to the accused had a "political character."[1]

Why were states so reluctant to hand over to their governments people far more threatening to those governments than common criminals, people among whom were potential or successful assassins of public officials and other assorted subversives many of whom would today be regarded as "terrorists"? One motive sometimes shared to a degree by reactionary states with those of a more liberal cast was a desire not to get involved in other peoples' conflicts. But liberal states like France and Britain doubtless had a second motive. Many of the persons protected by the political offense exception were champions of national self-determination for Poland or some sliver of the Balkans, or were seeking the overthrow of absolutism in Russia. These causes enjoyed numerous and influential sympathizers in liberal states, indeed echoed many of the slogans of contemporary liberalism. Whatever the accused may have done, it had been done in the name of liberty. Hence they were seen as potential martyrs to the liberal cause. Since, in the illiberal states, above all Russia, advocacy of liberal goals could itself be cause for punishment, harsh deeds were understandable.

In addition, states like Russia or the Ottoman Empire were not known for the quality of their criminal process. Those who had been convicted of crimes might therefore be innocent, and those who were merely accused might never have a fair chance to prove their innocence. Thus the practice of refusing to extradite for political offenses could be seen as a forerunner of the broader protection now available to refugees.

It was not only by their way of being that reactionary governments in Europe and the Middle East contributed, however inadvertently, to the gradual emergence of an international principle of safe haven. Beyond simply being their charmless selves, they contributed actively by means of energetic persecution that catapulted whole groups of people into a desperate search for new homes: supporters of the aborted liberal revolutions of 1848 in Germany and Hungary; various Christian minorities within the shrinking Ottoman Empire; Jews battered by pogroms in Russia. Acceptance of these fleeing masses by countries self-consciously populating themselves through immigration—countries like the United

States, Argentina, and Australia—contributed nothing to the principle of asylum for the persecuted. But countries like the United Kingdom that had more selective immigration policies also opened their doors. Reflecting the attitude of the liberal states was Britain's 1905 Aliens Act, adopted at the height of anti-Semitic pogroms in Russia. With respect to those "seeking to avoid prosecution or punishment on religious or political grounds or for an offence of a political character, or persecution involving danger of imprisonment or danger to life or limb on account of religious belief," the act created an exception to the prevailing policy of refusing entry to persons without the means to support themselves.

The turmoil spawned by the First World War spilled new waves of migrants across international frontiers. Some, like the Greeks of the Anatolian plateau, fleeing alongside the retreating fragments of the Greek national army, could return to the ancestral home. But two of the largest clusters of involuntary migrants, Russians escaping the Bolshevik Revolution and Armenians fleeing starvation and massacre in Turkey, had neither a realistic prospect of returning home nor a single evident sanctuary. Given the inextinguishable antagonism between them and the regimes in their former homes, in effect they were stateless, and thus under the existing scheme of things, stripped of legal protection.

Out of the international response to their condition appeared the first signs of the regime that would finally emerge in the wake of the next great war. In 1922, under a program initiated by the League of Nations, fifty-four states agreed to collaborate in the recognition of certificates of identity to be issued by international agencies under League auspices. These certificates would substitute for passports and enable the refugees to move on from the countries where they had first found protection. From then until the outbreak of the Second World War, similar agreements were executed first for the Armenians and then for certain other groups, principally refugees from Nazi persecution. These agreements did not commit states to give financial assistance to the refugees either directly or through the agencies authorized to provide identity and travel documents. The latter had to scramble for funds on their own. Nor did states commit themselves to provide documented refugees with residence and work permits. Each government remained at liberty to determine the targets and the extent of its philanthropy.

The one effort at extracting a broad commitment proved abortive. Only eight states were willing to ratify the 1933 Convention on the International Status of Refugees, which prohibited the parties from denying entry or expelling refugees, and of the eight, half gutted their nominal commitment with various reservations and declarations. Although the small formal steps taken by the League members on behalf of refugees left them in a largely prelegal condition dependent on the discretion of individual governments, as one of the leading authorities on refugee law has written, "the period was also remarkable for the very large numbers of refugees not in fact sent back to their country of origin, whether they fled Russia after the revolution, Spain, Germany or the Ottoman Empire."[2] He notes in this connection that following the collapse of Republican resistance to the Fascist armies in Spain, France within the space of just ten days admitted 400,000 refugees.

The Refugee Treaty System

The vast uprooting of peoples caused by Nazi invasions, by their attempt to exterminate the Jews, by their enslavement of peoples from occupied territories, and by all the other circumstances of the Second World War, once again left the victors with an acute refugee problem that the Sovietization of Eastern Europe rapidly intensified. The allies began even before the war's end to organize relief and rehabilitation for the millions of displaced persons. Shortly after the end of the war the emphasis began to shift from relief for all war victims to assistance and protection for a narrower category of persons designated as refugees from persecution, a shift codified in the 1951 Convention Relating to the Status of Refugees, which defined the persons who would be considered as falling within the mandate of the United Nations High Commissioner for Refugees (UNHCR), the agency created a year earlier by the General Assembly to assume relief and protective functions. A refugee was a person

[who] owing to [a] well-founded fear of being persecuted for reasons of race, religion, nationality, membership of a particular social group or political opinion, is outside the country of his nationality and is unable or, owing to such fear, is unwilling to avail himself of the protection of that country.

Although sponsored by a global organization and replete with universalistic rhetoric, the convention functioned within narrow temporal and geographic limits. The well-founded fear of persecution had to arise from events associated with the Second World War or "events occurring in Europe before January 1, 1951." These limits meant that the convention applied largely to refugees from Soviet bloc countries, an outcome clearly intended by the United States and its allies. Despite being one of the convention's chief architects, the United States refused in the end to commit, and thus continued to pursue its national interests and exercise its humanitarian impulses unrestrained, at least formally, by international norms.

This went on until 1967 when the United States ratified the Refugee Protocol that removed the temporal limits and extended the substance of the original convention to refugees throughout the world.[3] That substance amounts in the end to two norms. One is the rule of nonreturn or, in the generally used French phrase, "non-refoulement." Parties to the protocol undertook not to send an alien who had entered, by whatever means, back to the country of origin if he or she had the well-founded fear of persecution that defined a refugee under the protocol and the original convention. The only exception was for someone found by the state of potential refuge to represent a threat to its security. The other norm precluded punishment for illegal entry of persons who had entered in search of asylum.[4]

What about persons who arrive at the frontier and request asylum? Does the rule of non-refoulement apply to them? Though raised often enough, the question has never received a definitive response. Efforts to summon a consensus among United Nations members that persons claiming fear of persecution should not be summarily turned back at the border have not been successful. But despite the reluctance of states to commit themselves formally, in practice states have generally admitted persons who arrive at their borders with claims to protection that are not palpably without merit.

In assessing the extent of the formal intergovernmental commitment to assist and protect even those persons who satisfy the protocol's by no means generous definition (putting aside the matter of claims at the frontier), one needs to enumerate the obligations that states party to the protocol clearly have not assumed. They are not obligated to refrain from expelling anyone who can find sanctuary elsewhere or to provide more than temporary shelter for those whom they choose or are required to retain. Thus they have claimed the right to house their beneficiaries in detention camps, bar them from employment in the local economy, and expel them as soon as their fear of persecution ceases to be credible or an alternative place of refuge is found. States have not, moreover, assumed any obligation to assist refugees in getting to the point where the doctrine of non-refoulement may require the grant of asylum. They do not, for instance, have to instruct their embassies to process asylum applications, much less request persecuting states to allow the departure of their victims, or provide the persecuted with temporary sanctuary in the embassy. Finally, they have not assumed any obligation to accept the advice of the UNHCR or any other international agency about how to define the terms in the definition or about the procedures to be employed in assessing claims to refugee status.

Not only the obligations but the beneficiaries thereof are narrowly fixed even by a fairly generous construction of the protocol's definition, for it implies that the refugee has been individually targeted for persecution or is a member of a group that is virtually outlawed. Any Jew from Nazi Germany might have qualified as a refugee, but not any Mayan peasant in Guatemala today, even though violations of Mayan human rights are grave, persistent, and pervasive. Still, it has been the view of the United States, and probably would be of many other countries, that in cases like Guatemala, only certain activists may develop a well-founded fear of persecution. Construing the definition to embrace primarily those who, by their acts or associations, stand out from the general population and even from some minority regarded with suspicion or revulsion by the authorities implies a highly individualized assessment of asylum claims (that is, claims not to be summarily expelled or denied entry), a procedure that is impossible to implement in the face of sudden mass exodus.

The one other thing that must be said of the definition is that if, through an unimaginable investment of resources, states could fairly process the vast number of contemporary claimants who might fall within the protocol's definition, *they would still end up denying refugee status to a very large number of persons who might fairly be called "involuntary migrants."* The number will, of course, vary widely depending on one's conception of what should be deemed to make departure "involuntary." That conception might reasonably include persons fleeing their countries of residence because of a credible fear of imminent death or crippling, and regardless of whether the proximate cause of flight was 1) a threat directed at them personally, 2) a generalized condition of intense violence in their home country, or 3) hunger.

The de Facto System

State Practice

How have states coped, on the one hand, with a definition that excludes millions of persons fleeing for their lives and imposes extraordinary administrative difficulties and, on the other, with the periodic tidal flows of refugees that have marked the last four decades? Perhaps the first point one should note is that in most instances of mass flight, most of the refugees have managed to get into other countries and remain. Often they have done so with the knowledge and cooperation, however grudging, of the authorities. Sometimes they have entered illegally, infiltrating or pouring across borders and disappearing into local society. The several million persons who fled Afghanistan after the Soviet occupation, going mainly to Pakistan, exemplify the first set of cases. Exemplifying the second are the hundreds of thousands of Salvadorans who fled the war in that country during the 1980s and entered the United States. A second point is that only rarely have states attempted forcibly to halt the flow short of their borders. Probably the most notorious exception, prior to the 1994 Cuban exodus, has been the largely successful effort of the United States to interdict Haitian refugees. Malaysia briefly implemented a policy of intercepting Vietnamese boat people and towing them away from the shore, but a combination of criticism and pressure from Western countries and receipt of assurances from the critics that they would eventually resettle the Vietnamese restored Malaysia's previous policy of grudging tolerance. A third salient point about the coping process is that states of first refuge have often not even attempted individualized assessments. A fourth is that states that have taken large numbers of refugees and attempted individual assessments have usually found themselves accumulating a very large backlog.

A fifth indisputable point is that the degree of generosity evidenced by receiving states at any given moment varies widely, as one would anticipate where governments are making choices on the basis of perceived interests rather than as directed by a comprehensive and precisely articulated cluster of legal norms. No country more perfectly illustrates this point than the United States, which, almost without exception during the cold war, welcomed and aided persons who had left Communist countries, whether singly or en masse, while blockading Haitians and insisting on individual hearings and applying relatively rigorous standards of proof to Salvadorans and Guatemalans.

A sixth point is that once asylum seekers actually manage to enter a country, they have rarely been forced to leave. After trying for years to round up and expel the almost half million Salvadorans who originally entered or remained in the country illegally, the United States government finally agreed to grant them a temporary reprieve (of indefinite length). Forcible repatriation of substantial numbers of people from a particular country is rare. Even when it is not patently illegal, it tends to evoke criticism, as the Hong Kong authorities discovered in 1993 when they forcibly repatriated Vietnamese boat people found not to satisfy the convention definition. Although the United States was then engaged in physically intercepting Haitian refugees and returning them to the jurisdiction of that country's violent de facto government, it joined the chorus of condemnation.

An additional aspect of state practice over the past four decades is some degree of regional variation. The nations of sub-Saharan Africa have appeared particularly inclined to accommodate refugee flows. The appearance may reflect something more than administrative ineptitude and resignation in the face of the irresistible. When certain African states—for instance Ghana in the 1970s and Nigeria a decade later—decided to send voluntary migrants home (workers and small entrepreneurs attracted by temporarily more dynamic economies), they proved efficient, even ruthlessly so, in bundling the unwanted out of the country. That Africans actually feel either a higher degree of moral responsibility for involuntary migrants from other African countries or a much lower order of economic and social threat is at least suggested by the difference in breadth between the UN Refugee Convention's definition of refugee and the definition in the 1969 Convention on Refugee Problems in Africa adopted by members of the Organization of African Unity. The latter, while incorporating the UN definition, includes:

every person who, owing to external aggression, occupation, foreign domination or events seriously disturbing public order in either part or the whole of his [sic] country of origin or nationality, is compelled to leave his place of habitual residence in order to seek refuge in another place outside his country of origin or nationality.

African states have been prepared to pay a heavy price for their hospitality. In defense of apartheid, South Africa's white government violently harassed governments harboring activists of the African National Congress, combining overt incursions and aerial bombardment with all of the forms of clandestine terrorist violence. Whatever the roots of African tolerance for the forced migrant—cross-border ethnic ties, relatively attenuated national identities, less encroachment by refugees on developed urban areas, fewer social services to be strained and social goods to be consumed, greater empathy stemming from comparable vulnerability, stoic acceptance of the unavoidable, all have been suggested—its existence seems clear to this point.

As already noted, Europe's response to mass migration in the 1920s and 1930s displayed a similar willingness to assume responsibility in case of mass migration away from persecution and harshly authoritarian and intolerant regimes. Many of the migrants—particularly the Russians, Armenians, and Spaniards—were given not merely temporary refuge but the chance to integrate into the recipient country. Europe's migrants, like those of contemporary Africa, were not crossing perceived cultural/racial divides, divides maintained in part by illiteracy, primitive systems of global communication, and the cost and difficulty of long-distance travel. The revolution in international communication systems as well as in the diffusion of knowledge, and the radical reduction in the costs, availability, and speed of intercontinental travel, have bridged that divide. The swelling number of people crossing it has contributed substantially to a crescendoing demand among European electorates for sharp limits on all crosscultural immigration, regardless of the immigrants' motives and needs.

A final point about the international coping mechanisms. The seven phenomena sketched above reflect the choices, interests, and improvisations of individual states. Still, as I have suggested, the practice of individual states is not entirely unpatterned. They have influenced each other, naturally, and all have been influenced by the slender norms of the migration regime, primarily the rule of non-refoulement and, perhaps more diffusely, by the norms of the overlapping, far more elaborate regime of human rights. At a minimum, human rights norms limit national discretion over the treatment of migrants pending decisions about their status. The refugee convention and protocol prohibit punishment for applicants who have entered or stayed illegally. Human rights law and practice dictate that, however characterized, detention for an extended period *is* punishment and is thereby prohibited in the absence of precise charges (of activities previously determined to be criminal) and conviction after expeditious and fair trials.[5] In limiting the period of detention, human rights law correspondingly exerts pressure to accelerate processing of asylum requests in those states that are loathe to parole applicants into the society while their cases are being considered.

Human rights norms also affect the conditions of detention. Article 10 of the International Covenant on Civil and Political Rights states that "all persons deprived of their liberty shall be treated with humanity and with respect for the inherent dignity of the human person." Presumably the minimum standard of treatment must be higher when the persons detained are not charged with or even under suspicion of having committed criminal acts. The covenant is, moreover, subject to an interpretation that would prohibit any state from discriminating among persons seeking asylum, if not among migrants generally, on the basis of their race, color, sex, language, religion, political or other opinion, national or social origin. One may fairly dispute whether the past practice of the United States satisfies this legal prohibition.

Global Coping Arrangements

As they have been forced to wrestle with the mass migrations flooding over the formally neat arrangements of the refugee treaties, states have enlarged the jurisdiction and resources of the United Nations High Commissioner for Refugees. Indeed, from the moment at the beginning of the 1950s when they conceived the main formal elements of the present regime, the leading states have implicitly conceded a need to extend assistance and protection beyond the formal jurisdictional boundaries they had created through their definition of a "refugee." The very diplomats who approved the refugee convention recommended in a final act of the conference that states not apply the convention strictly.[6] In 1957, when the members of the Executive Committee of the UNHCR (dominated by representatives of the states who are the main voluntary contributors to the agency budget) could not reach agreement on the question of whether Chinese refugees in Hong Kong satisfied the convention definition, the General Assembly authorized the organization to use its "good offices" on their behalf. In subsequent resolutions the Assembly frankly eliminated the formal distinction between convention and non-convention refugees and authorized the UNHCR to act on behalf of "refugees who were in a situation 'analogous' to that of convention refugees because they were victims of man-made events over which they had no control."[7]

These resolutions have simply regularized the practice of the UNHCR, a UN agency respected for its will to act consistent with the spirit of its mandate, even when that has meant exceeding its original letter, and to anticipate ex post facto authorization from the General Assembly. By its consistent efforts on behalf of refugees fleeing unnatural disasters—mostly pogroms and wars—it has given the migration regime worldwide presence and coherence. Those efforts include establishing camps, providing and coordinating relief, interceding with host governments on the refugees' behalf, monitoring refugee settlements in an effort to protect their human rights, providing identity and travel documents, fostering rehabilitation and training and other measures designed to provide refugees with means of self-support, facilitating repatriation, and, where repatriation is not a viable option, seeking the integration of refugees in countries willing to accept them as permanent residents.

The means for immediate relief and for the beginnings of economic rehabilitation come primarily from the agency's own budget, supplemented by the efforts of some national aid programs and a plethora of mostly Western based nongovernmental organizations (often working with local NGOs) that, in addition to raising money from private sources, have become channels through which a growing proportion of governmental assistance flows. These NGOs are now key elements of the international regime, supplementing the resources and administrative infrastructure of the UNHCR and influencing the policies of their respective national governments. In dramatic cases like Rwanda, where the physical remoteness, scale, and velocity of migration bursts through the international safety net, probably the only available means for avoiding a holocaust is employment of the unrivaled logistical capacity of the U.S. armed forces.

Internally Displaced Persons. The UNHCR's explicit mandate from the General Assembly currently endows it with responsibility for materially assisting and protecting nearly 20 million people, an eightfold increase since 1970. Sizable number though it is, 20 million constitutes only a minority of the globe's involuntary migrants. An additional 25 million are displaced within their own countries, not so much ignored in most cases as actively molested: by their nominal government, by insurgents, or by more-or-less autonomous paramilitary formations. They are, in the words of a UN report, "persons who have been forced to flee their homes suddenly or unexpectedly in large numbers, as a result of armed conflict, internal strife, and systematic violations of human rights or natural or man-made disasters."[8]

Until very recently, if they were not the most wretched of the wretched, they were at least the most ignored and least protected. As far as protection is concerned, they fell and still fall outside the explicit mandate of the UNHCR, the only UN organization with the authority, means, and personnel for worldwide day-to-day monitoring and intercession on behalf of the endangered. With respect to assistance, while they are potential beneficiaries of both UN humanitarian agencies (like the United Nations International Children's Emergency Fund [UNICEF] and the United Nations Development Program [UNDP]) and NGOs (like CARE and OXFAM), these agencies lack a universally conceded right of access to a country for the purpose of helping displaced segments of its population. Legal formalities aside, providing assistance without the cooperation, much less with the veiled or open opposition of public authorities, is extremely difficult when it is possible at all.

Where the displaced are in countries that have ratified the 1949 Geneva Conventions and Additional Protocol II of 1977, the International Committee of the Red Cross (ICRC) is the one organization with a formal right to assist and protect, but only if displacement occurs in the context of a large-scale internal conflict. How large is often a matter of dispute, with the incumbent regime often insisting, even as it clings to a few square miles around the capital, that the problem is little more than banditry.

In some instances, the UNHCR has partially bridged this yawning gap in the international migration regime. It has done so either in response to special authorization from the General Assembly or as an incident of ministering to transborder refugees inside a country that has many internal ones. No one in either the humanitarian or human rights communities, including the High Commissioner for Refugees, has suggested that these ad hoc arrangements are in any sense satisfactory. Among other flaws, they have in a substantial number of cases confronted the UNHCR with awful dilemmas. In Bosnia, for instance, it has been torn between assisting people inside the country, partially with an eye to dissuading them from swelling the war induced refugee population of Central and Western Europe, and helping them to escape chronically perilous conditions (and in the process probably facilitating the policy of ethnic cleansing). In countries where external and internal migrants coexist and the latter are objects of government hostility, remonstrating with the government over its treatment of the latter may compromise cooperation in assisting and protecting the former. While by their acts and omissions, the official organs and leading states of the General Assembly have provided the UNHCR with moral dilemmas and conflicts of interest, they have denied it sufficient resources adequately to aid all the internally displaced where political conditions permit.

It was with an awareness of the virtual vacuum of protection for the internally displaced that the United Nations Human Rights Commission in 1992 requested and obtained from the secretary-general appointment of a representative to study the protection problem and prepare a report. In his first report a year later, the man chosen, a former Sudanese diplomat named Francis Deng, widely respected for his intellect and integrity, underscored the need to develop legal norms addressed explicitly to the perils of displaced persons and machinery for monitoring compliance.

Two kinds of norms are required. One would limit the means governments could adopt during states of emergency when, under the various human rights treaties, most rights (with the universal exceptions of life and security from torture and other forms of cruel treatment) are subject to suspension. This must be done since it is conditions susceptible to characterization as emergencies that produce internal displacement. The other would obligate states to allow humanitarian organizations to aid the displaced. Such a declaration would contribute to the widening conviction that where governments block humanitarian relief to persons in imminent danger of death from starvation or disease, it may be introduced without the consent of the government, even, *in extremis,* by force.

Parts of the machinery necessary to monitor enforcement of these norms are already in place. Humanitarian and development agencies like UNDP and UNICEF have field representatives in most potential national sites of mass displacement. They could be instructed to report violations to the Office of Humanitarian Affairs at the United Nations or to a specially created crisis anticipation and strategic planning unit attached to the Office of the Secretary-General. The same unit in New York could receive and collate data from human rights and humanitarian relief NGOs and national intelligence agencies. In addition, the General Assembly could institutionalize the system of human rights monitors like those hitherto deployed, in cases like El Salvador, to facilitate the settlement of internal conflicts. Further to the end of protecting the internally displaced, it could augment the resources available to the Human Rights Commission and its support staff at the Geneva based Human Rights Centre.

The Shrinking Refuge?

Refugee advocates, critical as they often are of existing arrangements and practices, fear that on balance the future will be worse. Western Europe, a long-established place of refuge for involuntary migrants, is the major immediate focus of concern. The consequences of growing hostility to foreign residents, particularly non-Europeans, in the various states and the reactive erection by national governments of stricter barriers to entry will, it is feared, be compounded by regional harmonization of migration controls generally and of asylum policies and procedures in particular. One critic argues with passionate exaggeration that the future is already here. "Under the guise of 'harmonization,' " he has written, "European governments have effectively renounced their commitment to an inter-regional system of asylum."[9] Asylum, as well as immigration in general, is coming under increasingly severe controls because, in the words of another scholar/advocate, "To a great extent the distinction between refugees, illegal immigrants, drug traffickers and terrorists has become blurred in the public mind and they are all seen to be problems which can only be resolved by stricter border controls."[10]

Harmonization of rules and procedures governing immigration and asylum is an inevitable incident of the effort to achieve completely free movement of persons, as well as goods and services, throughout the European Community (EC). Control over entry is so closely bound up with the idea of the nation-state and of the right of national self-determination, and lies so near to the heart of sovereignty, that its complete surrender to a supranational authority is bound to be resisted bitterly. To the extent enthusiasts for integration can hope to overcome resistance, it must be in part through achieving intergovernmental agreement on common external controls that maintain or even advance the preferences and interests embodied in each national control system. Since immigrants are not today the object of great solicitude from important segments of any national electorate, and restriction is a major theme in the domestic politics of most members, harmonization inclines naturally toward closure.

Most EC states severely limit ordinary immigration. Thus the rapid increase in immigrants in most states stems almost exclusively from clandestine migrants and asylum seekers. Even if Community members were united in the desire to maintain Europe as a major place of refuge and to generous compliance with the non-refoulement norm, measures to reduce illegal entry by so-called economic refugees would incidentally tend to inhibit asylum claims. Since asylum is increasingly identified as a main source of Europe's immigration problems, the incidental effects are likely to be ignored. At worst, they may be contrived.

One current technique for enforcing restrictions on ordinary immigration that may coincidentally thwart some asylum claimants is a uniform system of fines for common carriers that bring persons without entry visas to European points of entry. In addition, the act of assisting or conspiring to assist entry of persons without visas is being criminalized. The kind of intense persecution that drives legitimate bids for asylum will often erupt with little warning. Targets will sometimes have a slight window of opportunity for leaving the country. It may close long before an embassy concludes its evaluation of a request for refuge. Simply visiting an embassy may trigger the acts the latent victim fears. Ironically, common carrier penalties may have much less impact on economic migrants, for with the aid of family and friends who hope to follow, they may leisurely accumulate sufficient funds to support a plausible request for a tourist visa that will open the door to an illicit permanent stay.

Still, concern over the fines, however uniformly onerous, may be a little exaggerated. Many national governments have long required common carriers to check for visas if they are carrying passengers from countries whose citizens require them. Uniformity and an overall increase in severity of the fines seem unlikely to have much effect on the status quo. What is feared, I gather, is the imposition on common carriers of an obligation to go beyond a cursory check of visas. But the elements of the feared wider inquiry are unclear. That the passenger has a return ticket? Funds sufficient for maintenance during the visit?

The visa itself seems likely to remain the main obstacle. Hence a more serious concern is the prospective evasion of non-refoulement through refusal to grant or readiness to cancel visas to persons assumed to be seeking them in order to present a claim of asylum when they reach an EC country. What advocates fear is an agreement among all Community states that applicants must apply for asylum through one of the European embassies in their own countries.[11] On-site decisions diminish the opportunity for asylum in at least two ways: 1) they are reached by diplomats through an opaque, informal process (far from the censorious eyes of refugee advocates) rather than by quasi-judicial officials in a transparent, trial-type hearing that in some countries is subject to judicial review; 2) they deprive the applicant of non-refoulement protection, since it snaps into place only when he or she has reached another country (or at least is subject to its effective authority). Asylum may be denied, after all, simply because a country has set some numerical limit on the number of people it will take in a given year. But if the applicant is already in the country, the rule of non-refoulement temporarily trumps the limit; applicants are protected from expulsion until their fear has ceased to be credible.

It is not only the potential evasion of non-refoulement and the consequent peril for persons fearing persecution that animate critics of harmonization. Another source of concern is the larger number of people fleeing the generalized violence of civil wars and intercommunal brawls. While they qualify for assistance from the UNHCR, since in most cases they cannot demonstrate that they as individuals are, or are likely to become, objects of persecution, they do not, of course, satisfy the definition of the refugee treaties. Hence, in theory, their asylum applications will be rejected wherever they file, and, even if they filed in a Community member, once rejected they could not invoke non-refoulement to block deportation.

What in fact has generally happened to these "de facto" refugees, as they are sometimes called, is either of the following. Some countries have simply allowed them to remain indefinitely. In others, de facto refugees have had no need to test the generosity of the host government; rather, they have been able to rely indefinitely on the sluggish pace of asylum adjudication in most of Europe,[12] where petitions will be presented and defended with meticulous care by immigration lawyers and every possible appeal exhausted. What has hitherto been critical, then, is getting to Europe.

Heavy pressure for on-site processing is one of the measures directed specifically at potential refugees that tends to link harmonization with the prospect of a straitened European gate. Others are: 1) prohibiting multiple asylum applications (countries would treat a claimant's rejection by one Community member as binding on all the rest); 2) distributing applicants according to Community criteria rather than applicant preference, largely by making the country that admits or issues a visa to the applicant or possibly the country of residence (should it differ) responsible for hearing the claim; and 3) coordinating views about conditions in the home countries of the bulk of applicants toward the end of establishing uniform presumptions about the credibility of their claims.

As the system has functioned, an alien arriving in a member country by one means or another may apply for asylum. While awaiting decision, which together with appeals of an initial rejection can be years away, applicants in many countries are paroled into society and either allowed to work or provided with financial support. Under another possible scenario, the alien enters the

Community as a student or visitor with a visa from one or several Community members. (They are now working toward a common visa.) Deciding to seek asylum, the applicant may file simultaneously or serially in several or all member states or choose the one believed to be most generous in evaluating asylum claims and/or to have the most elaborate system of review. Each country makes an independent determination according to its procedures, presumptions, and sources of information.

If harmonization follows the lines sketched above, the applicant will be able neither to try his or her luck in a number of countries nor to choose the one with the best general record of approval or the best rate for applications from this individual's country of origin. Analysis of asylum decisions in cases involving persons from the same country with roughly similar sorts of claims shows a striking diversity of results. In the mid-1980s, for instance, "some 90 percent of Tamil refugees from Sri Lanka were recognized in Denmark. During the same period in Germany, however, the figures for Tamil refugees were 8 percent for 1984, 37 percent for 1985, and 20 percent for 1986."[13]

Integration and harmonization could have a benign effect on European Community asylum policies if they encouraged agreement on the equitable distribution of refugees among the members. Wider distribution of the refugees might help to exempt them from the increasingly indiscriminate popular hostility particularly toward non-European migrants. Candidates for asylum have evidenced distinct national preferences. The relative abundance of employment opportunities and welfare services, together with the relative liberality of asylum norms and practices, have no doubt influenced them. All of these elements have made Germany a favored port of call. In 1988, 1989, and 1990, 61, 54, and 62 percent, respectively, of all persons seeking asylum in the EC chose Germany as their point of entry. Had an allocation agreement already been in place, it might have moderated the accumulation of electoral pressure that finally moved the German government to narrow sharply the opening for asylum applicants. A combination of measures, including more summary procedures and refusal to consider for asylum persons coming to Germany through safe countries, has abruptly shrunk asylum applications. In short, through unilateral measures Germany is attempting to redistribute potential asylees.

It is conceivable that a Community-wide fair-sharing agreement, one incident of harmonization, will in some measure reduce the pressure felt in all countries to restrain migration. But the German experience may be read as a confirmation that countries can ward off refugees without benefit of multilateral arrangements. That will depend, presumably, on whether an increase in undocumented immigration rapidly succeeds the decline in entries effected through the avenue of asylum.

In any event, the natural momentum of harmonization is toward much tougher restrictions on entry. There is no blinking the fact that the elimination of internal barriers to movement unaccompanied by the general adoption of the more severe national standards and procedures could hardly elicit support from those member states most anxious to reduce their intake of persons from outside the Community.

The political forces driving restrictive policies in the latter countries seem far more compelling than the forces urging generosity in the countries hitherto occupying the liberal camp. There may be exceptions. The Dutch parliament has stated its determination to assure that country's compliance with its international commitments concerning refugees. The European Parliament and the Council of Europe also have spoken in favor of generosity. Nevertheless, in Europe the Parliament and the Council are nowhere near so revealing of regnant political sentiment as are national governments. In the Schengen Agreements and Dublin Convention, and in proposals developed by the ministers responsible for immigration, they have evidenced a commitment to restraint, a readiness to adopt most or all of the measures feared by refugee advocates, that closely tracks the growth of antiforeign sentiment within national electorates.

Whether the Community can effectively enforce a much more restrictive policy is unclear. Open requests for asylum have been increasing alongside informal immigration. According to UNHCR data, the number of people seeking asylum in EC countries rose from 420,000 in 1991 to 560,000 in 1992, with an estimated 400,000 in the first half of 1993. This increase has occurred in the face of what is overall a very high rate of rejection: on average, only about 9 percent of applications are accepted.[14]

Particularly since the Single European Act of 1986 envisioned the abolition of internal controls, but with antecedents in antiterrorist consultations begun in the mid-seventies, ministers and officials of the member states have been working to enhance cross-border cooperation among police and other law enforcement agencies. Within the framework of the Schengen Accord of 1985 and its 1990 Implementing Convention, working groups (including representatives of all Community members other than Denmark, Ireland, and the United Kingdom) have been developing schemes of operational cooperation in a wide range of areas including asylum, which has its own subgroup.

One product of their exertions is a project consisting of a central computer into which information will be poured automatically from national data banks. The resulting common data base will give government agencies access to identical information on wanted persons, "undesirable aliens," asylum seekers, persons to be expelled or extradited, and certain other categories of people. Specifically to facilitate implementation of agreed approaches to immigration and asylum matters, the states participating in the Schengen arrangements are establishing another system to store and share data concerning visas. With the coming into force of the Treaty of European Union in November 1993, joint enforcement planning is continuing as part of the overall Union administrative and consultative structure.

The pooling and exchange of information and other forms of cooperation are essentially opaque. The concerned officials are politically accountable only to national ministers primarily concerned with national security and law enforcement. It remains to be seen whether, in the event an individual discovers that he or she has been injured as a consequence of these activities, effective judicial review and restitution are possible.

Assessing the Regime

Is There an International Migration Regime?

Before turning to assessment of the regime, we need to step back and confirm its nature and proper scope. Arguably there is no international *migration* regime in the sense of a coherent cluster of norms and institutions that both reinforce and reflect accepted ways of dealing with some international relations issue. There is simply a *refugee* regime. At any given time, it affects directly only a small portion of humanity, and a somewhat larger portion of that subset of the species that is currently on the move away from ancestral homes or clearly would like to be. Beyond the refugee regime's jurisdiction lies a hodge-podge of the idiosyncratic law and practice of 180-odd nation-states assiduously pursuing their narrow interests, and normative fragments from other regimes, primarily the human rights one.

This is not a merely academic point. It connects with the question of whether the refugee issue ought to be kept as separate as possible from the immigration one. Once they begin to fuse in the public discourse of wealthy and stable states, where for the most part electorates are demanding sharp reduction in the intake of "foreigners," the prospect for refugees dims. Hence it is only if they can be kept on a separate track in the minds of electors and leaders that refugees can hope to find safe havens as the generality of immigrants confront a closing door.

Even in a country like Germany, where a right of asylum, enhanced by procedural guarantees, is built into the constitution, the separate track is proving difficult to maintain. The chances of overcoming that difficulty, in Germany or elsewhere, will vary in part with the sheer numbers of refugees who seek admission, and in part with the degree of success in handling two other factors. One is the ability to articulate a morally compelling distinction between the condition of refugees and other potential immigrants. Another is the ability of each concerned country to find ways of embodying that distinction in procedures that are seen to work. Managing to do either is decidedly problematical.

CHAPTER 8   283

The raw truth is that hundreds of millions of people (the figure
continues to rise) are threatened every day with death, mutilation,
crippling disease, starvation, and degradations of a hundred sorts.
They enjoy a firm guarantee that if they remain where they are,
their awful conditions will endure. How persuasive, ultimately, is
the moral distinction between X who credibly fears imprisonment
for writing editorials critical of the government, Y who is in flight
from chaotic tribal conflict in her homeland, and Z, a landless
Indian peasant with two young and malnourished children (surviving out of an original five) whose only means of employment,
weaving fish nets, has been destroyed by new technologies? The
less persuasive the distinction between X, on the one hand, and Y
and Z, on the other, the more the images of refugee and immigrant tend to merge. However, they also tend to merge when, in
an effort to soften the moral tension caused by distinguishing
sharply between X and Y/Z, as well as to provide X with maximum assurance of asylum, governments adopt spongy criteria and
quasi-judicial procedures, for together they guarantee a process
not only messy and prolonged, but one that, as it is colonized by
advocates, will grind more and more coarsely until asylum becomes little more than another avenue of immigration.

Critique of the Regime

Most academic scholars and human rights activists appear
united behind a wide-ranging critique of the present regime,
which they characterize as arbitrarily underinclusive in defining
who is to be excluded from its benefits, and arbitrary and capricious in treating those who are theoretically included. It is underinclusive, they argue, in terms of the liberal ideals that animate
it. Rooted in the perception of a common humanity, those ideals
impose moral obligations to help all human beings who, through
no fault of their own, are threatened with death or crippling injury
or otherwise fall below the minimum needed for the experience of
human dignity. It is, they argue, as immoral for a state to bar the
entry of people fleeing ethnic pogroms or civil wars as it is for one
person to ignore another seen bleeding by the roadside.
Nor can the cases be consistently distinguished in terms of

sharpness of need. A person able to demonstrate a "well-founded fear" of being targeted for execution, torture, or indefinite detention is not necessarily at greater risk than civilians occupying de facto free-fire zones in guerrilla-infested territory and collectively suspected by the government of lending aid and comfort to its enemies. Nor, for that matter, some might argue, is he or she more immediately threatened than peasants stripped of their crops by natural disaster and left to rot by a corrupt and incompetent government. And, one might add, their condition seems indistinguishable from that of persons, such as homosexuals in some countries, who suffer not from the positive acts of government officials but rather from their indifference and consequent failure to protect. Finding a failure of protection in a Brazilian city, a federal court judge ruled that a homosexual applying for asylum satisfied the statutory criteria.

The second facet of the critique is that even those who satisfy the narrow treaty based definition of refugee are frequently rejected, while, most conspicuously in the case of the United States, those who probably do not qualify are often admitted. Even after emigration from Cuba had begun to correspond fairly closely to decline in living standards there, the United States continued until the late summer of 1994 to admit virtually all Cubans who reached shore or a U.S. vessel. Even after the military government instituted a reign of terror against persons and social groups deemed hostile to it, and the economic sanctions sponsored by the United States aggravated chronic deprivation, most Haitians have been denied entry. Before the Haitians, Salvadorans and Guatemalans discovered the disadvantage of fleeing a right-wing regime and lacking politically influential predecessors already settled in the United States.

Gross anomalies occur because interpretation and application are left almost entirely to the discretion of individual states. Each government, only slightly restrained by human rights law, decides such matters as who will hear asylum cases. How will they be trained? What presumptions will they apply? What standard of proof should they employ? Can they use as evidence material, like confidential reports from the Foreign Office, not subject to critical examination by the applicant? To what extent, if any, are their decisions subject to judicial review? Does the applicant have a right to legal representation?

The treatment of applicants pending decision or after rejection on purely numerical grounds (the year's quota had been filled), execution of which is blocked by the rule of non-refoulement, is subject to an almost equally broad discretion. European governments have generally paroled persons into society; now, however, there is movement toward detaining them. American policy has varied, with geopolitical interests and domestic politics the critical determinants.

International human rights treaties impose a little order on procedures and treatment, but probably not enough to justify the claim that anything like the rule of law prevails in this area of national jurisprudence. Article 13 of the International Covenant on Civil and Political Rights (ICCPR) states:

> An alien lawfully in the territory . . . may be expelled therefrom only in pursuance of a decision reached in accordance with law and shall, except where compelling reasons of national security other wise require, be allowed to submit the reasons against his expulsion and to have his case reviewed by, and be represented for the purpose before, the competent authority or a person or persons especially designated by the competent authority.

It leaves largish room for interpretation. Is an alien who makes it to the immigration kiosk "in the territory"? How about one who is hauled out of a leaking boat on the high seas into a Coast Guard cutter? Should a public ship be deemed "territory"? Is an alien who enters ostensibly as a tourist and then, immediately after arrival, applies for asylum "lawfully" in the territory? In short, one could credibly argue that the article applies only to persons who have passed through immigration in possession of a valid visa obtained in good faith.

Even persons to whom the article applies are guaranteed neither a trial-type hearing nor a right of appeal. Subject to restrictions "necessary to protect national security, public order *(ordre publique)*, public health or morals," however, they enjoy under Article 12 of the International Covenant the right to liberty of movement. But a government inundated by asylum seekers might plausibly claim that their detention was necessary for public order.

Human rights norms do establish a protective floor below which governments cannot in any circumstances sink. They cannot lock people up in dangerous and noisome cells; they cannot detain people indefinitely if they are not shown to constitute individually a serious threat to national security or the rights of others; they cannot discriminate among migrants purely on the basis of their race and other ascriptive characteristics (although they probably could distinguish among them on grounds of the relative ease of assimilating peoples). Government officials carry these legal obligations around wherever they go, including the high seas and foreign military bases. The High Commissioner for Refugees has hitherto been the main organ of the international community available to monitor and urge compliance with these standards. Theoretically the newly established High Commissioner for Human Rights can, and certainly the office should, supplement the UNHCR's efforts.

A further threat to just administration of the international standard stems from the bonding of decentralized implementation and the rubbery language of the refugee treaties, for it gives states considerable flexibility as they set about translating the "credible-fear-of-persecution" norm into operational guidelines for asylum judges. Is fear "credible" only if, given the person's position, the feared event is likely to occur? Or must the scenario envisioned be sufficiently likely that a reasonable person positioned like the applicant might well feel fearful? Must the feared event be seen as imminent or something reasonably likely to occur if the individual, for instance, continues to write editorials critical of Islamic fundamentalism?

The word "persecution" establishes a wide field of play for contesting interpretations. What deprivations beyond death, torture, and detention suffice? Should a government or a society that requires women to cover their hair and wear black, sack-like garments be seen as persecuting any woman who prefers suits by Chanel to dresses by Khomeini? Does it matter how restrictions are enforced, whether by exclusion from public employment or publicly supported educational institutions, by caning, or by imprisonment? Can it not be argued (it has been by at least one scholarly commentator) that all women who wish to ignore one or more of the sexist rules of behavior characteristic of many, probably the great majority, of societies have a credible fear of punishment? Is it not also arguable that in such societies, women can be seen as being persecuted by virtue of their membership in a "social group." As I suggested above, could not homosexuals in many societies make a still stronger claim to living with a credible fear of persecution by reason of their membership in a particular social group?

The human rights community obviously inclines toward a broad view of persecution as the prospective violation of any human right, in other words, as a credible threat to punish some current status or membership or planned or desired activity protected by the human rights conventions. Most governments and asylum judges interpreting government policy have thus far adhered to a more restricted notion of persecution, and have doubtless done so out of an appreciation that the broadest credible interpretation would vastly increase the number of the world's refugees. But because a plausible but narrow construction denies refugee status to a great number of affecting cases, in liberal polities it is bound to be contested and, regardless of political outcome, to remain an enduring source of political tension, bureaucratic conflict, and moral confusion.

What Is to Be Done, if Anything?

Among the few things that can be confidently anticipated in today's chaotic world are a) chronic increase in the number of involuntary migrants punctuated not infrequently by mass exodus, and b) increased resistance among the electorates of wealthy states to existing, much less increased, arrival rates for migrants, however labeled. In the very long run, of course, the second phenomenon could change. It is, after all, not unlikely that most wealthy countries will be unable to stem the flow of undocumented aliens, and hence their populations will become more ethnically and racially diverse. Political competition in pluralistic societies will probably accelerate the process as political activists of recent and still expanding ethnic streams work the system in order to enlarge

their electoral base. Although this is less predictable, the rate of
ethnic diversification and the ease of communication between new
arrivals and their countries of origin could, in conjunction with
postmodern cultural forces in the most developed states, partially
neutralize the assimilative forces of the host societies. Rather than
Balkanizing and polarizing society, the resulting multiculturalism
might in turn thin out the distinction between the indigenous and
the foreign, between citizen and alien. While that pretty scenario is
imaginable for the very long term, in formulating policies now,
Western political leaders must assume an environment in varying
degrees unreceptive to the absorption of large numbers of migrants coming, as most invariably would, from across racial/cul-
tural divides.

One possible response of Western policy makers is to accept in
their essence the present normative and institutional arrangements
on the grounds that, for all their faults, they may be the best
politically sustainable means of assisting involuntary migrants, one
likely to function rather more coherently now that the cold war is
history.

One of the present regime's declared vices, its decentralization
and the consequent diversity of interpretation and enforcement,
may also be a virtue. For it provides, albeit higgledy-piggledy, the
flexibility required by often volatile shifts in the generosity of public sentiment in one or another country, and helps the international community as a whole avoid a grinding, polarizing, and
quite possibly futile effort to negotiate clearer standards and procedures.

Nor, despite what some enthusiasts of virtually open borders
seem to imply, is the regime morally incoherent. There is, in fact, a
quite sensible basis for not including in the refugee regime victims
of famine and lethal poverty. Since their agony results from the
mere indifference or ineptitude of public authority, not its active
hostility, assistance can be brought to them by compassionate governments and private groups. In other words, the danger can be
alleviated *in situ* by uncoercive means that do not challenge the
authority of governments or the sovereignty of states. In-place
protection of those targeted by governments conversely requires

coercion. The costs of coercion—to those who employ it, to innocent bystanders, and even in many instances to its putative beneficiaries—discourage its use and guarantee inconsistency to the extent it is used. Improbability of use makes deterrence unlikely. Coercion, moreover, will normally require more time to achieve its effects than the targets are likely to have. Flight will usually be the most efficacious alternative, almost invariably so where targets are too few to excite the moral passion normally requisite for the triggering of potentially effective intervention.

Excluding from refugee status persons fleeing the generalized violence of an internal conflict also can be justified on the basis of alternative means for achieving the protective end. In some cases samaritans can exercise the protective function by establishing safe havens within the country in uncontested areas to which noncombatants can flee. Where that is not possible, but where the conflict seems subject to fairly rapid resolution, the migrants require no more than temporary safety and sustenance rather than a new home. Discrete targets of persecution will often have no foreseeable opportunity to return in safety. Hence the countries to which they flee must contemplate them as permanent residents.

Not only does the present regime have distinct virtues, but it is also susceptible to considerable improvement short of radical reform. The governments that are its main supporters could help by enhancing the funding and expanding or clarifying the mandate of various UN agencies that do or could assist in protecting refugees, internal or external. The leading states could also act to strengthen the secretary-general's capacity to anticipate events likely to generate mass population displacement and to bring them expeditiously to the Security Council. In the meantime, they would remain at liberty to expand or contract the space for refuge in light of their individual perceptions of national interest.

Further enhancement short of root-and-branch change would entail reducing the incentives of states to plunge toward the lowest common denominator of refugee receptivity. Principally this would involve negotiating some burden-sharing mechanism. Without it, refugees will tend to flood into countries with the most liberal policies or those that are the most accessible geographically, thereby generating political pressures for tight ceilings and unrelenting enforcement that could in turn catalyze a free-for-all national competition to reduce access.

A second option, less innovative than may at first appear, is for the wealthy states to increase exponentially material support provided directly to migrants, and support for those developing countries willing to shelter and, where necessary, assimilate involuntary migrants *and* to cooperate in discouraging their onward movement to Europe and North America. By this means, if coupled with the automatic denial of refugee status to persons arriving from safe countries, or who could have found asylum in places nearer their country of origin, the Organization for Economic Cooperation and Development (OECD) states would effectively isolate themselves from consideration as likely venues for Third World refugees.

This policy option would rest on four premises. One, already enumerated, is that for the foreseeable future, generous asylum policies, even if limited to persons with a well-founded fear of persecution, will aggravate the divisions already roiling political life in many of the affluent democracies. A second premise is that significant but not implausible increases in support levels, particularly financial and logistical aid and technical assistance, for Third World governments that provide a haven of first instance will both persuade and enable those governments in the generality of cases to maintain refugees from neighboring countries indefinitely, and ultimately, where they cannot return home, to assimilate them. The third premise is that the described investments (if you will, the "inducements") would actually reduce the flow of crosscultural migrants rather than simply shifting asylum seekers from open applicants for admission into the category of undocumented infiltrators. The final one is that democratic electorates will believe the third premise and regard the hypothesized payoff as an efficient investment rather than a waste of resources that could otherwise fund more Draconian means.

In dealing with another widely perceived threat to society, crime, the American electorate has thus far been unwilling to see much less to respond positively to a somewhat analogous trade-off, that is, investment to alter the life chances of poor youth in order to reduce the social costs of crime and the financial costs of punishment. They have not bought the trade-off in large measure, I believe, because it has been impossible to demonstrate to their satisfaction a close causal relationship between a particular kind and size of investment and corresponding reduction in violent crime. If, at existing levels of knowledge and political sophistication, it has been impossible to sell that trade-off, can we have any confidence that the migrant trade-off would be bought, even assuming leaders could be found to sell it?

Perhaps not, yet it could be argued that this second option is already being tested, albeit on a very small scale. When, in the mid-1980s, the budget of the UNHCR reached a half-billion dollars, it was conventional wisdom among refugee experts that the limits of international support had been plumbed. In 1995 its budget was $1.5 billion and rising. Meanwhile, those Cubans testing the once generous asylum policies of the United States are finding a new home in Guantanamo, while in Germany, for years affluent Europe's greatest asylum donor, the once-long backlog of pending applications shrinks apace.

Notes

[1] The definition of political offense remains problematical. See, for instance, cases involving efforts by the United Kingdom to extradite alleged IRA terrorists from the United States: Matter of Doherty by Government of UK, 599 F.Supp. 270 (S.D.N.Y. 1984) and *Quinn v. Robinson,* 783 F. 2nd 776 (9th Cir. 1986), *cert. denied,* 107 S. Ct. 271.

[2] Goodwin-Gill (1983), p. 71.

[3] While 1967 is the date of its formal adhesion to the international regime, the United States continued operating outside it until 1980 when Congress at last adopted implementing legislation. Among other things, the legislation substituted the convention's definition of a refugee for the narrower one adopted by Congress shortly after the war.

[4] And this norm is qualified in ways that would seemingly permit states to punish for unauthorized entry a substantial number of persons who entered in search of asylum and possessed the requisite well-founded fear of persecution in their home country. In other words, unlike non-refoulement, this second norm is far from categorical.

[5] See, for example, the 1979 Report on the Situation of Human Rights in Argentina, prepared by the Inter-American Commission on Human Rights of the

Organization of American States (pp. 140–141), quoted in *The Inter-American Commission on Human Rights: Ten Years of Activities, 1971–1981* (Washington, D.C., OAS, 1982), p. 317. See also *Rodriguez-Fernandez v. Wilkinson,* 654 F. 2nd 1382 (10th Circuit 1981).

[6] Goodwin-Gill (1983), p. 13.

[7] Gunning (1989–90), p. 51. The entire article is a very useful account of the de facto expansion of the definition by the General Assembly, the UNHCR, and individual states.

[8] Analytical Report of the Secretary-General on Internally Displaced Persons, February 14, 1992.

[9] Hathaway (1993).

[10] Loescher (1989), p. 624.

[11] They also fear that, unlike the United States, the Community will decide not to process in-country asylum requests. The Refugee Convention imposes no obligation in this respect.

[12] This is not to imply that the process is any more expeditious in the United States.

[13] Kanstroom (1990), pp. 222–223.

[14] Benyon (1994), p. 497.

Bibliography

Adelman, Howard. ed. 1991. *Refugee Policy: Canada and the United States.* Toronto: York Lanes Press Ltd.

Bach, Robert L. 1985. "Cubans." In Haines 1985.

————. 1990. "Immigration and Foreign Policy in Latin America and the Caribbean." In Tucker, Keely, and Wrigley 1990.

Benyon, John. 1994. "Policing and European Union: The Changing Basis of Cooperation on Law Enforcement." *International Affairs* 70:3.

Bohning, W.R., and M.L. Schloeter-Paredes. 1994. *Aid in Place of Migration.* Geneva: International Labor Office.

Borjas, George. 1993. *Immigration Research in the 1980s: A Turbulent Decade.* La Jolla: University of California at San Diego.

Chiswick, Barry R. ed. 1982. *The Gateway: U.S. Immigration Issues and Policies.* Washington, D.C.: American Enterprise Institute.

————. ed. 1992. *Immigration, Language, and Ethnicity: Canada and the United States.* Washington, D.C.: American Enterprise Institute.

Chorabjian, Leon S. 1982. "Armenians and Middle-Eastern Americans." In Roucek and Eisenberg 1982.

Clark, Rebecca L., Jeffrey S. Passel, Wendy N. Zimmermann, and Michael Fix. 1994. *Fiscal Impacts of Undocumented Aliens: Selected Estimates for Seven States.* Washington, D.C.: The Urban Institute, September 1994.

Deng, Francis M. 1993. *Protecting the Dispossessed.* Washington, D.C.: The Brookings Institution.

Divine, Robert. 1957. *American Immigration Policy, 1924–1957.* New Haven: Yale University Press.

Dominguez, Jorge. 1990. "Immigration as Foreign Policy in U.S.-Latin American Relations." In Tucker, Keely, and Wrigley 1990.

———. 1992. "Cooperating with the Enemy? U.S. Immigration Policies toward Cuba." In Mitchell 1992a.

Dowty, Alan. 1987. *Closed Borders: The Contemporary Assault on Freedom of Movement.* New Haven: Yale University Press.

Fagen, Richard F., R.A. Brody, and T.J. O'Leary. 1968. *Cubans in Exile: Disaffection and the Revolution.* Stanford: Stanford University Press.

Fix, Michael, and Jeffrey S. Passel. 1994. *Immigration and Immigrants: Setting the Record Straight.* Washington, D.C.: The Urban Institute, May 1994.

Fuchs, Lawrence H. ed. 1968a. *American Ethnic Politics.* New York: Harper Torchbooks.

———. 1968b. "Minority Groups and Foreign Policy." In Fuchs 1968a.

George, Alexander L. 1991. *Forceful Persuasion.* Washington, D.C.: U.S. Institute of Peace Press.

Gibney, Mark. 1991. "U.S. Foreign Policy and the Creation of Refugee Flows." In Adelman 1991.

Goodwin-Gill, Guy S. 1983. *The Refugee in International Law.* Oxford: Clarendon Press.

Gordenker, Leon. 1987. *Refugees in International Politics.* New York: Columbia University Press.

Gordon, Linda. 1993a. "The Demography of Refugees." Paper presented at the annual meeting of the Population Association of America, Cincinnati, Ohio, April 1, 1993.

———. 1993b. "Political Asylum Statistics, 1991–92: A Time of Transition." Washington, D.C.: U.S. Department of Justice, Immigration and Naturalization Service, Statistics Division, Office of Strategic Planning. Unpublished mimeo, October 1993.

——— 1993c. "Information on the Alien Population in the United States." Washington, D.C.: U.S. Department of Justice, Immigration and Naturalization Service, Statistics Division, Office of Strategic Planning. Unpublished mimeo, October 1993.

Gunning, Isabelle. 1989–90. "Expanding the International Definition of Refugee: A Multicultural View." *Fordham International Law Journal* 35.

Haines, David W. ed. 1985. *Refugees in the United States: A Reference Handbook.* Westport, CT: Greenwood Press.

Hathaway, James. 1993. "Harmonization for Whom? The Devaluation of Refugee Protection in the Era of European Economic Integration." *Cornell International Law Journal* 719.

Higham, John. 1963. *Strangers in the Land: Patterns of American Nativism, 1860–1925.* New York: Atheneum.

Hobsbawm, E.J. 1990. *Nations and Nationalism since 1780.* Cambridge: Cambridge University Press.

Homer-Dixon, Thomas. 1994. "Environmental Scarcities as Causes of Violent Conflict: Evidence from Cases." *International Security* 19:5–40, Summer 1994.

Huddle, Don. 1993. *The Net Costs of Immigration to California.* Houston: Rice University Press.

Huntington, Samuel P. 1993. "The Clash of Civilizations?" *Foreign Affairs* 72:22–49.

Jonas, Manfred. 1990. "Immigration and U.S. Foreign Policy: The Interwar Years." In Tucker, Keely, and Wrigley 1990.

Kanstroom, Daniel. 1990. "The Shining City and the Fortress: Reflections on the Eurosolution to the German Immigration Dilemma." *Boston College International and Comparative Law Review.* 16:201.

Kaysen, Carl, Robert A. Pastor, and Laura Reed. eds. 1994. *Collective Responses to Regional Problems, the Case of Latin America.* Cambridge: Committee on International Security Studies, American Academy of Arts and Sciences.

Keely, Charles B. 1993. "The United States of America: Retaining a Fair Immigration Policy." In Kubat 1993.

Keely, Charles B., and Richard C. Barrett. 1992. *The Office of the United States Coordinator of Refugee Affairs.* Washington, D.C.: Center for Immigration Policy and Refugee Assistance, Georgetown University.

Keely, Charles B., and Sharon Stanton Russell. 1994. "Responses of Industrial Countries to Asylum-Seekers." *Journal of International Affairs* 42:399–417, Summer 1994.

Koehn, Peter H. 1991. *Refugees from Revolution: U.S. Policy and Third World Migration.* Boulder: Westview Press.

Kraly, Ellen Percy. 1990. "U.S. Refugee Policies and Refugee Migration since World War II." In Tucker, Keely, and Wrigley 1990.

Kubat, Daniel. ed. 1993. *The Politics of Migration Policies.* New York: Center for Migration Studies.

Loescher, Gil. 1989. "The European Community and Refugees." *International Affairs* 65:617–624.

Loescher, Gil, and John A. Scanlan. 1986. *Calculated Kindness: Refugees and America's Half-Open Door, 1945 to the Present.* New York: The Free Press.

Loescher, Gil, and Laila Monahan. eds. 1989. *Refugees and International Relations.* New York: Oxford University Press.

Lutz, Wolfgang. ed. 1994. *Alternative Paths of Future World Population Growth. What Can We Assume Today?* London: Earthscan.

Mathias, Charles McC. 1981. "Ethnic Groups and Foreign Policy." *Foreign Affairs* 59:975–998.

Mitchell, Christopher. ed. 1992a. *Western Hemisphere Immigration and United States Foreign Policy.* University Park, PA: Pennsylvania University Press.

———. 1992b. "Introduction: Immigration and U.S. Foreign Policy toward the Caribbean, Central America, and Mexico." In Mitchell 1992a.

———. 1992c. "U.S. Foreign Policy and Dominican Migration to the United States." In Mitchell 1992a.

Moynihan, Daniel Patrick. 1994. *Pandaemonium.* New York: Oxford University Press.

O'Grady, Joseph P. ed. 1967. *The Immigrants' Influence on Wilson's Peace Policies.* Lexington: University of Kentucky Press.

Ranis, Gus. 1994. "International Migration and Foreign Assistance: The Case of the Philippines." In Bohning and Schloeter-Paredes 1994.

Reed, Laura, and Carl Kaysen. eds. 1993. *Emerging Norms of Justified Intervention.* Cambridge: American Academy of Arts and Sciences.

Reimers, David M. 1982. "Recent Immigration Policy: An Analysis." In Chiswick 1982.

Rico, Carlos. 1992. "Migration and U.S.-Mexican Relations, 1966–1986." In Mitchell 1992a.

Robbins, Carla Anne. 1992. "Dateline Washington: Cuban-American Clout." *Foreign Policy,* Fall 1992.

Rogers, Rosemarie, and Emily Copeland. 1993. *Forced Migration: Policy Issues in the Post–Cold War World.* Medford, MA: The Fletcher School of Law and Diplomacy, Tufts University.

Rogers, Rosemarie, and Sharon Stanton Russell. forthcoming. *Toward a New Global Refugee System.*

Roucek, Joseph S., and Bernard Eisenberg. eds. 1982. *America's Ethnic Politics.* Westport, CT: Greenwood Press.

Russell, Sharon Stanton. 1992. "International Migration and Political Turmoil in the Middle East." *Population and Development Review* 18:-719–727.

Russell, Sharon Stanton, and Charles B. Keely. forthcoming. "The Diplomacy of Multilateral Efforts to Harmonize Asylum Policy among Industrial Countries, 1984–1993." In Rogers and Russell forthcoming.

Schoultz, Lars. 1992. "Central America and the Politicization of U.S. Immigration Policy." In Mitchell 1992a.

Simmons, Alan. ed. forthcoming. *Migration, Human Rights and Economic Integration.* Staten Island: Center for Migration Studies.

Singer, David. ed. 1992. *American Jewish Yearbook 1992.* New York: American Jewish Committee.

Skerry, Peter. 1993. *Mexican Americans: The Ambivalent Minority.* New York: The Free Press.

Stepick, Alex. 1992. "Unintended Consequences: Rejecting Haitian Boat People and Destabilizing Duvalier." In Mitchell 1992a.

Teitelbaum, Michael S. 1984. "Immigration, Refugees and Foreign Policy." *International Organization* 38:229–250.

Tucker, Robert W. 1990. "Immigration and Foreign Policy: General Considerations." In Tucker, Keely, and Wrigley 1990.

Tucker, Robert, Charles B. Keely, and Linda Wrigley. eds. 1990. *Immigration and U.S. Foreign Policy.* Boulder: Westview Press.

United Nations. 1994a. *Trends in the Total Migrant Stock.* Database maintained by the Population Division of the Department for Economic and Social Information and Policy Analysis of the United Nations Secretariat.

———. 1994b. *World Population Monitoring, 1993.* New York: United Nations (ESA/P/WP.121).

United Nations Economic Commission for Europe (UN/ECE). 1994. *International Migration Bulletin.* Geneva: United Nations. No. 4, May 1994.

United Nations High Commissioner for Refugees. 1993. *The State of the World's Refugees: The Challenge of Protection.* London and New York: Penguin Books.

———. 1994. "Populations of Concern to UNHCR: A Statistical Overview 1993." Geneva: UNHCR, Division of Programmes and Operational Support.

United States Department of Justice. 1993. *1992 Statistical Yearbook of the Immigration and Naturalization Service.* Washington, D.C.: U.S. Government Printing Office.

U.S. Committee for Refugees. 1993. *1993 World Refugee Survey*. Washington, D.C.: U.S. Committee for Refugees.

Weiner, Myron. 1992/93. "Security, Stability and International Migration." *International Security* 17:91–126.

———. ed. 1993. *International Migration and Security*. Boulder: Westview Press.

Zlotnik, Hania. 1994. "Migration to and from Developing Regions: A Review of Past Trends." In Lutz 1994.

———. forthcoming. "Who Is Moving and Why? A Comparative Overview of Policies and Migration Trends in the North American System." In Simmons forthcoming.

Zolberg, Aristide R. 1990. "The Roots of U.S. Refugee Policy." In Tucker, Keely, and Wrigley 1990.

———. 1992. with the assistance of Ursula Levelt. "Response to Crisis— Refugee Policy in the United States and Canada." In Chiswick 1992.

Zolberg, Aristide R., Astri Suhrke, and Sergio Aguayo. 1989. *Escape from Violence: Conflict and the Refugee Crisis in the Developing World*. New York: Oxford University Press.

Zucker, Norman L., and Naomi Flink Zucker. 1987. *The Guarded Gate: The Reality of American Refugee Policy*. San Diego: Harcourt, Brace, Jovanovich.

Final Report
of the
Eighty-Sixth American
Assembly

At the close of their discussions, the participants in the Eighty-sixth American Assembly, on "World Migration and U.S. Policy," at Arden House, Harriman, New York, November 10–13, 1994, reviewed as a group the following statement. This statement represents general agreement; however, no one was asked to sign it. Furthermore, it should be understood that not everyone agreed with all of it.

International migration is rising to the top of the foreign policy agenda. The novel focus of this American Assembly, therefore, is global migration as it affects and is affected by U.S. foreign policies. The underlying theme is that migration has joined global economic trends, sustainable development, the environment, and population growth as an important foreign policy issue.

Deeply disturbing emergencies (Iraq, Bosnia, Algeria, Haiti, Cuba, Rwanda) have forced policy makers in many countries to confront—in a crisis mode—the complexities of "ethnic cleansing" and of refugee protection, asylum, and temporary safe haven. Similarly, global economic integration, new communications and transportation networks, the availability of rights and benefits to migrants, freer exit from former Communist countries, and domestic debate about the costs and benefits of immigration have forced attention to policies regulating voluntary migration for economic, family, and other reasons.

In global terms, international migration movements have been large and on the rise over the past decade, and the numbers designated as refugees and displaced persons have increased sharply. Of course, people have always migrated, and immigration has been a formative element in American history. Many believe that protecting the tradition of U.S. commitment to legal immigration is an important goal because such migration provides significant economic, social, and cultural benefits. At the same time, many believe that we face new conditions and that some of the underlying premises of American immigration and refugee policy are no longer valid. The terrain is shifting, and is quite unfamiliar for the public and for foreign policy professionals alike. Frameworks for considering these changes have not yet been well formulated, and policy-making structures taking them into account have only begun to be developed.

In many of the industrialized countries to which migrants and refugees have been moving there has been increasing public resistance to their arrival, fueled in part by a perception that governments are no longer able to control their borders. Typically, public opinion makes little distinction among those who are refugees, asylum seekers, legal or illegal migrants. Some see international migration as a boon, others recognize both its benefits and costs, and others see it increasingly as threatening. Some believe that new conditions require new trade-offs among humanitarian, economic, and family admissions, while others are opposed.

Perceptions of threat posed by migration may or may not reflect reality. However, they are strongly felt and cannot simply be dismissed. In the framing of policy, both perceptions and reality matter.

In general, threat perception grows when immigration numbers grow and when there is a convergence of insecurity about underlying economic and social conditions with the sense that control has been lost by governmental institutions responsible for managing international migration.

Hence the *domestic setting matters:* unemployment, or the fear of unemployment; disappointed expectations about standards of living; claims for public expenditure; race and ethnicity issues; changing cultural values.

The *international setting matters:* instabilities following the end of the cold war; forced migration and "ethnic cleansing"; flagrant violations of human rights; the reappearance of genocide; rapidly growing populations and deteriorating environments; increasing economic differentials and stagnating economies; and new visibility for these via global communication channels.

The *characteristics of the migration itself matter:* migration flows seen as large, rapid, and uncontrolled; heavy concentrations of migrant groups in particular regions, cities, or neighborhoods; anxieties about rapid ethnic and racial change in regions of settlement; views about whether migrants are integrating; concerns over illegal entry or residence; and whether migrants are identified with violence, crime, terrorism, or drugs, or seen as hardworking contributors to society.

These concerns are apparent in many countries, both industrialized and developing. They wax and wane over time; differ among countries, cities, and neighborhoods; and vary markedly among different subgroups of the domestic population. Actions of political leaderships can moderate or exacerbate the expressions of such concerns, but do not explain them.

The American people, their political leaders, and their government face compelling questions. They must decide what means are available to the United States—unilaterally and in conjunction with other states and with international organizations—to respond in an effective and humane manner to the international movements of people, in the context of increasing resistance to their entry. They must determine how to weigh the diverse interests and concerns of different groups among the American population. They must determine if foreign and related trade and economic policies are consistent or inconsistent with the policies framed to deal with international migration. In any case, it is important that we have the ability to control the composition and magnitude of migration to the United States.

U.S. Foreign Policy and
Its Impact on Migration

U.S. foreign policy frequently affects migration to the United States and other countries. Unilateral, bilateral, and multilateral policies may stimulate or reduce movements of people from one country to another. In recent examples, diplomacy and military intervention reduced migration from Cuba and Haiti. Policies that have increased migration include involvement in civil wars in Central America and elsewhere, economic embargoes, and the encouragement of the individual right of departure, as in the former Soviet Union and Cuba. Foreign policy relationships may also affect whether migrants seek and gain entry into the United States as, for example, in the case of the Vietnamese refugees.

In some cases, U.S. foreign policy positions are adopted with full recognition of the migration ramifications. More often, however, this is not the case. Not enough executive branch personnel responsible for the formulation and implementation of foreign policy have the expertise to identify and assess the migration impacts of their actions. The same is true of congressional staffs. Nor, until the last few years has there been interest in these issues among senior policy makers in the Department of State and the National Security Council. This Assembly welcomes the steps that already have been taken to ensure systematic incorporation of global immigration concerns into the formulation of U.S. foreign policy. Much more, though, must be done.

Substantial discussion has taken place during the past decade on the use of trade, investment, and aid policies to reduce migration. Although in the long term sustainable development of developing countries will likely decrease the potential for regulated and unregulated migration, in the short term economic development can be expected to enhance the potential for increased migration. Therefore, while this Assembly supports sustainable development endeavors in their own right, it cautions against justifying them solely on the basis of their short-term deterrent effect on migration. Building support for trade, investment, and aid policies on unrealistic expectations of an immediate deterrent to migration can cause negative reaction to these policies when the expected results do not quickly emerge. The Programme of Action of the United Nations International Conference on Population and Development, agreed to by over 170 nations in Cairo in September 1994, contains many useful recommendations for promoting the kind of human and social development that will contribute to reducing migration potential over the long term.

Identifying instruments of U.S. foreign policy that can reduce unwanted migration over both the short and long terms should be given high priority. For example, promotion of human rights, minority rights, and the achievement of democracy could provide increased political stability in countries that have been or could become important sources of forced migration. Diplomatic pressures are an important tool in persuading foreign governments to avoid creating conditions that compel their citizens to emigrate.

This Assembly recommends development of more systematic processes for incorporating assessments of the impact of foreign policy decisions on domestic and international migration. Appropriate experts from the Departments of State and Justice, including the Bureau for Population, Refugees, and Migration and the Immigration and Naturalization Service, should be involved in foreign policy deliberation relating to migration. A curriculum on migration and refugee issues should be incorporated into the standard training for diplomats. Systematic assessment of migration impacts will raise awareness of these consequences of foreign policy decisions, leaving it to policy makers to determine the weight to give to these impacts in making their decisions. Moreover, consideration should be given to strategies to upgrade and enhance interagency coordination in the formulation of U.S. policies bearing on migration.

U.S. Immigration and Refugee Policy as an Instrument of Foreign Policy

Generally, U.S. immigration and refugee policies should advance broad national interests. Throughout the period of the cold war, these policies were used to support specific foreign policy objectives. Migration policy was intended in part to stabilize friendly governments (e.g., El Salvador) and to destabilize unfriendly ones (e.g., Cuba). For example, individuals leaving Communist states were defined as refugees and therefore received preferential treatment.

In the post–cold war era, many of the foreign policy underpinnings of U.S. immigration and refugee policies require reconsideration, some of which has already begun. This Assembly believes that cold war criteria should cease to apply in determining U.S. refugee admissions policy. However, this Assembly acknowledges that a short transition period is necessary to move migrants from refugee resettlement categories into legal immigration ones because of the number of people already in the system.

Decisions about granting asylum to individuals in the United States should be governed by current American law, which provides that foreign policy considerations should not prejudice the applicant's protection from possible harm by return.

Legal immigration and temporary admissions policies can promote U.S. foreign policy interests, particularly in the area of international economic and trade policies. New trade arrangements such as the North American Free Trade Agreement (NAFTA) and the most recent round of the General Agreement on Tariffs and Trade promote the freer movement of goods, services, and capital, and should promote economic growth in the United States and abroad. The United States should examine its immigration policies in the light of the actual operation of the international economy, such as balancing interest in increasing our competitiveness with interest in the protection of U.S. workers.

International migration is increasingly perceived in the United States and other countries as a threat to domestic well-being. The concern stems, in part, from a failure to manage and control immigration in a way that deters illegal entry. It is in the domestic and foreign policy interest of the United States to demonstrate tangible evidence of a reduction in current and prospective illegal immigration.

The Intersection between Immigration Policy and Foreign Policy

Two examples illustrate the intersections between immigration policy and foreign policy and demonstrate lessons for both.

U.S.–Mexico Migration

Migration between Mexico and the United States is one of the most important issues on the bilateral agenda. In part because of its proximity, Mexico is the largest contributor to both legal and illegal immigration to the United States. Mexico is also a key trade partner of the United States, made more important by the conclusion of the NAFTA.

The interconnections between foreign policy and immigration policy are evident in a number of recent developments involving the two countries. In the debate over the NAFTA, the relationship between migration and trade was expressed most vividly by President Salinas's remark that Mexico could export either tomatoes or tomato pickers. Although debatable in terms of immediate effect, the potential for a reduction in migration pressures was an important factor in building domestic U.S. support for the agreement. In addition to the NAFTA, new relationships have developed on border management, including a pledge from the U.S. government that Mexico would be consulted prior to the erection of additional fences along the border. Other items on the bilateral agenda include cooperative efforts to reduce border violence, the smuggling of migrants, the transit of nationals of third countries through Mexico to the United States, and the development of secure means to ease legal entries for family visits and shopping. A more controversial item has been the Mexican government's open opposition to Proposition 187 in California, which seeks to deny education, health, and social services to illegal immigrants by requiring service providers to identify all persons suspected of being in illegal immigration status.

Regional Safe Haven

The U.S. experience in responding to the recent boat exodus from Cuba and Haiti provides pointed examples of a strong interconnection among migration, foreign, and domestic policy concerns. In both instances, the United States aimed to prevent large-scale out-migration while providing protection to people whose flight from their country is at least partly motivated by fear of violence and repression, in addition to economic reasons. The United States opted for a policy that provides safe haven in third countries and at the U.S. naval base in Guantanamo, Cuba, sending a clear message that people with a genuine fear of persecution or violence would find protection, but those who leave their countries in order to immigrate to the United States would remain in camps or voluntarily return home. Before this policy was implemented, many poor Haitians were forcibly returned to Haiti where they were subject to increased danger of political persecution.

U.S. policy makers engaged in active diplomacy with other countries to create a regional response to these movements of people. The U.S. effort also won the support of the UN High Commissioner for Refugees (UNHCR), which legitimated the concept that satisfactory protection could sometimes be provided in regional safe havens.

A workable safe haven requires that individuals will be protected temporarily, then return to their country of origin when conditions permit. Haitians have returned in substantial numbers, but the future of the detained Cuban population remains to be determined.

To a large degree the use of regional safe havens was adopted because of the nature and loose enforcement of current U.S. asylum law. After extended individual status determinations, even many rejected asylum seekers are not returned to their countries of origin. This consistent failure to enforce decisions in asylum cases undermines confidence in the rule of law in the migration area. When persons who fled civil disruption have received safe haven in the United States, similar problems of return exist. Current U.S.

asylum and domestic safe haven policies should be changed in two directions: to provide for prompt return of those whose asylum applications are rejected, and, in conjunction, to consider building a safe haven capacity in the United States itself.

Bilateral Policies

The United States has a direct interest in the migration policies of other countries because they may have destabilizing effects either regionally or globally; may result in the direct flow of peoples to the United States; and may affect the content, credibility, and effectiveness of international norms. The United States has the clearest interest in engaging countries regarding refugee policies where there is an international humanitarian consensus. The three conditions under which the United States is justified in taking a strong position with other countries are where 1) there is a clear violation of international law (e.g., when a state engages in mass expulsions of its citizens); 2) an emergency requires coordinated efforts and quick response; and 3) the goal is to engage other states in offering their assistance.

On immigration and citizenship policies, the U.S. interest (and the legitimacy of its interventions) is less clear, although it is important that the United States not ask of others what it is unwilling to do in its own domestic policy. There is legitimate interest when the immigration enforcement and emigration policies of other nations produce significant unwanted migrant flows to the United States. In keeping with the emerging international norm that sees a state's mistreatment of its citizens as a cause for action, citizenship issues that involve the rights of specific groups or create the possibility of statelessness are also appropriate subjects for bilateral engagement.

The right of exit should remain an important object of bilateral negotiation, and must carry with it the related right to return. It is also appropriate to seek to persuade governments to limit departures of economic migrants where the exiting persons will violate the immigration laws of the state of destination. Such diplomatic efforts are less appropriate when the government in the country of origin restricts orderly departure, when people are fleeing conditions of civil conflict, when substantial numbers of those leaving by irregular means appear to have refugee characteristics, or when it is unclear whether those leaving are seeking unlawful entry into the United States. All diplomatic efforts should consistently reflect our continued support for the protection of bona fide refugees.

In general, it is legitimate for the United States to concern itself with the immigration and nationality policies of other countries when the United States is likely to feel their direct effects (such as those policies pursued by Mexico or by the Caribbean states) or when such policies are likely to have regional destabilizing effects (such as the policies of the Baltic states toward Russians living within their borders).

Strengthening International Institutions

The United States is in a position to take a leading role in international discussions of migration issues. U.S. policies and practices will significantly influence the evolution of international institutions and standards of behavior on refugee and immigration issues. Although there is a reasonable consensus regarding the treatment of refugees per se, there is a strong need for new norms and arrangements for other forms of forced migration, including internally displaced persons, individuals fleeing violence and repression, and those leaving because of natural disasters and environmental degradation. Also needed are international norms for responding to these complex migrations, such as temporary protection and safe haven. Here regional agreements seem the most promising starting point.

The UNHCR has dramatically increased its capacity to respond to crisis situations involving not only refugees but also internally displaced persons. Rising ethnic divisions, religious conflicts, environmental degradation, and the growing number of "failed" states have increased the challenges that the UNHCR must face. However, the gap between needs and available resources remains large and is growing. Support for the UNHCR is a vital U.S. concern; it can grow if the public sees evidence of successful efforts and the benefits of effective cooperation with other countries.

Similarly, the foreign policy interests of the United States would be served by increasing the capacity of international institutions to address the underlying causes of mass migrations, intervene more effectively when they occur, and deal with their consequences.

International intervention is most effective when international institutions can respond to early warning signals of crisis. Policy makers often have information that would make it possible to take preventive steps, but the lack of coordination and communication, and the political resistance to responding before a problem becomes a full-blown crisis, make prevention difficult to achieve, despite the evidence that prevention is less costly and saves lives. The United States and other countries have been more willing to respond to mass migration crises after they occur than to attempt to prevent them, and have been more willing to fund humanitarian relief than peacekeeping and peacemaking efforts.

Sovereignty remains a fundamental element of the international system of states. Yet, under certain circumstances—particularly when human rights violations and mass exodus may result in regional or international instability—humanitarian intervention in the internal affairs of states is justified. Intervention may include international diplomatic efforts, establishment of safe zones and other techniques to guarantee the delivery of relief to displaced persons, economic sanctions, and, as a last resort, military intervention.

The recent experience with both regional safe havens for Haitians and military intervention to resolve the reasons for their departure underscores the need to develop effective regional, not just global, structures for responding to crises. Needed are regional structures with effective capacity for early warning, emergency response, and readiness to address underlying causes of migration.

Conclusions

International migration patterns, and reactions to them, have changed dramatically over the past decade, and have been punctuated by crises. These new conditions require new thinking.

Most promising are approaches to incorporate migration issues constructively and systematically into the process of foreign policy formulation, and vice versa. The ultimate foreign policy decision maker is "we the people" through our political institutions. In this spirit this American Assembly makes the following recommendations:

Domestic Policy Instruments

- Promote a calm, well-informed, searching public discussion of all facets of the impact of immigration on our country, in the context of changing global economic and political conditions.
- Define a better process and structure in the executive branch to consider the impact of immigration policy on the domestic, political, economic, and social interests of the nation.
- Assess the role of legal immigration and temporary admissions in fostering the performance of the U.S. economy in the context of global economic integration.
- Develop effective and credible domestic policies to significantly reduce illegal migration into the United States.
- Urge members of the executive, judicial, and legislative branches to resist the temptation to resolve "temporary" problems via ad hoc exceptions to U.S. immigration and refugee laws.

Foreign Policy Instruments

- Assure that the migration implications of alternative foreign policies are fully assessed.
- Develop expertise and resources within the U.S. government for systematic assessment of the migration impacts of foreign policy choices.
- Better anticipate future migration crises and prepare creative approaches, such as safe havens, to deal with them in a humane, effective manner, consistent with international legal norms.
- Assure that the U.S. military is adequately prepared for future emergency humanitarian actions.
- Consult actively with other governments about global and regional responses to migration crises, including developing new international norms and arrangements.
- Develop coordinated policies with other governments for deter-

ring unauthorized migration, including the sharing of information about international criminal organizations engaged in illegal migrant trafficking.

- Engage energetically in diplomatic negotiations with countries producing large illegal migration flows to the United States to design strong innovative approaches to deal with the causes of such movements.
- Support sustainable development programs (including efforts to protect the environment, stabilize population growth, and improve living standards) that can help ameliorate conditions leading to migration pressure.
- Reinforce the capacities of international institutions to prevent and to respond more effectively to humanitarian crises.

Participants
The Eighty-Sixth American Assembly

DEBORAH AMOS
ABC News
New York, NY

†DIEGO C. ASENCIO
International Consultant
Diego Asencio & Associates,
  Inc.
Palm Beach, FL

PAULINE H. BAKER
Research Associate & Director,
  Project on Modern Ethnic
  Conflict & International
  Diplomacy
Institute for the Study of
  Diplomacy
Georgetown University
Washington, DC

FRANK D. BEAN
Ashbel Smith Professor of
  Sociology
Population Research
  Center
The University of Texas at
  Austin
Austin, TX

ROY BECK
Washington Editor
The Social Contract
Washington, DC

RICHARD E.
  BENEDICK
Senior Fellow
World Wildlife Fund
Washington, DC

DANIEL BOB
Special Assistant
Asian & Pacific Affairs
Office of Senator William V.
  Roth, Jr.
Washington, DC

**MUZAFFAR CHISHTI
Director
Immigration Project
International Ladies Garment
  Workers Union
New York, NY

JOSH DEWIND
Program Director
International Migration
  Program
Social Science Research
  Council
New York, NY

SERGIO DÍAZ-BRIQUETS
Senior Associate
Casals and Associates
Arlington, VA

ANNE DONOHUE
Senior Producer, Special
  Projects
Monitor Radio, the broadcast
  edition of the *Christian Science
  Monitor*
Boston, MA

PAMELA S. FALK
Author and Foreign Policy
  Analyst
New York, NY

TOM FARER
Professor of Law and
 International Relations
The American University
Washington, DC

BARBARA D. FINBERG
Executive Vice President
Carnegie Corporation of New
 York
New York, NY

KATHRYN FLEWELLEN
Migration Project Director
National Immigration Forum
Washington, DC

JAMES O.
 GOLDSBOROUGH
Foreign Affairs
 Correspondent
San Diego Union-Tribune
San Diego, CA

LEON GORDENKER
Professor Emeritus
Center of International Studies
Woodrow Wilson School of
 Public & International
 Affairs
Princeton University
Princeton, NJ

OTIS L. GRAHAM, JR.
Department of History
University of California, Santa
 Barbara
Santa Barbara, CA

KATE L. GRANT
Professional Staff Member
Committee on Foreign Affairs
U.S. House of Representatives
Washington, DC

LUCAS GUTTENTAG
Director
Immigrants' Rights Project
American Civil Liberties
 Union Foundation
New York, NY

GEORGE B. HIGH
Executive Director
Center for Immigration
 Studies
Washington, DC

RICHARD C. HOTTELET
America and The World
Wilton, CT

*JANE S. JAQUETTE
Chair
Department of Diplomacy &
 World Affairs
Occidental College
Los Angeles, CA

HAL KANE
Worldwatch Institute
Washington, DC

CARL KAYSEN
Professor of Political Economy,
 Emeritus
Defense & Arms Control
 Studies Program
Massachusetts Institute of
 Technology
Cambridge, MA

CHARLES B. KEELY
Herzberg Professor of
 International Migration
Department of
 Demography
Georgetown University
Washington, DC

ROGER KRAMER
Director, Division of
    Immigration Policy &
    Research
Bureau of International Labor
    Affairs
U.S. Department of Labor
Washington, DC

MALCOLM LOVELL
President
National Planning
    Association
Washington, DC

*ABRAHAM F.
    LOWENTHAL
Director
Center for International
    Studies
University of Southern
    California
Los Angeles, CA

DAVID A. MARTIN
Henry L. & Grace Doherty
    Professor of Law
F. Palmer Weber Research
    Professor of Civil
    Liberties & Human
    Rights
School of Law
University of Virginia
Charlottesville, VA

PHILIP L. MARTIN
Department of Agricultural
    Economics
University of California-
    Davis
Davis, CA

*SUSAN MARTIN
Executive Director
U.S. Commission on
    Immigration Reform
Washington, DC

†BRUNSON MCKINLEY
Senior Deputy Assistant
    Secretary
Bureau of Population,
    Refugees, & Migration
U.S. Department of State
Washington, DC

†DORIS M. MEISSNER
Commissioner
Immigration & Naturalization
    Service
U.S. Department of Justice
Washington, DC

ELIZABETH MIDGLEY
President
Working English
Washington, DC

HARRIS N. MILLER
Immigration Services
    Associates
Washington, DC

MARK J. MILLER
Department of Political
    Science & International
    Relations
University of Delaware
Newark, DE

CHRISTOPHER
    MITCHELL
Center for Latin American &
    Caribbean Studies
New York University
New York, NY

JEANNETTE MONEY
Department of Political
  Science
University of California-Davis
Davis, CA

FRANK MORRIS
Dean
School of Graduate Studies
Morgan State University
Baltimore, MD

KATHLEEN NEWLAND
Senior Associate
International Migration Policy
  Program
Carnegie Endowment for
  International Peace
Washington, DC

JEFFREY S. PASSEL
Director
Program for Research on
  Immigration Policy
Urban Institute
Washington, DC

**ROSEMARIE ROGERS
Professor of International
  Politics
The Fletcher School of Law &
  Diplomacy
Tufts University
Medford, MA

SHARON STANTON
  RUSSELL
Research Scholar
Center for International
  Studies
Massachusetts Institute of
  Technology
Cambridge, MA

RICHARD RYSCAVAGE,
  S.J.
Arrupe Scholar
Refugee Studies Programme
University of Oxford
Oxford, UNITED
  KINGDOM

JURGEN SCHMANDT
Professor, LBJ School of Public
  Affairs
Director, Center for Global
  Studies
The Woodlands, TX

ENID C.B. SCHOETTLE
National Intelligence Officer
  for Global & Multilateral
  Issues
National Intelligence Council
Washington, DC

PETER H. SCHUCK
Yale University Law School
New Haven, CT

PETER SKERRY
Woodrow Wilson Center
Washington, DC

**CORDIA A. STROM
Minority Counsel
Committee on the Judiciary
Subcommittee on Immigration
  & Refugee Affairs
U.S. Senate
Washington, DC

GEORGES VERNEZ
Director
Center for Research on
  Immigration Policy
RAND
Santa Monica, CA

WARREN ZIMMERMANN
Senior Fellow
RAND
Washington, DC

HANIA ZLOTNIK
Population Division
United Nations
New York, NY

ARISTIDE R. ZOLBERG
University-in-Exile Professor
Graduate Faculty
New School for Social
  Research
New York, NY

*Discussion Leader
**Rapporteur
†Delivered Formal Address

317

About The American Assembly

The American Assembly was established by Dwight D. Eisenhower at Columbia University in 1950. It holds nonpartisan meetings and publishes authoritative books to illuminate issues of United States policy.

An affiliate of Columbia, the Assembly is a national, educational institution incorporated in the state of New York.

The Assembly seeks to provide information, stimulate discussion, and evoke independent conclusions on matters of vital public interest.

American Assembly Sessions

At least two national programs are initiated each year. Authorities are retained to write background papers presenting essential data and defining the main issues of each subject.

A group of men and women representing a broad range of experience, competence, and American leadership meet for several days to discuss the Assembly topic and consider alternatives for national policy.

All Assemblies follow the same procedure. The background papers are sent to participants in advance of the Assembly. The Assembly meets in small groups for four or five lengthy periods. All groups use the same agenda. At the close of these informal sessions participants adopt in plenary session a final report of findings and recommendations.

Regional, state, and local Assemblies are held following the national session at Arden House. Assemblies have also been held in England, Switzerland, Malaysia, Canada, the Caribbean, South America, Central America, the Philippines, and Japan. Over one hundred sixty institutions have cosponsored one or more Assemblies.

Arden House

The home of The American Assembly and the scene of the national sessions is Arden House, which was given to Columbia

University in 1950 by W. Averell Harriman. E. Roland Harriman joined his brother in contributing toward adaptation of the property for conference purposes. The buildings and surrounding land, known as the Harriman Campus of Columbia University, are fifty miles north of New York City.

Arden House is a distinguished conference center. It is self-supporting and operates throughout the year for use by organizations with educational objectives. The American Assembly is a tenant of this Columbia University facility only during Assembly sessions.

Index